Class-Conscious Coal Miners

SUNY series in Labor Studies

Jeff Schuhrke and Richard Wells, editors

Class-Conscious Coal Miners

The Emergence of a Working-Class Movement in Central Pennsylvania

ALAN J. SINGER

Cover image of the WPA poster promoting Pennsylvania; Library of Congress.

Published by State University of New York Press, Albany

© 2024 State University of New York

For information, contact State University of New York Press, Albany, NY
www.sunypress.edu

Library of Congress Cataloging-in-Publication Data

Name: Singer, Alan J., author.
Title: Class-conscious coal miners : the emergence of a working-class
  movement in central Pennsylvania / Alan J. Singer.
Description: Albany : State University of New York Press, [2024] | Series:
  SUNY series in labor studies | Includes bibliographical references and
  index.
Identifiers: LCCN 2023043084 | ISBN 9781438497716 (hardcover : alk. paper) |
  ISBN 9781438497730 (ebook) | ISBN 9781438497723 (pbk. : alk. paper)
Subjects: LCSH: Working class—Pennsylvania—History—20th century. |
  Working class—Political activity—Pennsylvania—History—20th century. |
  Minors—Pennsylvania. | Labor unions—Pennsylvania—History—20th century.
Classification: LCC HD8083.P43 S56 2024 | DDC 305.5/62/09748—dc23/eng/20240111
LC record available at https://lccn.loc.gov/2023043084

10 9 8 7 6 5 4 3 2 1

Contents

Illustrations

Tables

Maps

Acknowledgments

I began this project as a doctoral dissertation at Rutgers University in the 1970s. My key question then and now is how to explain the militancy and class consciousness of bituminous coal miners in Central Pennsylvania and the United States. Their militancy and class consciousness stand out in the history of the American working-class, and an understanding of the factors that contributed to their development became even more essential in the second and third decades of the twenty-first century as private-sector unions and subterranean coal-mining virtually disappeared and working-class white voters, including voters from what were formerly coal-mining regions of the country, overwhelmingly supported conservative ethno-nationalist political candidates. In 2016 and 2020, two-thirds of the voters in Cambria County, Pennsylvania cast their presidential ballots for Donald Trump who promised, without any plan or regard for environmental impact, to restore the American coal mining industry.

I would like to thank the many people whose contributions helped make this book possible. Essentially, they breakdown into three cohorts: people and institutions that assisted in the original project in the 1970s, people who aided in continuing research, and people and institutions that helped this book reached fruition five decades after the project began. I was distracted too many times while studying the United Mine Workers of America and the Central Pennsylvania bituminous coal miners, and unfortunately many of the people who helped me along the way are dead.

This study owes an enormous debt to the historians who influenced my approach to the study of the working class and history in general. They include, but are not limited to, W. E. B. Du Bois, Edward Thompson, and Herbert Gutman for their seminal histories of working-class life and political struggles; Eric Hobsbawm, Robin Blackburn, and Marcus Rediker for their comprehensive approach to history that imbeds the daily lives and struggles of ordinary people into explanations of broader historical events; and E. H. Carr and Marc Bloch, who in their work explored the very purpose of studying history. Carr argued, "The historian is engaged on a continuous process of moulding his facts to his interpretations and his interpretations to his facts" (34–35), a process that I attempt to engage with in this book. Carr recognized that the past and present form a continuum and that questions about the present shape the historian's interpretations of the past. I hope this book does justice to Carr's approach.

Professors Gerald Grob (1931–2015) and Norman Markowitz of the Rutgers University History Department served as mentors while I was in graduate school and as members of my doctoral committee. Norman became a lifelong friend and thinking partner. Andor Skotnes, a fellow history department graduate student at Rutgers University in the 1970s, as well as a lifetime social justice activist, has helped me clarify ideas about working-class struggle at different points over the years. A number of residents of the Nanty Glo, Pennsylvania area shared their experiences, personal records, and hospitality with me. They included Katherine and Paul Martin, Clair Cook, Frank Brushko, Johnny Hill, Joe Shulick, Dave Braken, John Szekeresh, Russell Teeter, Frank Hocevar, Cyril Halovich, Charles Zankey, William "Spider Bill" Ray, and Esther Gelotte. William Martin, who edited the local newspaper, introduced me to people in Nanty Glo, assisted in interviews, provided me with credibility, and helped examine town records and local newspapers.

Very early in this project I was fortunate to come across unpublished doctoral dissertations by Edward Wickersham and Clark Everling that helped clarify my research questions and avoid pitfalls along the way. Everling and Gerald Grob directed me to available sources and explained the complex organization of the United Mine Workers of America (UMWA) archives that I stumbled into when they were opened up to the public after Miners for Democracy took control over the international office of the United Mine Workers Union in 1973.

The staffs of these libraries provided valuable and gracious assistance: Tamiment Institute, Bobst Library, New York University; Alexander Library, Rutgers, the State University of New Jersey; Butler Library Oral History Archive, Columbia University Center for Oral History; Stapleton Library, Indiana University of Pennsylvania; Lilly Library, University of Indiana at Bloomington; Pittsburgh University Library; Catholic University of America Library; Library of Congress; New York Public Library; Nanty Glo Public

Library; Axinn Library, Hofstra University; and Cambria County Historical Society.

John Laslett involved me in *The United Mine Workers of America: Model of Industrial Solidarity?* (Pennsylvania State University, 1996), which celebrated the union's one-hundredth anniversary. For this project, Melvin Dubofsky pointed me in productive directions and graduate student assistants at Hofstra University—Lynda Costello-Herrera, Katherine Simons, and Christine Bogart—assisted in organizing research material and editing.

When I visited the Central Pennsylvania coalfields in the 1970s to conduct interviews, I focused my attention on men and their experience in the mines and during strikes, and I lost the opportunity to learn more from the women who lived through these times and participated in these struggles. I owe much to the groundbreaking work of Mildred Allen Beik who introduced me to the importance of understanding the entire community through her communications and her book on *The Miners of Windber* (University Park, PA: Pennsylvania State University Press, 1996). In this book I draw on her work to flesh out research missing from my study of Nanty Glo. Robert Bussel's biography of Powers Hapgood, *From Harvard to the Ranks of Labor: Powers Hapgood and the American Working Class* (University Park, PA: Pennsylvania State University Press, 1999), helped fill in gaps in my chronology and clarify my ideas on the role of leadership.

During the course of the entire multidecade project, I received intellectual support and challenges from a cohort of community organizers and teachers I first met and started working with in the late 1960s. They include Tina Bernstein, Arthur Camins, Martin Eisenberg, Rhonda Azous Eisenberg, Anita Fisher-Faulding, Steve Faulding, Mel Grizer, Howard Harris, Rosemarie Hernandez, Susie Hoffman, Joe Kling, Prue Posner, and Judith Yanowitz Singer. Susie Hoffman proofread the original dissertation in the early 1980s.

During the last phase of my work on class-conscious Pennsylvania coal miners, I received assistance from support staff at Hofstra University, including Pearlita King, Janice Chopyk, Debra Willett, Preet Dhiren Shah, and Jasmine Torres, and I continually drew inspiration from colleagues, including Amy Catalano, Sean Fanelli, Doris Fromberg, Andrea Libresco, Maureen Miletta, Maureen Murphy, and Eustace Thompson, from family members, Heidi, Rachel, and Solomon, their spouses, Martin, Richard, and Pete, my grandchildren Sadia and Gideon, and my colleague/life partner Felicia Hirata. David Tarlo and Norman Markowitz took on the arduous task of proofreading the manuscript and pointing out passages that needed clarification. SUNY Press reviewers Mildred Beik, Rosemary Feurer, and Carl

Weinberg were instrumental in helping to transform a doctoral dissertation into a book.

Chapters in this book include material previously published in the articles "Class-Conscious Coal Miners: Nanty-glo versus the Open Shop in the Post–World War I Era," *Labor History* 29, no. 1, Winter 1988; "John Brophy's 'Miners' Program': Workers' Education in UMWA District 2 (Central Pennsylvania) during the 1920s," *Labor Studies Journal* 13, no. 4, Winter 1988; "Communists and Coal Miners: Rank-and-File Organizing in the United Mine Workers of America during the 1920s," *Science and Society* 55, no. 2, Summer 1991; and as a chapter in *The United Mine Workers of America: Model of Industrial Solidarity?* (Pennsylvania State University, 1996), edited by John Laslett.

Glossary for General Readers

anthracite—"hard coal" mined in northeastern Pennsylvania, primarily a home-heating fuel

base-rate/tonnage rate—miners were pay by the ton for coal mined, non-mining laborers were paid a daily base rate

bituminous—"soft" coal mined in Appalachian area and farther west and used in industry, by rail lines, and power plants

blacklist—a list maintained by coal companies, and sometimes by the UMWA, of miners suspected of causing trouble who should not be hired

blue-sky locals—union locals with few working miners where unemployed miners were able to see daytime blue skies

boney—a slang term for rock and dirty coal separated from marketable coal

boring-from-within—radical workers and groups who work inside established unions

business unionism—belief that union officers were professional managers who would work with companies and the government to make coal production more efficient and protect the livelihood of miners

captive mines—mines owned or controlled by the companies that used their coal production in their industries

Central Competitive Field (CCF)—coal mines under union contract in Illinois, Indiana, Ohio, and Western Pennsylvania

checkweightman—a union miner assigned to make sure coal is weighed accurately

class consciousness—awareness of class position with beliefs based on class position

coke—processed high-carbon coal used in steel production

dead work—unpaid work usually widening mine shafts and placing roof supports district autonomy—belief that authority rests with district officials, not the international union

dual union—a new and separate union competing with an established union

hand-picked coal—dislodging and loading coal with a pick and shovel

labor chautauqua—camp meetings modeled on traveling church revivals

pit or bank committee—formal or informal union subdivision in a single mine

rank-and-file—ordinary members of the union, not officers

scab—a strikebreaker

slate—layers of rock often mixed in with coal seams

tipple—above ground platform where coal is weighed and transferred into rail cars.

wildcat—an unauthorized strike

yellow-dog contract—an agreement that a worker will not join a union

---

Note on Spelling: The spelling of Nanty Glo, Pennsylvania appears differently in sources. I use Nanty Glo except when referring to the *Nanty-Glo Journal*. In some sources, the Central Pennsylvania Coal Producers' Association is referred to as the Central Pennsylvania Coal Operators' Association. I use "Producers'" in all cases to avoid confusion.

Introduction

In the spring of 1934, Gilbert Seldes, a feature writer for the Hearst newspaper syndicate, was forced to detour through the Central Pennsylvania coal mining town of Nanty Glo (previously called Nanty-glo). He wrote about what he saw in an article published in the *New York Evening Journal* and reprinted with an outraged response in the *Nanty-Glo Journal.*

> I wish that every congressman and every writer on economics and every supporter and every enemy of the New Deal or Old, would go to Nanty-glo and stay there a few days. I came upon it myself, by accident; a detour sent me through it. I have seen nothing more hideous. The center of town has a movie house and the usual red brick stores—perhaps two city blocks or three all together. The rest is given over to houses for people to live in, to call Home—houses to which young men bring young wives, in which they raise children—long rows of low gray wooden shacks, jammed one against the other, dilapidated, violently ugly—the whole thing a scene out of some half-lunatic painter's imagination, unspeakably desolate. There are houses of a better class. Instead of gray clapboard they seem at a distance to be either of yellow brick, through which some fungus has eaten its way, or of wood painted and scaled off. They are, however, bigger than the others, and their front porches stand right over long trains of coal cars proceeding into the mine. . . . I know also that coal companies, like all others, were made for profit, and that if a company could put up a row of cheap houses it was not only doing well for itself but quite possibly was giving the miners a better habitation than the huts they might build for

1

themselves. Granting all that, I still do not believe that human beings ought to live in houses such as these, in an ugliness which they themselves may soon forget but which must have some effect upon them. . . . My feeling is that it is not a good thing for America that any Americans should live in houses not equal to a good pigpen. . . . And the houses of Nanty-glo were not (meant for human beings to live in). They were meant for slow death. (Seldes, May 17, 1934: 5)

The *Nanty-Glo Journal* editorial claimed that the town had been done a grave injustice by Seldes and argued that Nanty Glo was not as bad as the slums of New York City. However, it did recommend that since the bituminous coal mines were only working a couple of days a week, and since others saw Nanty Glo this way, community residents should volunteer to beautify the borough (Eldridge, May 17, 1934: 4).

Nanty Glo, Pennsylvania received national media attention again in 1943, when *Life* magazine featured interviews with Nanty Glo mine workers and pictures of the borough in an article on the United States government's wartime takeover of the bituminous coal industry. According to the article, "LIFE sent photographer Alfred Eisenstaedt to Nanty Glo, a typical drab little coal town" to document the "dangerous . . . dirty and depressing" life of the coal miner. One photograph caption described how the "coal dust . . . seeps into everything . . . Miners' bleak, box-like houses are soot-covered, and the washed clothes are soon smudged" (*Life*, 1943a: 26–29). In addition, the *New York Times* intermittently covered Nanty Glo miners from May 1943 through April 1945, as they launched work stoppages in violation of federal wartime no-strike policies and against the official union leadership.

In 1920, Nanty Glo, which means "streams of coal" in Welsh, was a bituminous coal mining town of over 5,000 people located in the Blacklick Valley of Cambria County in Central Pennsylvania—approximately twelve miles northeast of Johnstown and sixty miles east of Pittsburgh. The history of Nanty Glo, Pennsylvania, its geographic circumstances, demographic patterns, and the presence of a nucleus of bituminous coal miners willing to explore new and often radical ideas, all contributed to the development of a sense of class-conscious community during the 1920s, 1930s, and 1940s.

There are four major grades of coal mined in the United States. Anthracite, also known as hard coal, has a limited geographic range, primarily

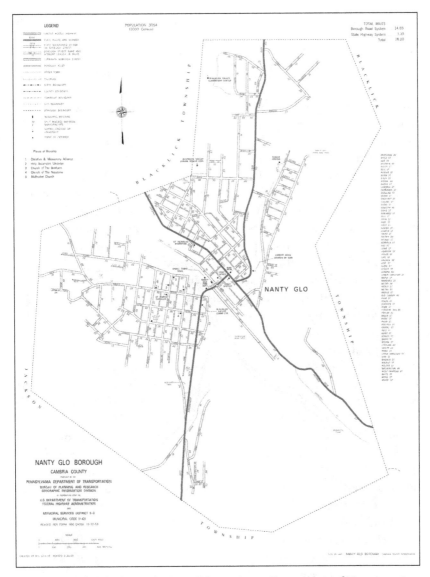

Map I.1. Nanty Glo Borough. Source: Pennsylvania Department of Transportation, "Nanty Glo Borough," February 20, 2009. https://gis.penndot.gov/BPR_pdf_files/ Maps/Type5/11421.pdf.

in northeastern Pennsylvania. It was the most widely used home-heating fuel in northeastern American cities from the late nineteenth century until after World War II. Bituminous, or soft coal, deposits are extensive in the northern and southern Appalachian basin, including Central Pennsylvania, and westward to the Mississippi River. It was the primary fuel used by American industry in factories, for steam-powered railroads and ships, and in electrical power plants. Anthracite and bituminous coal were both traditionally mined in underground shafts and anthracite and bituminous coal miners were members of the UMWA; however, they were different industries serving different markets. Subbituminous and lignite are considered lower-grade coal. They are more prevalent in the American south and west and were not widely mined or used in the United States until the second half of the twentieth century. Seams tend to be close to the surface and are accessed by stripping away top layers of soil and rock using earth-moving machinery (Schweinfurth, 2003; Henderson & Kleiner, 1976).

In this study of bituminous coal miners, class-consciousness is defined by worker understanding and action as they respond to the conditions they face at work and in their communities. Working-class consciousness is a collective identity that includes recognition that improvement in an individual's social and economic position is dependent on improvements and empowerment for the group as a whole. From this perspective, working-class consciousness is fluid rather than something to be achieved and a permanent condition. There is no false consciousness, a concept debated by Marxist theorists, especially in the post–World War I period, only levels of class identity and action. Requisites for the emergence of a class-conscious working-class movement in Central Pennsylvania included the conditions faced by workers and their families, the immediate circumstances that generated the movement, a set of ideas people could identify with, leadership committed to more radical solutions, and the existence of organizations to support militant activism (Miliband, 1971; 1977; Eyerman, 1981: 43–56).

This conception of class-consciousness rejects arguments for American exceptionalism forwarded by Selig Perlman in *A Theory of the Labor Movement* (1928). Perlman believed American workers possessed a "trade union mentality" or job consciousness and rejected social ownership and control of industry, an ideology he attributed to "social and economic conservatism, bred in the American Community." According to Perlman, attempts to infuse a more radical ideology into the labor movement reflected efforts by intellectuals to dominate unions and he anticipated that a mature labor movement in a democratic free enterprise system would reject both revolutionary changes and even significant social reform. This study contradicts the Perlman thesis and demonstrates that the class consciousness, militant unionism, and political action of Central Pennsylvania bituminous coal miners was not imposed from the outside by radical intellectuals but resulted from the nature of their work and their experience combating the 1920s open-shop drive (Perlman, 1928).

The class consciousness of the Nanty Glo and other Central Pennsylvania miners was forged out of conflict and a spirited contentiousness; class conflict with the region's coal corporations and steel and railroad barons; political conflict with agents of the coal companies and local merchants for control over the municipal government and police force; ideological conflict with the national leadership of the United Mine Workers of America over the direction of the union; and internal conflicts over ethnic and religious differences. Even when John Brophy, a longtime Nanty Glo resident, was president of UMWA District 2 (Central Pennsylvania) from 1917 until 1927, there was periodic conflict between Nanty Glo miners and the District office. During World War I, Nanty Glo Local 1386 protested the unwillingness or inability of both the District and UMWA international leadership to effectively challenge unpaid manual car-pushing forced on miners because of narrow coal seams in the region. These were some of the underlying conditions that led to the emergence of the class-conscious movement. Brophy and other District 2 officers provided an ideological framework, the leadership, and organization structure necessary to sustain a class-conscious movement. They were often joined by activists and organizers affiliated with socialist groups and the Workers (Communist) Party, groups that supported, but did not control the miners' movement (Singer, 1988a; 1988b; Singer, 1991).

This class-conscious working-class movement emerged among bituminous coal miners after World War I (1919–1928). Despite, or perhaps because of, intense anti-union campaigns in the 1920s and the Great Depression of the 1930s, they were among the most militant workers in the United States during World War II. Their class consciousness had roots in the traditional values and experiences of American bituminous coal miners. In the 1920s it was articulated as the "Miners' Program," which included organization of unorganized miners into a national union; creation of a labor political party; nationalization of the bituminous coal industry; and promotion of rank-and-file democracy in the UMWA. The program went beyond traditional American Federation of Labor "bread-and-butter" trade unionism as it drew from more radical socialist proposals. A labor party would defend the civil liberties of the working class and challenge domination of the country by what they viewed as business controlled political parties. A nationalized coal industry would be operated in the public interest while protecting the lives and livelihood of coal miners (Gutman, 1976; Goodrich, 1925).

The leadership of this class-conscious movement came from two groups. The first consisted of lifelong miners and union officials who turned toward militancy and leftist alternatives, convinced that none of the existing political options offered coal miners a chance for a better life. The second included communists and independent left-wing progressives from outside the mine workers' union who shared similar goals and provided philosophical direction, organizational skills, and financial assistance to the miners. Both groups viewed participation in the bituminous coal miners' struggle as a vehicle for affecting broader change in the American labor movement and the United States (Singer, 1991: 132–57).

Between 1922 and 1928, the leaders of this movement struggled to wrest control of the UMWA from John L. Lewis and a business-unionist faction committed to cooperation between labor, management, and government to maintain a stable and profitable industry while defending the position of the UMWA in unionized fields. This faction's power rested on the ability of the international office to negotiate a uniform labor contract encompassing the main bituminous coal producing fields, known as the Central Competitive Field (CCF). The business-unionist program included three basic points. First, the CCF agreement would serve as a national standard for industrial relations in the industry. Second, contracts would be enforced against both recalcitrant operators and insurgent miners. Finally, an effort would be made to commit the federal government to a plan to cartelize the industry and reduce the amount of coal produced as well as the number of miners. During the period Lewis and other union officials testified before federal investigating bodies and endorsed legislation that would have exempted the bituminous coal industry from antitrust regulations. Lewis also attempted to involve Secretary of Commerce Herbert Hoover in plans to encourage cooperation between bituminous coal operators' associations and the UMWA. District 2 Central Pennsylvania was considered an outlying district not party to the CCF agreement because of narrow coal seams, although the district's contracts with coal companies followed the CCF agreement (Laslett, 1996: 104–50).

By the 1920s, after a quarter century of internecine struggle between international officers and the union's powerful semi-autonomous districts, the former became dominant in the UMWA. During this struggle the international officers developed an effective machine to ensure control over the districts. They used appointed international organizers to circumvent hostile district officials, and exploited control over the union's newspaper, the *UMWA Journal*. They also created interim district offices staffed with officers loyal to the International faction in newly organized fields and bankrupt or besieged established districts.

Between 1908 and 1920, opposition to the international faction came from a diverse and fluctuating coalition committed to district autonomy and democratic unionism, which included greater rank-and-file participation in union decision-making. From the 1908 retirement of John Mitchell as union president through John L. Lewis' election over Robert Harlin for the union presidency in 1920, the coalition vied for control of the union's international machinery. Its leaders included local and district business unionists politically opposed to the international faction; trade union socialists, at least nominally committed to the broader program for the union; and rank-and-file militants who rejected the international's enforcement of contract provisions against the union's membership. This group believed the international office was undermining effective struggle against operators who were violating union contracts and was trying to preserve the CCF agreement at the expense of the outlying and unorganized fields. The ability of the International officials to secure CCF contracts during and after World War I, the increasingly national scope of the industry, and the growth of a militant rank-and-file opposition, broke up the early district autonomy-based coalition by the 1920s. The coalition's factions then either drifted into the international camp or joined the developing class-conscious movement (Singer, 1982: 3–4).

While it was successful in maintaining control over the UMWA machinery, the international faction was unable to counter the sustained opposition of the coal industry and American industrial capital during the 1920s. The ability of nonunion fields to provide a large percentage of the nation's coal needs and a coordinated and well financed open-shop drive in the union fields brought massive long-term underemployment and unemployment to the unionized areas. From a high of nearly 400,000 members in 1921, the union's membership in the bituminous coal industry declined to under 100,000 members in 1929, mostly concentrated in Illinois.

During the 1920s, the coal operators, with the support of American industrial and finance capital, sought to rationalize and mechanize bituminous coal production in a union-free industry. They used ethnic and racial tensions to undermine the miners' sense of group solidarity and challenged the miner's craft skills and work-related values, which were supported by traditional work patterns and active pit committees. The open-shop drive was spearheaded by the major producing groups in the bituminous coal fields and was supported by the leading forces of corporate and finance capital in the country, including U.S. Steel, the automobile industry, and the Mellon, Morgan, and Rockefeller empires (Laslett, 1996).

The open-shop drive had its most devastating effect on the rank-and-file miners. The operators concluded that the strength of the union rested on the skilled miner's control over production at the mine face. The miners' skill, in addition to traditional patterns of labor and community, contributed to the development within the miners of an ideological conception of themselves as independent artisans with the right to make work judgments, production decisions, and defend their standard of living through militant locals. During the open-shop drive operators used the weakening of the international union to mechanize production and make traditional skills obsolete, reorganize established work patterns, and systematically emasculate pit committees (Goodrich, 1925).

The international machine strengthened its grip on the union structure at the same time that union membership was declining and the miners' way of life was under siege. After 1922, the union was unable to conduct a nationwide strike, and miners in the CCF became more dependent on the negotiating ability of the international officers to secure a contract. After 1924, the opposition was unable to mount an effective challenge at machine-dominated union conventions. By 1926, the machine's control over union institutions was complete. The remnants of the rank-and-file movement organized the Save the Union Committee and supported District 2 President John Brophy in a campaign to unseat Lewis, but Brophy was defeated in a disputed election where tens of thousands of blatantly falsified ballots were cast for Lewis. Following the election, Lewis banned Brophy and his supporters from the UMWA as dual unionists. The Save the Union Committee worked to rebuild the rank-and-file movement and the union until 1928. At that time, the remaining active leadership of the committee had dwindled and now consisted mainly of Workers' (Communist) Party members. It ceased struggling within the skeletal remains of the Lewis controlled UMWA and unsuccessfully attempted to organize a new union in areas the UMWA abandoned. The decision to form a new union isolated the remnants of the movement from the main body of American labor. Generally, only blacklisted miners, or locals hopelessly engaged in strikes against operators not dependent on the production of the struck mines, joined the National Miners' Union. Ultimately, this decision meant the end of the miners' program in the UMWA and the bituminous coal industry (Laslett, 1996; Brophy, 1964).

The same industrial conditions that spurred rank-and-file militancy and promoted class-consciousness, overcapacity, underemployment, and an operator open-shop drive supported by the federal government, ultimately overwhelmed bituminous coalminers and virtually destroyed the UMWA, exposing the folly of the business unionist strategy of collaboration with hostile corporate management to rationalize coal production.

By 1930, UMWA membership had precipitously declined and Lewis had successfully expelled most of his remaining opponents from the union. Starting in 1933 a more militant Lewis, but one still committed to labor as a junior partner with industry and union leaders as managers of labor, helped launch American Federation of Labor organizing drives and the founding of the Congress of Industrial Organizations. At that point, many 1920s radicals became key organizers in the push for industrial unionism (Bernstein, 1971; Dubofsky & Van Tine, 1977: 155–279).

Deindustrialization in the United States and the continued shift from bituminous coal to other fossil fuels as sources of energy in the post–World War II era, led to a collapse of both the industry and the United Mine Workers union. Nanty Glo and other coal towns were devastated. Class consciousness lingered, but it was dissipated, especially across generations. The change in circumstance produced a change in political consciousness. By the first decades of the twenty-first century, Central Pennsylvania had become a bastion of political conservatism.

Class-Conscious Coal Miners is organized into five parts. In part 1, "Bituminous Coal Industry," chapters 1 through 4 look at the industry and conditions faced by bituminous coal miners. They lay the basis for understanding the development of a class-conscious miners' movement in the 1920s. Chapter 1 examines the early history of the UMWA, its organizational structure, and the tension between more radical union districts and an international office generally committed to a cooperative form of business unionism. This tension created space for local opposition movements to emerge in the union. Chapter 1 also introduces the concept of the "Miner's Freedom," the way the organization of work and artisanal traditions in the bituminous coal industry supported the development of working-class consciousness. A key source for understanding the ideas of the workers and communities examined in this chapter is the folk music of the bituminous coal miner.

Chapter 2 focuses on the irrationality of production in the bituminous coal industry, its impact on the UMWA and bituminous coal miners, and efforts by the international office to stabilize conditions in the industry through cooperation with bituminous coal companies. Chapter 3 discusses ethnic division in the coalfields and the ways coal companies manipulated their workforces in efforts to undermine worker solidarity. Chapter 4 introduces the importance of community in isolated coalfields to support worker struggles and the crucial roles played by women in building and sustaining community during intense labor conflict.

Part 2, "Rank-and-File Miners," chapters 5 through 7, examines the growing rank-and-file bituminous coal miners' movement in the 1920s that fought a two-front battle, challenging the business unionists in control of the UMWA international office and an anti-union open-shop drive by coal companies. Chapter 5 documents the rank-and-file rebellion in a number of the UMWA Districts that started with opposition to a World War I wage freeze and a no-strike pledge agreed to by the international office and included efforts to prevent the consolidation of power by John L. Lewis as the autocratic leader of the business unionists and president of the UMWA. Chapter 6 offers a closer look at the emerging opposition to Lewis centered in UMWA Central Pennsylvania District 2 and Pittsburgh area UMWA District 5. District 2 President John Brophy championed the "Miners' Program" as a way to stabilize the industry and protect the rights of workers. The program included support for strikes in nonunion coalfields to force operators to sign fair contracts. In District 5, radical miners allied with communist organizers tried to build a broad opposition movement to challenge Lewis and business unionist control over the UMWA international office. Chapter 7 details how rank-and-file bituminous coal miners fought against an open shop drive initiated by major corporations and supported at the highest levels of the federal government. This battle included fights on the floor of the UMWA annual conventions where representatives of rank-and-file miners tried, unsuccessfully, to change the direction of the union and make it less accommodating to mine operators.

Part 3, "Nanty Glo," chapters 8 and 9, looks at the battle to sustain the UMWA in one Central Pennsylvania coal mining community, Nanty Glo, the home base of John Brophy in UMWA District 2. Chapter 8 focuses on the history and demographics of Nanty Glo. Chapter 9, based on interviews with retired miners and their family members, details the struggle by Nanty Glo miners to defeat the open-shop drive, including combating

Ku Klux Klan activity that was supported by coal operators to undermine local union organization.

Part 4, "Save the Union," chapters 10 and 11, examines the struggle by opposition forces to gain control over the UMWA international office. Chapter 10 examines the 1926 UMWA Presidential campaign where John Brophy, running on the Miners' Program with support from left-wing groups inside and outside the union and the labor movement, challenged John L. Lewis. Lewis was declared reelected and retained control over the union in a highly questionable vote outcome. Chapter 11 describes the Save the Union Committee led by Brophy and miners aligned with the Workers (Communist) Party following the disputed election. The campaign faltered and Brophy and his closest supporters withdrew, unwilling to participate in what they saw as dual unionism.

In part 5, "Revival and Collapse," chapters 12 and 13 examine the impact of the Great Depression, World War II, the postwar collapse of the bituminous coal industry, and the steep contraction in UMWA membership, on the class consciousness of bituminous coal miners. Chapter 12 examines the labor resurgence, as John L. Lewis takes advantage of the political climate during the New Deal to rebuild the UMWA and found the Congress of Industrial Organizations (CIO), and looks at tension between the leadership of the UMWA and the federal government and decisions by miners to go on strike in violation of federal policy and the international office's no-strike pledge. Chapter 13 analyzes the impact of the postwar collapse of the bituminous coal industry on Central Pennsylvania mining communities, the loss of working-class class consciousness, and the growing conservatism of voters in the area as work and the miners' union no longer shaped their political views.

Part 1

Bituminous Coal Industry

Chapter 1

Ideological and Structural Conflict in the United Mine Workers of America

History and Structure of the UMWA

The UMWA is an international union because it has locals and districts in both the United States and Canada. The early history of the United Mine Workers of America (UMWA), its organizational structure, and tension between union districts and the international office created space for opposition movements to emerge in the coalfields. The bituminous coal miner's traditional conception of himself as a free artisan, what miners called the "Miner's Freedom," provided the ideological and social underpinning for opposition groups within the United Mine Workers of America and was a source of conflict between rank-and-file miners and the business-unionist policies of an international union machine committed to enforcing industrial discipline and developing labor-management cooperation. The traditional values of the rank-and-file miner also laid the foundation for an ideological challenge to management's right to reorganize and mechanize production and strengthened local resistance to the direction of the union's international leadership. This notion of a "Miner's Freedom" was a key component of the bituminous coal miner's working-class consciousness (Goodrich, 1925; Gutman, 1976; Montgomery, 1979; Braverman, 1974).

Conflict was built into the structure of the UMWA, contributing to the transformation of rank-and-file unrest into a class-conscious movement with a program for reorganizing the bituminous coal industry. In May

1921, Adolph Germer, a leading American Socialist and a former UMWA district official, wrote to UMWA President John L. Lewis, that the union was divided into three hostile camps. The factions were rooted in the division of union responsibilities between district offices and an international office and the failure of the international union to secure a uniform national contract and organize miners in nonunion southern and western coalfields. The factions included a business-unionist international group, headed by Lewis and imbedded in the union's international machinery; a broad district-based coalition of the major opposition groups in the union, including socialists, demanding district autonomy as a means of combating the centralization of power by the international faction; and a small group of independent radicals who were perceived as threatening the stability of the union by attacking the sanctity of the contract and organizational discipline. These were indigenous radicals who migrated into the UMWA from earlier more militant groups, including the Knights of Labor and the Industrial Workers of the World. During the 1920s the latter group emerged as the principle ideological and political counterweight to business unionism in the UMWA, as it rallied rank-and-file opposition to the policies of John L. Lewis (Everling, 1976: 149).

The international office of the UMWA pioneered in industry-wide bargaining. It supported cooperation between labor, management, and government for maintaining profitable operation of the bituminous coal industry by restricting productive capacity. A business-unionist faction developed within the international office committed to a narrow concept of the union as the bargaining agent for membership. In their view, union officials were industrial managers working with corporate executives to promote efficiency and prosperity. The contract, not a militant trade union, protected the worker. Additionally, adherence to the contract established the responsibility of the union and ensured the stability of the industry. Active rank-and-file movements and the expansion of membership in nonunionized western and southern fields, threatened the international faction's control of the union. Because of this, the international faction worked to divide its opponents, suppressed union democracy by rigging elections, and undercut the traditional concept of a "Miner's Freedom" (Lewis, 1925; Bernstein, 1966; Calhoun, 1928).

The base of power of the international faction was the Central Competitive Field (CCF) and an increasingly national market for coal. The CCF was a joint bargaining unit incorporating the industry's major unionized fields in Illinois, Indiana, Ohio, and Western Pennsylvania. CCF contracts set the standard for the entire industry and securing the contract cemented the authority of the international business-unionist faction. However, because this faction was so closely wed to the CCF, stiff operator resistance and poor contracts placed the more powerful districts in a position to challenge the centralization of power in the international office.

The strength of the district-based coalition rested on the continuing role of district offices in contract negotiations, the responsibility of the districts for administering the broad range of services generally identified with a trade union, and close ties between the district-based coalition and socialists in the UMWA and the broader trade union movement.

In many of the outlying fields the basic contract negotiations were on the district level. In these areas marketing often resisted national trends and bituminous coal production remained primarily for local or regional needs. In addition, the negotiation of a standard national contract in areas producing for the national market was hindered by the wide range of mining conditions, the different widths of coal seams, and diversity in coal volatility, chemical composition, and hardness. Each district was required to maintain a bargaining unit to negotiate supplemental agreements covering specific local conditions (Wickersham, 1951: 94).

When the UMWA was founded in January 1890, from the merger of the National Trades Assembly #135 of the Knights of Labor and the National Progressive Union affiliated with the American Federation of Labor, it was an amalgam of semiautonomous districts. Neither of the predecessor unions had succeeded in establishing a truly national body. It was not until a successful strike in 1897 secured a joint conference with the bituminous coal operators that the foundation was laid for the formation of the Central Competitive Field and a stronger national organization (Everling, 1976; Wickersham, 1951; Laslett, 1996: 29–50).

At its inception, the strength of the UMWA rested on the strength of the individual districts. Even as the international office assumed an increasingly important role in contract negotiations, the districts continued to distribute strike relief, police contract provisions, organize nonunion miners within their jurisdiction, lobby for state regulatory legislation, provide welfare benefits, offer legal services, run educational programs, and publish newspapers. Supporters of the district-based coalition, particularly in the more powerful districts like District 12 (Illinois), believed the districts were capable of operating independently without interference from centralized authority in the international office. This intensified the demand for district autonomy and opposition to the international faction (Wickersham, 1951: 35–38; Everling, 1976: 37).

From the founding of the UMWA in 1890 until the 1920s the main conflicts within the union emerged as conflicts between a coalition of districts and the international office. Yet despite the ability of the district coalition to successfully challenge the international office, developments within the industry prevented it from redirecting the union. These developments included the increasing importance of coal production for a national market, and integration of the industry through the formation of bituminous operator associations, corporate conglomerates, regional transportation networks, and the CCF national contractual standard. Institutional ties between business, government, and labor officials during World War I also reinforced the centralization of authority in the international office of the union. Even when candidates endorsed by the district-based coalition were elected to national office, the conditions of the industry coupled with the seductions of political office, drew officials pledged to district autonomy into the international group (Everling, 1976: 78–91).

In his 1921 letter to John L. Lewis, Adolph Germer predicted that the international faction and the district-based coalition would remain the principle protagonists within the UMWA during the next decade. Germer failed, however, to examine internal inconsistencies that contributed to the weakening of the district group. Germer identified the "Big Four"—Frank Farrington and John Walker of Illinois, Alexander Howat of Kansas, and Robert Harlin of Washington—as the force behind the district group. However, while the "Big Four" were united in opposition to the international faction and John L. Lewis, they held radically different concepts of the role of the union (Everling, 1976: 149–51).

Frank Farrington, president of UMWA District 12 (Illinois), was a business unionist who shared the ideas of the international faction, but opposed Lewis because of his own political ambition. Walker and Harlin identified as socialists and endorsed a UMWA platform calling for a campaign to organize unorganized miners, the formation of a labor party to advance the interests of the working class, and a general call for government intervention in the bituminous coal industry and possible nationalization of the mines. However, they were willing to make political deals with the business unionists in order to gain union office. Walker, a former president of the Illinois district, and president of the Illinois State Federation of Labor, accepted the international faction's concept of the union's role in managing workers and he helped stifle rank-and-file militancy during World War I (Everling, 1976: 75–78; Weinberg, 2005: 91).

Howat, as president of UMWA District 14 (Kansas), defined his job as organizing workers into militant action. He rejected the sanctity of the contract, which he viewed as restricting the worker while allowing business a free hand. Howat also endorsed struggles for local union democracy and wildcat strikes in other districts, undercutting the position of his fellow coalitionists (Gagliardo, 1941).

Starting in 1919, increasing rank-and-file militancy broke up the district-based coalition. After World War I, rank-and-file strike sentiment, pent up by a wartime no-strike pledge, exploded in a series of wildcat strikes, and then a national strike in violation of a federal injunction that neither the districts nor the national offices could control. As an example of the tension within the coalition, Farrington appealed to Lewis for the authority to suspend membership rights of wildcat strikers, while Howat supported the Illinois wildcatters and led strikes in violation of the contract in Kansas (Gagliardo, 1941: 3–20; Everling, 1976: 133).

In 1921, bituminous coal operators launched an open-shop drive in West Virginia that radically altered the situation in the industry. The campaign aimed at driving the UMWA out of the coalfields by undermining the miner's control of the work process. In a 1924 report on an interview with the superintendent of the Utah Fuel Company, *Black Diamond*, an industry periodical, presented the point of view behind the mushrooming anti-union sentiment among operators. The goal of the operator was to gain absolute control over production by destroying the tradition of the independent free artisan, which was perceived of as the backbone of the union. According to *Black Diamond*, the task of the open-shop drive was to destroy the "psychological base" of the UMWA, which was basically a craft union built on the skill of the miner. The open-shop drive drove a final wedge into the district-based coalition as it confronted unionists with either continuing to support the international office's program of developing support for labor-management-government cooperation, or joining with "independent radicals" in a campaign to reorganize the industry by increasing the workers' role in production (Olds, February 2, 1924: 3).

During the 1920s, the open-shop drive spread throughout the entire bituminous coal industry. Operators violated UMWA contracts or refused to negotiate with the union when old contracts expired. They moved to break union locals and reorganize and mechanize bituminous coal production. When the UMWA international office retreated in the outlying fields and tried to hold the line in the CCF, many rank-and-file miners turned to the developing working-class conscious miners' movement for leadership. This movement was led by a new generation of independent radicals, communists, and some district officials committed to building on the traditions of the Miner's Freedom and challenging both the business unionists and the operators with a new program and vision for the industry.

Ideological Roots of Class Consciousness

The roots of the ideology of the rank-and-file American coal miner were in the coalfields of England and Wales. The expansion of the American bituminous coal industry after the Civil War created a demand for skilled coal miners that lured thousands of miners across the Atlantic. These British Isle miners brought with them, as part of their values and ideology, a tradition of trade union activism with a record of achievement dating back to the 1840s and the Chartist movement. Their experience included involvement in an active union movement with both local and national organizations, involvement in the beginnings of the British Socialist movement, and a strong sense of a miners' community. The nature of coalmining meant that other European bituminous coalminers migrating to the United States also brought with them experience with union activism and a level of class consciousness (Galloway, 1898; Cole and Filson, 1967: 464–68, 492, 552; Laslett, 1970: 19; Rosen, 1943: 441; Weitz, 1989).

In the United States these immigrant miners found a rapidly expanding coal industry which doubled output and employment each decade from 1870 to 1910, and a fledgling coal unionism operating without many of the traditional legal restrictions imposed on unions in England. In this setting the work values and trade union ideology of British Isle miners helped develop a class-conscious working-class ideology. Crucial in the development of this ideology was conflict between the miner and the operator over the organization of coal production, and the miner's fight to retain his industrial independence. In this fight, especially after 1900, the miner often found himself fighting against attempts by the UMWA international office to limit independence and maintain work discipline. The relatively early introduction of mechanized coal mining in the United States challenged the miner's conception of his role in production. The early hand-picked coal miner considered himself a skilled craftsman. His assistant or loader was often a son or other relative whom he was teaching the craft. Apprenticeship included learning the customs of the trade as well as the skills involved (Shurick, 1924: 5, 42–49; Evans, 1918; Dix, 1977: xiii; Rosen, 1943: 161).

The British miner's ability to pass along his traditions to new generations of coal miners was aided by the uneven development of factory-style coal production in the United States. Mechanization was spread out over half of a century, from 1880 through 1930. In a number of important coalfields bituminous coal mining remained essentially a cottage industry into the 1920s. This allowed the miner's traditions and values to be nourished, even while they were under attack. In traditional mining, the miner worked in teams in rooms spread out over miles of underground passages, largely without effective supervision. An 1890 survey of mine occupations conducted by the Pennsylvania Department of Internal Affairs in Allegheny County tabulated one foreman for every 114 miners. Because of the difficulties of supervision, mining continued to be organized around principles of piecework, and the pace of work was left to the determination of the individual miner. Even when cutting machines began to replace hand-picked mining, the first machine undercutter was introduced in Hocking Valley, Ohio, in 1876, production imitated old work patterns. The need to load coal by hand placed a break on management's ability to reorganize production underground. Mechanization was further complicated because conditions underground varied greatly from one coal seam to the next and from one mine to the next. Machines were not as adaptable as the skilled bituminous coal miner (Dix, 1977: 14–21).

The significance of the miners' control of the workplace was understood by the coal companies. A study by the Illinois Bureau of Labor in 1888 reported that operators were attempting to organize mines into underground factories. Their strategy was to use machines to subdivide the job of the miner and make the operator less dependent on the skill of his work force. According to the study, machine mining "relieves him (the operator) for the most part of skilled labor and of all the restraints which that implies. It opens him to the whole labor market from which to recruit his work force." For the operators, mechanization would make it possible to sweepingly alter work procedures, hire unskilled workers, and pay a lower wage scale (Dix, 1977: 19).

While coal-mining machines increased profits where they were easily adaptable to mining conditions, aggregate levels of productivity for machine mining measured in tons per man-day were not appreciably better than hand-picked mines. From 1901 to 1917, hand-picked mining was more productive in thirteen out of seventeen years, even though machines tended to be introduced in mines with the most easily accessible coal. The advantage of machine mining in its early years lay less in its productivity and more in its ability to permit operators to hire less skilled and more pliant nonunion workers. Machine tenders and loaders replaced skilled miners. The introduction of machines in a mine gave the company an opportunity to put workers on notice; new machines set standards for production and let workers know that the company was prepared to do without its experienced miners in the event of labor unrest (Dix, 1977: 28).

Ultimately, the nature of coal production, the difficulties of supervision, and particularly, the wide range of mine conditions hampered factory-style reorganization of the mines. Because mechanization was spread out over such a long period of time, the miner, instead of experiencing the reorganization of production as a hopeless situation that offered the displaced craftsman little alternative, was able to organize based on work traditions and customs in a struggle to sustain his concept of life and community. The bituminous coal miners were able to organize an industrially advanced industrial union, which they hoped would preserve an essentially preindustrial artisanal organization of work. Their union would give them the ability to keep the Miner's Freedom alive and teach it to new groups of miners.

The artisanal tradition of the miner contributed to the strength and the organization of the early UMWA. Many of the traditions of the industry enforced by local unions had their origins in preindustrial patterns of work. Once a miner had established a place in the mine as his own, the place was his as long as his tools remained there, even if he did not appear for work over an extended period of time. The miner established his own pace of work and was often able to end his day when he decided he had mined sufficient tonnage. British Isle miners brought with them a tradition of piecework output based on their needs rather than market place demands. Workers expected a fair day's pay for a day's work. They were unlikely to increase their weekly output even when they were able to mine their accustomed volume of coal in a shorter workweek. A West Virginia miner, heir to both the southern agrarian tradition and the artisanal tradition of the coal miner succinctly summarized the miner's attitude toward attempts by industry to reorganize traditional patterns of work. When asked why he had given up a more highly paid factory job to return to the mines as a relatively unskilled loader, he replied that in the mine he set his own pace, was visited only once a day by a foreman, and in the mine "they [supervisors] don't *bother* you none" (Goodrich, 1925: 16, 41–43, 66–68, 107–8).

Underground hand-picked bituminous coal miners were paid by the ton of coal loaded and weighed at the mine's above ground tipple. This payment system added to the miner's sense of himself as an independent artisan. The day rate was for laborers working both underground and above-ground. The shift away from hand-picked mining to machine cutting and loading meant a shift to greater corporate control over work and shifting more underground miners from the tonnage rate to the day rate. That shift made coal mining more like factory work and was experienced as an attack on the Miner's Freedom.

Tonnage rates were more difficult for the UMWA to negotiate than day rates because every region and every mine had different underground conditions. That contributed to the importance of union locals and districts in negotiating wages. In some ways, the $7.50 day rate, equivalent to about $115 today, established in the Central Competitive Field starting in 1922 was at least partly symbolic as a wage standard because most underground miners were still being paid according to tonnage rates. When underground coal miners were covered by the day rate, it usually meant the mine had shifted to mechanized production.

UMWA locals played the major role in the miners' fight to sustain this sense of freedom. In 1904, for example, the UMWA District 2 (Central Pennsylvania) convention debated a contractual clause proposed by the operators and accepted by the district's leadership. Its purpose was to impose greater factory discipline in the mines; it called on the miner to remain at the mine face a full eight hours per shift. The delegates vigorously opposed this clause as a violation of work customs and their traditional right to stop work when they were tired and had earned enough. The rank-and-file miners succeeded in having the clause stricken from the contract. Union local pit or bank committees fought vigorously to prevent operators from reassigning miners to new tasks arbitrarily. Workers whose jobs were threatened were defended no matter what the infraction. In one case, a pit committee defended a locally renowned loafer, arguing that the contract did not dictate how hard a man must work (Goodrich, 1925: 16, 66–70).

The miner's ability to make decisions about how to utilize his time and efforts most efficiently also contributed to his sense of freedom on the job. In 1920, 20 percent of the coal mined in the United States was still hand-picked, and even in machine-cut mines, decisions about when to drill blasting holes and how heavy the charge should be were still left to the judgment of the individual miner. A time study conducted by the United States Coal and Coke Company at a West Virginia mine using machine undercutters in 1911 and 1912 illustrates the decision-making component of the miner's work. In the study, only 50–65 percent of a miner's actual work efforts were geared to loading coal cars for shipment. Other tasks included picking down loose coal, cleaning coal by separating out rock, drilling blasting holes, setting charges, laying tracks for coal cars, timbering roofs for support, and clearing out the workplace. Most decisions about what to do and when to do it were left up to the individual miner. In hand-picked mines, an even greater range of options was left to the judgment of the individual miner (Goodrich, 1925: 28).

For industrialists, the miner's perception of himself as a free artisan was a major source of consternation. In December 1921, *Industrial Magazine* warned factory managers to avoid hiring former miners. In the mines "the possibility of constant supervision or of surprise visits does not exist. The coal miner is accordingly trained to do as he pleases. . . . Transport such a man into a factory where production is speeded and no imagination is required to picture what will happen . . . he chafed under the necessary restrictions of employment . . . resents all suggestions as to his working methods, resents all efforts to compel continuous application, and assumes in general a hostile attitude to all supervision." Examining this phenomenon from a different perspective, John Brophy, the former president of UMWA District 2, who served as the CIO Director of Organization during the initial organizing drives in the mass production industries, viewed the exodus of union miners into the war preparation factories during World War I as the foundation for developing unions in the mass production industries (Goodrich, 1925: 17–18; Albertson, 1955: 8).

Other factors in the miner's experience helped to reinforce his self-image as a free artisan. The British miner, as noted above, brought with him a tradition of political activism, trade unionism, and socialist ideas. In an oral history conducted as part of the Columbia University Oral History Project, John Brophy argued that much of the democratic tradition of the UMWA on the local level is attributable to the British experience, which he believed gave the miner a basic familiarity with formal organizational structure and parliamentary procedure. Oral traditions, community life, and religion all played roles in creating a sense of class identity and building the consciousness of the miner. The boney pile orator, so named because the underground slate waste heaps were his speaker's platform, was a miners' institution. While the men rested, waited for coal cars, or ate, far from the ears and eyes of supervision, the boney pile orator explained issues, recounted stories, detailed traditions, initiated new miners, and organized all miners within hearing (Laslett, 1970: 194; Albertson, 1955: 185; Goodrich, 1925: 55–56).

The isolation of mine communities contributed to the miner's sense of himself as a class apart. All village life was organized around the mine.

Population expanded and contracted with the affairs of the mine. Miners, passing skills from father to son, formed a virtual hereditary occupational caste. High rates of diseases of the respiratory system, causing early aging, chronic sickness, and death in the coal fields, contributed to a glum solidarity in the mining community. The constant risks of accident, and the fear of the mine whistle signaling disaster, held mine communities together (Rosen, 1943: 214).

Preindustrial religious customs often contributed to a sense of solidarity and helped prepare new Eastern and Southern European immigrants to accept the miner's idea of unionism. In 1910 Slavic miners in District 5 (Western Pennsylvania) crucified a mine boss accused of spying on the men and reporting them for dismissal. In 1910 and 1911, striking Italian and Slavic miners in the district paraded through town carrying church symbols reminiscent of peasant protests. At least in some cases, rather than religious tradition undercutting unionism, they inspired protest in the name of traditional rights (Gutman, 1976: 65–66).

Musical Legacy

The bituminous coal miners have a long legacy of folk music that illustrates both continuity and change in their values. The ballad "Two-Cents Coal" was traced by UMWA folklorist George Korson to 1878. It shows the miners' class identification and a traditional sense of justice as a coal operator is vanquished by an act of God. The ballad retells the history of the harsh winter of 1876, when coal operators cut the prevailing piece rate to two cents a bushel, or approximately fifty cents per ton. Miners and their families tottered on the brink of starvation. Vengeance came when an ice flow on the Monongahela River broke, the mine tipple was destroyed, and the two-cents coal sank into the river. "Two-Cents Coal" celebrates the values of the workingman and contrasts them with the tyrannical and greedy boss. It is an early American miners' song and it depends on God to avenge the miner who is not yet organized to defend himself. The song concludes as follows:

> It's to conclude and finish,
> Let us help our fellow man,
> And if our brother's in distress
> Assist him if you can,

To keep the wolf off from his door,
And shelter him from the cold,
That he never again shall commit the crime
Of diggin' two-cent coal. (Korson, 1943: 402)

The oral tradition of the miner, particularly the Welsh tradition of the minstrel and the community songfest, often combined religious practices and class protest. Through songs, miners, often barely literate in English could share ideas and experiences. The role of religious music in the struggles of mining communities is illustrated by the song "Oh Stranger Listen." It was written and performed by a choral group of miners, and their wives and children, during a District 2 (Central Pennsylvania) battle against a company open-shop drive in the 1920s. It was performed at labor tent meetings, modeled on the church chautauqua, and organized to lift the spirit of strikers and educate them on issues. These meetings transcended sectarian religious and cultural boundaries. English- and foreign-language speakers and entertainers shared the platform and helped to involve Slavic and Italian miners in the program. The song itself is a simple prayer to strangers not to come to scab, and new arrivals are invited to join the strike.

Oh stranger, why did you come here
To take our homes and bread away;
Oh won't you leave your work today
And join us now we pray.
Won't you join us, won't you join us,
In fighting for our rights today,
We're going to win, you know we will,
So join us now we pray. (*Illinois Miner*, October 31, 1925)

The miners' folk songs also document changing attitudes and militancy. In "The Miner's Lifeguard," the miner no longer is dependent on God for his protection, though the boss is still viewed as tyrannical and greedy. In this song, traced by Korson to West Virginia, circa 1900, "God provides for every nation when in union they combine"; class organization implements God's will. Originally the tune was Welsh, and it was adapted in this country from a hymn, "Life Is Like a Mountain Railway." In the song, the miner's life is compared to a sailor's, bounced around on the waves of life. He is chastised for believing that he can change his situation by himself, or for expecting it to change by itself. He is called to action and union. The original hymn asks God to guide the pilgrim. "Miner's Lifeguard" charges the miner to organize.

> In conclusion, bear in memory,
> Keep the password in your mind;
> God provides for every nation,
> When in union they combine.
> Stand like men and linked together,
> Victory for you will prevail,
> Keep your hand upon the dollar
> And your eyes upon the scales. (Korson, 1943: 413)

Internal Conflict and Corporate Integration

With the merger of the Knights of Labor National Trade Assembly #135 and the National Progressive Union (AFL) in 1890, a national coal miners union was superimposed on local, district, and regional organizations. During the decade of the 1890s, responsibility for enforcing operator compliance with contracts and the organization of new members remained in the hands of the locals and districts. This pattern of district autonomy within a national structure remained a source of conflict between 1890 and 1930, as district officials battled the international office for authority in the union. Initially the new national union experienced some organizing success as its membership grew to 53,000 coal miners in 1892. However, the UMWA suffered badly in the national depression, starting in 1893. It was not until a successful strike in 1897 that the union forced a joint operator-union conference that established a uniform collective bargaining unit for Illinois, Indiana, Ohio, and Western Pennsylvania. This unit, the Central Competitive Field served as a national contractual standard through 1928, and was the main weapon of the international officers in their struggles for dominance over the district autonomy forces (Laslett, 1996; Coleman, 1943: 54–74).

Prior to the formation of the CCF, the organization of the districts was largely left to the initiative of district leaders, and in areas not included in the 1898 contract, union organizing continued to remain largely a local responsibility. District 2 (Central Pennsylvania) bordered the main productive region, but narrow seams made the extraction of its coal more costly so it was not included in the CCF agreement. Following the collapse of the district union in a strike in 1894, District 2 was not reorganized until 1899, when William P. Wilson, a leader of the old Knights of Labor National Assembly, called a district-wide organizing convention. The district organization remained weak, and in 1906 a lost strike led to the widespread blacklisting of union members (Albertson, 1955: 55–60).

Regional autonomy, while strenuously defended by district offices, offered the rank-and-file bituminous coal miner at best a mixed "blessing," especially in those districts not covered by the CCF agreement. Outlying districts received a measure of independence in their dealings with local and state regulations, regional mine conditions, and coal markets. However, independence also meant the lack of significant support from the international union on matters considered of urgent local importance. In District 2 miners vehemently opposed unpaid car-pushing, a practice requiring bituminous coal miners to physically push coal cars out of the mine rooms. In narrow seams, electric transport systems could not be run up to the mine face without removing tons of slate and raising the costs of production. Because District 2 coal tended to supply eastern shipping and railroad markets and was not in direct competition with the Great Lakes industrial belt served by the CCF, the issue received little attention from the international union. Operators in the outlying fields often preferred to remain outside the national accord because it was more difficult for union locals to enforce contract provisions. In December 1916, District 2 miners elected a slate of officers committed to eliminating car-pushing. The officials succeeded in forcing operators to sign a supplemental pact promising to end the practice within a reasonable length of time. However, the operators continued to stall, and the district never had the strength to force the issue (Brophy, 1964: 45, 104; UMWA MA District 2 File; District 2 Papers, 1917: Box 2).

At times the semblance of autonomy virtually trapped districts into enforcing contracts against their membership, while they remained helpless to insist that operators abide by the agreements. At the same time that the operators in District 2 were evading the supplemental pact settlement on car-pushing, district officials were forced to clamp down on wildcat strikers to maintain the integrity of the union. District officials distributed a flyer in August 1917, charging that "strikes of this character strike directly at the foundation of our organization, the Trades Agreement." Unless wildcat strikes were abandoned, "the force of the union, the collective power of the workers," would be "dissipated and wasted through such tactics" (District 2 Papers, 1917: Box 2).

While autonomy permitted the growth of localized socialist and radical movements throughout the union, local struggles were often sabotaged by an international office determined to prevent the creation of powerful opposition centers. In Kansas, militant leaders of District 14 were openly undercut by the international union in the district's battle against the state of Kansas's efforts to impose compulsory arbitration in all labor-management disputes (Gagliardo, 1941:135–40; Wickersham, 1951: 68–71).

The international office was generally content to see weak district organizations dependent on the power of the international union. A powerful district like District 12 (Illinois), located in close proximity to its markets, and with nearly 100 percent of the miners in its jurisdiction organized, was frequently in a position to negotiate a better wage agreement than the CCF. Ambitious Illinois leaders like district presidents John Walker and Frank Farrington used their position to challenge incumbent international officers and maneuvered for national office. In 1909 Walker, and in 1922 Farrington, pulled the district out of the CCF. In 1922, Farrington was accused of fomenting wildcat strikes in Illinois to maintain pressure on him to negotiate a better contract than the CCF (Wickersham, 1951: 35–38; Everling, 1976: 37).

Decentralized administration had the potential to splinter districts. In the same fashion that powerful districts challenged the authority of the international, powerful subdistricts challenged the district offices. In 1907, the Belleville subdistrict in Illinois had 20,000 members, 25 percent of District 12's membership. The Belleville miners were largely English-speaking with roots in the British Isles and a strong socialist tradition. Their strategic position as the largest subdistrict of the union's largest district gave socialists a powerful platform in the union. Other subdistricts and locals, particularly Springfield in Illinois and Charlesroi in District 5 (Western Pennsylvania) became hotbeds of rank-and-file militancy that challenged conservative district machines during and after World War I. From the point of view of the business unionists in the international office, conflict between rank-and-file dissidents and the district offices played two crucial roles. First, the District acted as a buffer protecting the international union from rank-and-file insurgency. Second, internal district battles undercut potential rivals to the international faction. Bituminous coal miners were caught in the political interplay of district and international groups (Laslett, 1970: 214; Weinberg, 2005: 171, 174).

The 1900–1920 period witnessed the gradual but steady movement toward domination of the union by its international office. A number of factors, both internal and outside the union, supported the growth in power of the international office, the business-unionist machine that controlled it, and the business-unionist ideology that dominated it. One factor supporting the growth of the international office was the relatively easy access to the bituminous coal industry. Bituminous coal was plentiful and coal seams ran unpredictably under vast acreages. Initial capital costs were lower than industries requiring plant construction. As a national transportation network made the marketing of bituminous coal to distant cities more feasible, it was increasingly necessary for miners and operators to find some way to regularize production. Because of this, the UMWA international office ended up playing a pioneering role in industry-wide bargaining and cooperation between labor and management standardizing wages and work rules, and over the introduction of new technology. This role supported the development of the business-unionist ideology of the international office (Hinrichs, 1923: 9–21, 246).

As early as 1885, organized bituminous coal miners had recognized the significance of the national market for coal and the need for a national union to serve the miner. The preamble to the constitution of the National Federation of Miners, a precursor of the UMWA, stated, "Local, district, and state organizations have done much towards ameliorating the condition of our craft in the past, but today neither district nor state unions can regulate the markets to which their coal is shipped. . . . In a federation of lodges and branches of miners' unions lies our only hope. Single-handed we can do nothing, but federated there is no power of wrong that we may not openly defy" (Baratz, 1955: 76). The tendency was for operators to maintain unprofitable production during depressed periods or forfeit routes and markets to competitors. For the operators, the most effective way of continuing to produce was to cut expenses by undercutting wage scales. The result was harsh interregional competition, overproduction of coal, and a downward wage spiral. Unionized miners in organized districts were at the mercy of wage rates in the nonunion fields. In a declining coal market, the wage patterns for nonunion fields set the pattern for the industry. Districts were virtually powerless to combat this, and union locals found themselves in direct competition with neighboring mines operating non-union. In 1921, miners in the unionized Fairmont, West Virginia field were forced to accept a relatively low union wage rate of 43.2¢ per ton because the nearby Whitmore Mine #3 operated nonunion and paid its miners 30¢ per ton. During the 1920s open-shop drive, the West Virginia fields were among the first where the UMWA was broken (Hinrichs, 1923: 9–21, 246).

The formation of the CCF supported the international office's belief that the UMWA had to play an organizational role in an industry marked by highly competitive, small and scattered operators. However, soon after the organization of the CCF in 1898, the union was supplanted as the major force for stabilization of the industry by a growing movement among coal producers and consumers to consolidate small operations into larger units. Included in this movement was the proliferation of holding companies controlling the production of coal from a large number of mines; the domination of smaller concerns by distributors who they depended on to market their coal; and railroads, who as shippers and coal consumers, could dictate terms to the companies on their routes. Captive mines, owned or managed by railroads, power utilities, and the steel industry, accounted for roughly seventy-five million tons of bituminous coal annually between 1910 and 1920. By the 1930s, captive mines, controlled as much as one-third of the nation's annual bituminous coal production, and an even greater amount of tonnage was committed in long-term contracts. The growing coordination of production increased the role of the UMWA international office in contract negotiations, while undermining the union's role as a force for stabilizing the industry (Baratz, 1955: 88–89; Parker, 1940: 6–9; Christenson, 1962: 43–46, 81; Putney, 1935; *Yale Law Journal*, 1935).

The federal Interstate Commerce Commission (ICC) also played an important, though unexpected, role in the tendency toward the centralization of union authority in the international office. ICC's actions designed to stimulate competition in the industry enhanced the position of the groups in the UMWA demanding increased power for the international office. Discriminatory shipping rates that favored long-distance shippers from the southern fields meant that unionized mines closer to industrial markets subsidized production in the nonunion fields. These trends were sped up during World War I, when the War Industries Board routed Pennsylvania coal eastward, and southern coal into the traditional Pennsylvania Great Lakes markets. International union officials, in response to discriminatory shipping rates, placed an even greater emphasis on the Central Competitive Field as a national contractual standard and increased the lobbying role of the international office in an attempt to influence federal policies (King, 1924: 155–64; Sharfman, 1937; Fritz & Venstra, 1935).

Because the conflict between the international office and district organizations placed them in an adversary relationship, developments that supported the growth of the International office, tended to undercut the district structure. Even local democratic movements aimed at district bureaucracies tended to strengthen the hold of the international officers on the union. Because periods of economic prosperity in the industry stimulated the leadership of powerful districts to challenge central authority, the relative position of the international office improved during periods of economic decline. At these times, when the union was besieged by hostile government and management actions, the stabilizing role of the international office in the industry, and its lobbying and collective bargaining functions, became more crucial.

Business Unionism

Crucial to the emergence of the UMWA international office bureaucracy as the power center of the union was the development of its business-unionist ideology. This ideology rested on three principle tenets. Business unionists viewed union leadership as a distinct managerial stratum, separate and independent from the union's membership. They placed the highest priority on maintaining the Central Competitive Field bituminous coal contract as a basis for establishing the responsibility of the union and laying the framework for labor-management cooperation. They substituted centralized administration by professional union officials for union democracy and rank-and-file participation in union office.

The founders of the United Mine Workers union expressly argued for the fraternity of miners and union officials. When John Mitchell was sworn in as union president in 1898, he pledged to the miners, "When I have finished my term of office I shall return to Illinois and take my pick among you." However, during Mitchell's tenure as UMWA president this idea changed. Union officials began to conceive of themselves as part of an independent stratum of managers, removed from the mines and the membership. John Mitchell never returned to work in the mines, and when he retired as UMWA president in 1908, he sought and received a sinecure from the National Civic Federation as an expert on labor relations (Van Tine, 1973: 44; Laslett, 1996: 107).

Gradually the idea evolved that the union officialdom was a breed apart from the rank-and-file miner. By 1908 the *UMWA Journal* was advising the miners that the union's leadership consisted of "men who are making a study of organized labor and know how to advise the lay member." In 1917 the *UMWA Journal* explained how union officials were "trained in the school of experience" to defend the worker's point of view in industrial conflicts "convincingly" and "with national, yes, international scope." No longer simply miners up from the ranks, union office was a career, and the *UMWA*

Journal tried to convince the membership that its leadership was a special group capable of matching wits with the best brains that management could hire (Van Tine, 1973: 53; *UMWA Journal*, June 4, 1917, June 26, 1917).

As the leadership was "professionalized," the international office attempted to stifle opposition by penalizing political disagreement. In 1909, the UMWA constitution was amended to make it an offense punishable by six months' suspension from membership and two years barred from union office, for "any member guilty of slandering or circulating, or causing to be circulated, false statements against any member of the United Mine Workers." In effect, UMWA officials were no longer to be viewed as representatives of the rank-and-file miners who were accountable to the membership for their point of view and decisions. They were experts, hired by the union, to bargain with management's experts on an even par (Van Tine, 1973: 85).

Once the union's international leadership had been set up as union managers, and divorced from the rank-and-file miners, the entire concept of the role of the union's leadership was altered. John Mitchell, UMWA president from 1898 through 1908, was committed to the idea of cooperation between labor and management to resolve the problems of the bituminous coal industry. As a member of the National Civic Federation, which included among its ranks Ralph Easley, Elbert Gary, George Perkins, August Belmont, Andrew Carnegie, and John Hays Hammond, Mitchell defended trade unions as responsible partners in production. As a manager of labor, Mitchell also saw no contradiction between his job as a union official and the advancement of his private political and economic fortunes. In 1908, Mitchell used his position on the NCF to present himself as a potential Democratic candidate for vice president or as a contender for governor of Illinois. After leaving the union in 1908, he went on the full-time payroll of the NCF, and from there to a series of minor political patronage positions (Morris, 1979: 5–24).

While he was still UMWA president, Mitchell entered a series of deals with officials of companies under contract to the union. Mitchell, along with Central Competitive Field operators from Peabody Coal, Mount Carmel Coal, General Wilmington Coal, Western Coal, Big Muddy Coal, and Bolen-Darnell Coal, was a heavy investor in the Egyptian Powder Company, which supplied blasting powder to miners. Mitchell also used his name, and made union membership and field organizers available, to sell miners health and accident insurance, as well as his own brand of cigarettes. In a plan that both bordered on illegality and was blatantly a conflict of interests, Mitchell was involved with a group of Illinois operators in a scheme to trustify Illinois bituminous coal. In return for his cooperation as UMWA president, Mitchell was offered the option to buy coal acreages that would be included in the trust (Morris, 1979: 5–24).

The pattern that Mitchell established of combining a career as a union official with entrepreneurial practice and government service eventually permeated the ranks of the business-unionist leadership of the UMWA. The miners increasingly discovered former union officials sitting on the other side of the table during contract negotiations. T. L. Lewis, the immediate successor to Mitchell as UMWA president, later became the labor commissioner of the New River, West Virginia Coal Operators' Association, and in 1922 spearheaded an open-shop drive that evicted striking miners from company housing. John White, who followed T. L. Lewis in office, resigned his position during World War I to become one of the joint heads of the federal Fuel Labor Board. The entrepreneurial spirit was not confined to the international office. In 1926, Frank Farrington, powerful president of District 12 (Illinois), justified signing a contract to work for the Peabody Coal Company while still a UMWA district official as his right to seek new and lucrative employment after years of service. Farrington claimed that in his new position he would be able to "continue my efforts to ameliorate the position of the workers and to promote a clearer understanding and goodwill between the men and the owners" (Everling, 1976: 111; Wickersham, 1951: 35; *New York Times*, August 30, 1926: 1).

World War I gave many district and local officials an opportunity to use government committees to establish close ties to management. Charles O'Neill, elected vice president of District 2 (Central Pennsylvania) in 1916, became an area production manager for the Clearfield District of the United States Fuel Administration during the war. In 1918, he used his position to help found the Central Pennsylvania Coal Producers' Association. O'Neill was appointed its general secretary and represented the operators in wage negotiations with the district's miners until 1930 (*National Cyclopedia of American Biography*, vol. 37, 1951, 479; U.S. Senate Committee on Manufactures, 1921: 714–25).

As the leadership of the union became more separate and distinct from the membership, business unionists became increasingly wary of rank-and-file initiatives. The business unionists believed that the willingness of operators to accept the legitimacy of the union as a positive force for industrial stability, and their own constructive position in the industry, rested on the sanctity of the Central Competitive Field contract. Increasingly the offices of the union were used to discipline recalcitrant district-based factions, rank-and-file protest movements, and local pit committees that challenged this view of the contract. From 1908 to 1923, the union's policy committee was so intimately involved with the concerns of the CCF agreement that it virtually ignored other pressing issues facing the industry and failed to develop a long-term strategy for the union as other energy sources entered the market, mechanization increased, and operators shifted production to nonunion coal fields. This total commitment to the CCF helped to develop a partnership mentality, as union and management joined together to crush the independence of the rank-and-file miner (Everling, 1976: 25–26).

As early as the 1902, international convention President Mitchell explained this view of the contract. According to Mitchell, "When a contract is made and signed, if we expect the operators to carry out those provisions that are advantageous to us, we in turn, must carry out just as explicitly those provisions which are unfavorable to us." Mitchell did not hesitate to enforce this point of view on the miners. In 1904, when two local unions covered by the standard contract struck over local issues, the international union revoked their charters, blacklisted their members, and circulated the blacklist among operators in the district (Van Tine, 1973: 81).

The international office's commitment to the ideas of union responsibility and labor-management cooperation were so imbedded in Mitchell's philosophy that when the union's contract expired in 1906, he refused to sanction a strike when negotiations with operators continued past the deadline. Eventually Mitchell sacrificed the CCF agreement in favor of district-wide accords, rather than support a strike. When this decision divided the union at the 1907 UMWA convention, Mitchell defended his actions claiming, "I am trying as best I can to promote a feeling of friendly business relations between the employers and ourselves." As part of this "friendly business relationship," the international office was committed to the resolution of industrial disputes through a grievance procedure detailed in the contract. The *Monthly Bulletin of Decisions* of the Illinois Coal Operators' Association documented over 10,000 grievances in Illinois from 1909 to 1925 in mines under their jurisdiction, which could not be resolved at the mine face and were handled through the appeals mechanism of the grievance machinery (Phelan, 1994: 288; Bloch, 1931: 134–35).

Despite the fact that the procedure often proved unable to resolve local disputes between mine locals and operators, the UMWA forced rank-and-file miners to follow it. Typically, the source of a dispute was management's right to hire and fire employees and the authority of management to unilaterally introduce new machinery and labor-saving devices. The standard contract included the clause "the right to hire and discharge, the management of the mine and the direction of the working force, are vested exclusively in the operator, and the United Mine Workers of America shall not abridge this right." The only exception was in cases of discrimination and blacklisting. Discrimination and blacklisting, however, were hard to prove, particularly because local pit committees were barred from taking class actions and could only proceed on the claims of individual miners. Further, the ability of the committees to investigate charges was limited by the "exclusive" right of management to run the mine. Local committees could not tour the mine to investigate infractions, and they were contractually obligated to advise members of the local union against striking. If a pit committee violated these strictures, the committee and the local union officials were removed by the joint action of operators and the district union (Bloch, 1931: 177–87).

The rank-and-file's challenge to this conception of labor-management cooperation was the unauthorized or wildcat strike. Mitchell and his successors vigorously condemned them. Mitchell told the 1902 convention, "It is, nevertheless, true that in some instances individual operators and local unions have sought to obtain temporary advantage by evading, if not deliberately repudiating, some provisions of our joint agreements. Against such practices on the part of either miners or operators, I have constantly and vigorously advised. There is no argument that employers use with more telling effect against trade unions than the thoughtless violations of contract provisions upon the part of their members. . . . It is doubly incumbent upon us to carry out religiously the letter and spirit of such agreements." In 1914, UMWA president John P. White reiterated these sentiments, declaring, "The success of our movement depends largely, if not wholly, upon a rigid enforcement of all contracts that have been legally entered into. One of the worst evils with which our organization has to contend, and one that brings sharp criticism, is the local and unauthorized strike" (Bloch, 1931: 307–8).

During World War I, the business-unionist concept of labor-management cooperation was integrated into the basic agreements between the union, the industry, and the federal government. In return for positions on government planning bodies, the international office agreed to a penalty clause that mandated automatic fines against striking miners. The clause authorized operators to deduct two days' pay for every day missed directly from the paychecks of striking miners. No fines were levied against operators who violated the contract or federal guidelines. The ability of the UMWA leadership to separate itself from the union's members, and to enforce its view of the contract on the rank-and-file miners, depended on the creation of a well-organized bureaucracy and political machine to run the union's international office. Starting in 1899, John Mitchell began to assign union organizers on the international payroll as campaign workers to elect loyal slates to district and local union office (Bloch, 1931: 294; Van Tine, 1973: 152).

Mitchell also used the *UMWA Journal* as the official organ of the faction in control of the union's international office, closing the paper to opposition points of view. In 1904, in an editorial, the *UMWA Journal* declared that opposition to the union's "official" position on the interstate contract was tantamount to treason against the union. The *UMWA Journal* was also used to tout the view that the union's officials had a valuable expertise that entitled them to special compensation. To support this position, the *UMWA Journal* celebrated the entrepreneurial spirit and reported on the upward mobility of former union officials. In 1905, it warmly informed readers of the appointment of Robert Watchorn, a former Secretary-Treasurer of the UMWA, as an immigration official in Newark, New Jersey, and as a vice president of the Union Oil Company. William P. Wilson, miner and politician, union official and secretary of Labor in Woodrow Wilson's cabinet, was another Horatio Alger, celebrated for trading off the influence secured as a UMWA official to achieve upward social mobility (Van Tine, 1973: 104, 177; *UMWA Journal*, March 10, 1904, July 6, 1905).

After Mitchell retired as UMWA president, his successors continued to develop the international office's political machine. T. L. Lewis secured his position as UMWA president by centralizing the supervision of district organizers in his office and using the organizers to bypass district offices in his dealings with operators and miners. While Mitchell had worked closely with nominally pro-union businessmen affiliated with the National Civic Federation and the Central Competitive Field, T. L. Lewis, in his battle against the district-autonomy coalition, found allies among nonunion operators associated with Alfred Hamilton of Pittsburgh. Through close ties to Hamilton, Lewis was able to replace a popular and powerful District 5 president with a more pliable candidate. Eventually, Lewis antagonized too many powerful forces in the union and he was defeated in his bid for reelection in 1910 by a candidate representing the district-autonomy coalition. John P. White, who was a compromise choice from relatively weak District 16 (Iowa), was elected on a platform promising to limit the use of international organizers to nonunion fields or to unionized fields with the consent of district officials (Everling, 1976: 39–42).

This reversal for the international machine was only temporary. Once in office White began to accept many of the business-unionist premises of

Mitchell and T. L. Lewis, particularly the need to restrict the militancy of the miners and to encourage cooperation with management. By 1914 White had endorsed an end to the policy of "no contract, no work," supported a plan to make the UMWA conventions more manageable by reducing the number of delegates, opposed militant strikes in Kansas and Colorado, and worked to defeat socialist candidates for district office in Illinois District 12. He employed John L. Lewis as chairman of the 1916 international convention to stifle district and socialist opponents during floor debates. White's political odyssey was bolstered by increasing production and union membership stimulated by World War I. New locals, particularly in the outlying fields, tended to increase the authority of the international office. With a weak tradition of unionism, they were especially dependent on the negotiations in the Central Competitive Field. When President Woodrow Wilson offered the international leadership positions on the United States Fuel Administration and other war-related supervisory boards, he added to the unwillingness of business unionists to jeopardize their relationship with business and government and contributed to their growing conservatism. When John White resigned from the UMWA presidency in 1917, he left to become labor adviser to the Fuel Administration (Everling, 1976: 79–80, 92, 118–29).

By the end of World War I, the international machine and the business-unionist ideology had become so entrenched in the UMWA that in 1919 John L. Lewis, as acting UMWA president, would call off a strike popular among the membership to secure the relationship of the international union with the government in the postwar period. By 1920, the international union's staff had swollen until 202 people were on the payroll, earning a combined $408,324 in salary and $368,323 in expenses per annum. This international machine, with a developed business-unionist ideology antithetical to the rank-and-file miner's traditions of artisanal independence, entered the postwar period committed to working in concert with government and management to modernize and centralize the bituminous coal industry by destroying the "Miner's Freedom" (Van Tine, 1973: 138; Green, 1921: 80–85).

In John L. Lewis, business-unionism found its ultimate champion. James Wechsler in a 1944 biography of John L. Lewis described him as a "labor baron." In their biography of Lewis, Melvin Dubofsky and Warren Van Tine (1977) characterized him as a "union tyrant." Lewis, however, preferred to think of himself as an executive who managed labor in partnership with business leaders (286).

Chapter 2

Chaotic Production and the Inadequacies
of the Business-Unionist Program

Inadequacies of the Business-Unionist Strategy

Conditions in the bituminous coal industry during and after World War I
and the complicity of business unionists in the UMWA international office
with coal operators created the conditions for the emergence of a militant
class-conscious rank-and-file movement. Increased demand for bituminous
coal during World War I to meet the energy needs of expanding industries
and fuel ships meant increased production and the opening of new mines
and coalfields. After the war, with the demand for coal sharply reduced
and the industry plagued by overcapacity, business unionists in control of
the UMWA international office continued to pursue a policy of trying to
stabilize conditions in the industry through cooperation with coal companies
and the government, only to discover that bituminous coal companies were
not interested in cooperation and were determined to destroy the union. In
the postwar period, the international office also faced new challenges from
District officials and rank-and-file groups opposed to the centralization of
union authority and in favor of organizing drives in nonunion coalfields
as the best way to defend the miners' interests in the industry (Everling,
1976: 114–29; Wiebe, 1967: 98–101).

The business-unionist strategy was based on the mistaken belief that
the problems impacting miners were seriously injuring all sectors of the
industry and could be resolved through labor-management cooperation and
the rationalization of the production and the distribution of bituminous coal.
Chaotic conditions in the industry were blamed on the seasonal demand

Table 2.1. United Mine Workers of America Districts, ca. 1920

1	Anthracite (Schuylkill, PA)
2	Central Pennsylvania
3	Anthracite
4	Southwestern Pennsylvania
5	Western Pennsylvania (Pittsburgh region)
6	Ohio
7	Anthracite (Lehigh, PA)
8	Indiana
9	Anthracite (Wyoming, PA)
10	Washington
11	Indiana
12	Illinois
13	Missouri
14	Kansas
15	Colorado
16	Maryland
17	West Virginia (central)
18	British Columbia
19	Southeastern Kentucky (Harlan County)
20	Alabama
21	Arkansas
22	Wyoming
23	Western Kentucky (Union County)
24	Michigan
25	Missouri (west)
26	Nova Scotia
27	Montana
28	Virginia
29	West Virginia (south)
30	West Virginia (north)

Source: Created by the author.

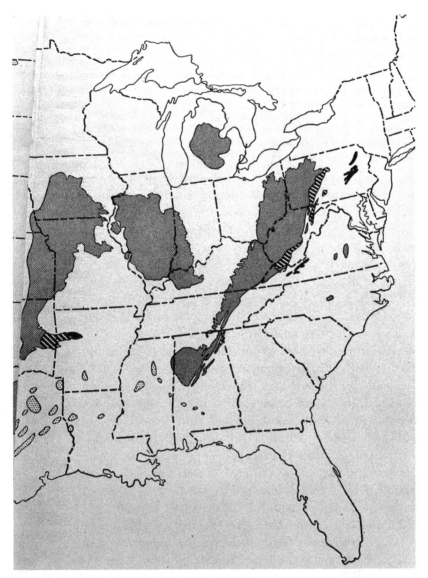

Map 2.1. Coal Fields of the Eastern United States. Central Pennsylvania UMWA District 2 is shown with diagonal stripes. *Source*: Marius Campbell (1917), *The Coal Fields of the United States*, United States Geological Survey (Washington, DC: Department of the Interior). Public domain.

for coal, railroad car shortages during peak seasons, regional competition for markets, and easy entrance into production for large numbers of small producers because of low capital costs and abundant coal supplies. The union leadership failed to understand that chaotic production was the logical outcome of overcapacity in the industry and had benefits for coal producers. In a series of reports, U.S. Bureau of Mines geologists concluded that if all other problems were resolved, and all U.S. coal production was put on an organized and rational basis, the only achievement would be a more rationally oversaturated market. The business unionists in the international office also refused to confront the possibility that overcapacity played a positive role for the major coal producers and consumers, and that the industry, if it desired, was capable of policing itself without the assistance of the UMWA. One of the leading causes of overcapacity, the plethora of small- and medium-sized mines entering and leaving production, freed large companies from the cost of maintaining their own surplus capacity for periods of high demand (Tryon & McKenney, 1922: 1009–13; Tyron and Hale, 1924: 453, 503; U.S. Bureau of Mines, 1927: 592, 613; Soule, 1947).

Chaotic production permitted large producers to diversify their coal holdings and to experiment with mechanized production. They were able to expand their holdings in the nonunion fields, depressing union wage rates in their unionized operations, and allowing them to take advantage of discriminatory shipping rates that favored long-distance southern shippers. In an industry divided between union and nonunion operation, companies were free to experiment with different types of machinery at various sites without interference by the union miners. Piecemeal mechanization both undercut the union's ability to police or to oppose the introduction of new machinery in violation of existing contracts and work practices, and pro-tected large corporations from making heavy capital investments in untried machinery (Parker, 1940: 6–7, 25–29; Dix, 1977: 16–20, 23–25; Goodrich, 1925: 56–100, 160–66; *Coal Age*, December 16, 1926).

The existence of large numbers of small and marginal independent coal producers provided a buffer between large producers and the miners' union. Smaller producers fought wage increases that could price them out of the market, and in their struggle to remain in business they invested in machinery that undermined their relationship with the union. Increased overhead costs required the small operator to continue production even when demand for bituminous coal plummeted, exacerbating the problem of overcapacity. In 1925, the United States Coal Commission reported that the cost per ton of coal at a mechanized mine operating at 80 percent capacity for one month rose by 5 percent above the costs of a mine running at its maximum capacity. When the mine worked only 20 percent of the time during a prolonged industrial slump, the cost per ton rose by 50 percent over regular costs. Because of this, mechanization required marginal and unprofitable companies to continue operation at close to maximum capacity. These companies often hung on the brink of disaster and pressed the union for contract concessions and a lower wage scale. Even when these companies went bankrupt, their property was rarely out of production for long. The mines reopened when the demand for coal increased, and the cycle was repeated (Parker, 1940: 6–25, 45–50; Everling, 1976: 12–14; Lewis, 1925: 27; Ringer, 1929: 111–17).

The greatest burden of overcapacity and overproduction fell on the men who mined the coal. Overcapacity meant that the average American bituminous coal miner was idle for as many as 100 workdays each year. Idleness, however, was not inherent to bituminous coal production; unemployment in the United States was far greater than in Western and Central European bituminous coal-producing countries. While the average American bituminous coal miner worked only 232 days in 1913, his Austrian counterpart worked 320 days, Prussians 317 days, and French, British, and Belgium miners about 290 days. The demand for bituminous coal in the United States consistently slumped to between 70 and 75 percent of capacity, and even heightened wartime production and labor shortages left the average miner idle for 65 scheduled workdays in 1917 and 59 workdays in 1918 (Tryon & McKenney, 1922: 1009–11).

When control in the industry was needed, the large operators and consumers were able to enforce it through formal and informal means. To avoid Interstate Commerce Commission regulations governing the relationship between the rail lines and coal suppliers, the railroads were masters at masking corporate ties. In testimony before the Senate Interstate Commerce Committee in 1922, Frank J. Warne, a statistician for the railway workers brotherhoods, described how the railroads were able to control large numbers of mines by owning coal lands and leasing out the actual mining operations. Railroads also used a system of interlocking directorships to control coal properties. To avoid violating federal antitrust laws, railroad company directors owned stock in the coal companies as individuals. Warne traced a complex web emanating from the Pennsylvania Railroad system. The Norfolk and Western and Baltimore and Ohio Railroads, parts of the Pennsylvania Railroad system, used interlocking directorships to control extensive mine operations in West Virginia, south-central Pennsylvania, and western Maryland. Norfolk and

Western directors controlled the Pocahontas Coal and Coke Company in West Virginia, while Baltimore and Ohio directors held 52 percent of the stock in the Consolidation Coal Company. Consolidation, in turn, owned the Fairmont, Somerset, and Metropolitan Mining Companies in Central Pennsylvania and Clarksburg Fuel, Northwest Fuel, Pittsburgh and Fairmont Fuel, and Southern Coal and Transportation in West Virginia. In other testimony before the Senate Interstate Commerce Committee hearings, W. Jett Lauck, representing the UMWA, attempted to untangle the affiliations of Thomas DeWitt Cuyler. Cuyler was a coal-mine company director and head of the Association of Railroad Executive with business ties to the New York, New Haven, and Pennsylvania Railroads and Bankers Trust, Guaranty Trust, and Equitable Trust banks—all parts of the J. P. Morgan financial empire (Warne, 1922: 1246–849; Lauck, 1922: 2207–307, 2245).

Railroads also used long-term contracts to maintain control over production. These contracts provided the railroads with guaranteed supplies in the event of tight coal markets, while protecting the railroads from losses during coal market gluts. In 1919 and 1920, the railroads used this method to control approximately 22 percent of bituminous coal tonnage. Between them, the major railroads, the steel companies, and the utilities consumed 56 percent of the nation's bituminous coal production in 1925. This gave them a powerful lever on the industry. The railroad's role in the bituminous coal industry was further explored in a report prepared by the American Federation of Labor's Railroad Employee Department. The report documented efforts by the Morgan financial empire to control railroads and bituminous coal production through interlocking directorships in the major New York banks (Shurick, 1924: 195; Christenson, 1962: 81; *Illinois Miner*, November 3; August 4, 1923).

In addition to exercising control over coal company boards of directors and shipping lines, large producers had an informal, but significant leadership role in coal operator associations, which enabled them to influence the smaller more dependent operators. The most important group, the National Coal Association, was divided into thirty-eight district organizations representing over 500 companies producing over 60 percent of the commercial bituminous coal tonnage by 1923. In *The Miners' Fight for American Standards*, John L. Lewis charged that this association, originally organized by CCF union operators during 1917, was dominated by open-shop advocates after 1922 (Parker, 1940: 9; Lewis, 1925: 27; *Illinois Miner*, November 3, 1923).

The Central Pennsylvania Coal Producers' Association provides an example of the role played by trade associations in preserving the large corporation's control of the industry. The Board of Directors of the CPCPA combined the large and small operators within the area corresponding to the UMWA District 2. The President of the Board was Thomas H. Watkins, president of the Pennsylvania Coal and Coke Company, which was part of a corporate network including the Pennsylvania Railroad with ties to national banking syndicates. Unlike the smaller operators in the regional association, whose main offices were located in and around the Pennsylvania coalfields, Watkins' office, and corporate headquarters were located in New York City. Through Watkins, the association transcended the isolation and parochialism of the small mining town. The secretary of the association, who was its chief operational officer, had been a former vice president of the UMWA district, and served as a member of the United States Fuel Administrator's office during the war. The minutes of the board meetings of the association show that its members were receiving regular reports on wage rates in neighboring union and nonunion fields, on the status of open-shop and union drives in the region, and on internal situations that might weaken the resistance of the UMWA (Central Pennsylvania Coal Producers' Association, 1921; Watkins, May 4, 1921: 27–32, 39–43; Watkins, July 21, 1923).

The level of control of the bituminous coal industry by the large producers, coal consumers, and railroads prior to World War I, should have led the business unionists in the UMWA to reconsider their long-term strategy of convincing the operators to work with the union in rationalizing the industry. However, UMWA officials were blinded by their own commitments to stability and rationalized production. When America entered World War I in 1917, the UMWA international office overestimated the willingness of the industry and the government to accept labor as an equal partner in production. During the war the large operators used the 1917 Lever Act (Food and Fuel Control Act) and their positions in government regulatory agencies to tighten their grip on the industry and accumulate record profits. At the end of the war, the UMWA international office hoped to continue wartime cooperation and was unprepared for and vulnerable to attacks by open-shop operators (Zeiger, 1969: 27).

Wartime Partnership

A major reason that the union was willing to accept a program of long-term cooperation between labor and management was the pervasiveness of the business-unionist philosophy in the international office prior to the war. Even when the district autonomy-based coalition succeeded in electing officers committed to a policy of organizing miners outside the Central Competitive Field, these officials still shared the business-unionist assumptions that the miner's deteriorating position in the industry was the result of chaotic conditions in the industry and could be cleared up through union-management cooperation. The socialists in the district autonomy group, who campaigned for the eventual nationalization of the mines, also based their call on the need to rationalize production. They ignored the part that overcapacity and mismanagement played in preserving the large producers' domination of the industry. In general, both major factions within the union leadership shied away from identifying conflict between labor and capital as a fundamental issue in the industry. Leading business unionists in the miners' union often echoed the philosophy of the operators. At government hearings on the Lever Act, designed to empower the Federal Trade Commission to reorganize and oversee the bituminous coal industry in the event of war, the union matched the operators in free market rhetoric. John L. Lewis, representing union President John White, testified before a Senate Committee that the Federal Trade Commission (FTC) was not competent to run the industry and accused the government of condemning the miner to "involuntary servitude" (Calhoun, 1928: 320–28; Everling, 1976: 117).

At first the union leadership believed that the higher prices, wages, profits, and steady work provided by a war-stimulated economy would be a permanent boon to the industry. In September 1917, the *UMWA Journal* reported a labor shortage in the mines of 25,000 men caused by workers leaving for higher wages in the munitions plants. The paper advertised for 15,000 miners in Western Pennsylvania, 3,000 in Indiana, 12,000 in Ohio, and 10,000 in Illinois. Once the Lever Act was approved, and the Wilson administration began to lobby for UMWA support, the business unionists maneuvered for positions on the Federal Regulatory agencies. They also discovered that they could use their relationship with government agencies to cement the hold of business unionism over the UMWA, and reinforce the idea that industrial cooperation, now expanded to a tripartite body including labor, management, and government, would permanently solve the problems of the industry (Everling, 1976: 119; Wickersham, 1951: 35; *UMWA Journal*, September 20, November 1, 1917).

Two important federal decisions convinced the union to cooperate with the War Industries Board that was created to direct the wartime economy. The Fuel Administrator ruled in favor of enforcing the Central Competitive Field agreements negotiated in September 1917, and invited labor participation in the United States Fuel Administration. In November 1917, UMWA President John White was appointed labor representative and joint head of the Labor Bureau of the Fuel Administrator's office. In return the union, beginning with the November 8, 1917 issue of the *UMWA Journal*, began praising the government's role in regulating the industry. Throughout the war, Frank Hayes, who succeeded White as UMWA president, proudly referred to the "progress achieved through the Federal Fuel Administration" (*UMWA Journal*, November 8, 1917; April 1, 1919).

While the union's wartime stance increased the stature of the UMWA international office, the miners' paid a high price for this recognition. In exchange for the Fuel Administration's acceptance of the Central Competitive Field contract, the union agreed to a directive outlawing the right to strike for the duration of the war. At the 1917 Washington Conference, which established federal overseership of the industry a dollar a day per man penalty was instituted for all wartime work stoppages. Despite the fact that the conference set no penalties for cases where operators refused to comply with contractual agreements, or provoked miners, former-UMWA President White pressed for acceptance of this clause at the next UMWA convention. White argued that the clause was consistent with the union's own ideas on the sanctity of the contract. Despite stiff opposition, White's position was confirmed by the delegates. The penalty clause placed a powerful weapon in the hands of both the operators and the union's administration. They now had government sanction to discipline radicals and dissidents and to undermine the "Miner's Freedom" in the name of maintaining the war effort (Everling, 1976, 120–22; UMWA Proceedings, 1918, vol. 1: 295).

Emergence of John L. Lewis

Another factor in the international office's commitment to labor-management cooperation was the emergence during the war of John L. Lewis, certainly one of the more perplexing figures in American labor history. Lewis' iron-fisted control over the UMWA in the 1920s, his ruthlessness toward opponents, and his willingness to sacrifice the interests of coal miners in the nonunion fields to advance his own position both spurred rank-and-file radicalism and helped to destroy it (Laslett, 1996: 104–50).

Lewis viewed himself as a manager of labor who should be accepted as an equal partner by corporate executives. He was a master of bureaucratic manipulation and political infighting, enabling him to rise in the central union without a district base of support. As union president, he used UMWA field organizers to assemble detailed spy reports on potential opposition and abandoned striking miners in nonunion fields to secure CCF agreements with coal companies. He was a failed U.S. presidential kingmaker and switched political parties when slighted, ignoring the wishes of union workers and unable to change their allegiances. Lewis abandoned institutions he was instrumental in creating, such as the Congress of Industrial Organizations (CIO), when he was unable to dictate their policies. Yet Lewis was also capable of seizing the moment in the 1930s to revive the UMWA and promote industrial unionism, and he was flexible enough to recruit former enemies on the left as field organizers and central office support staff. He characterized himself in a 1940 speech to a hostile CIO national convention when he stepped down as its president. "Your cheers do not enthuse me over much. And your curses discourage me not at all. You know when you first hired me I was something of a man" (Laslett, 1996: 104–50; Dubofsky & Van Tine, 1977: 366–67; *UMWA Journal*, December 1, 1940: 15).

John L. Lewis' father and grandfather were bituminous coal miners and Lewis worked in south-central Iowa mines for a short time as a teenager and young adult. He quickly left the mines to run a grain and feed business and then entered local politics. In 1907, he was defeated in a campaign for mayor of Lucas, Iowa, and his business collapsed during a national economic panic. Lewis and his extended family relocated to a company town in the central Illinois coalfields where he, his father, and his brothers went into the union business, establishing a political machine that allowed them to take control over UMWA Local 1475 (Dubofsky & Van Tine, 1977: 3–19; Alinsky, 1949: 18–19).

During the next decade, Lewis rose from relative obscurity to become the dominant figure in the international faction and seize control of the union machinery. In 1909 and 1910, Lewis supported John Walker and district-autonomy forces in UMWA state and national elections. Walker was elected president of the Illinois UMWA District 12, and as a reward Lewis was appointed an Illinois state lobbyist for mine safety and a special American Federation of Labor lobbyist. Lewis used these positions to integrate himself into Woodrow Wilson's 1912 presidential campaign and union organizing drives in Pennsylvania, Ohio, and West Virginia. Lewis made valuable contacts with business leaders and government officials, contacts that enhanced his standing in the union hierarchy and improved his personal financial position, often at the expense of miners in nonunion fields. In 1915, when John Walker challenged John White for the UMWA presidency, Lewis sided with White and helped secure his reelection. The decision to support White contributed to Lewis' rapid ascendancy in the UMWA hierarchy. In January 1917, he was appointed union statistician. Later he became business manager of the *UMWA Journal* and was appointed to the board of a federal agency responsible for the regulation of wartime coal production. When White resigned the union presidency to take a position in the Fuel Administrator's office, Frank Hayes succeeded him and the UMWA Executive Board appointed Lewis as vice president. Hayes was a popular figure among union members, but a poor administrator, which enabled Lewis to control the day-to-day operation of the UMWA. In 1918, Hayes and Lewis were elected over a Walker-Kennedy ticket that was trying to revive the district autonomy coalition. Hayes was later incapacitated by bouts of alcoholism enabling Lewis to become acting-UMWA President (Dubofsky & Van Tine, 1977: 18–42; Brophy, 1964: 134–37; Lauck, 1952).

Under the leadership of Hayes and Lewis, the international union traded cooperation and a no-strike pledge for access to previously non-union southern and western fields. While the Fuel Administration would not sponsor the growth of the union in these regions, it made organization easier by requiring the nonunion operators to pay the union scale for the district. Wage equalization and an organizing drive headed by Lewis increased UMWA membership to 400,000 miners in 1918. By the end of the war years, Colorado and Alabama were 40 percent organized and new inroads had been made in organizing miners in West Virginia, Eastern Kentucky, Tennessee, and Maryland (Everling, 1976: 123).

Two negative features overshadowed UMWA expansion during the war years. First, the UMWA remained a coalition of fragmented outlying districts, revolving around the CCF contract. The business unionists in the international office were convinced that they had entered a new era of rational production and government sponsored cooperation between labor and management. Consequently, they did not press for the expansion of the Central Competitive Field contract into a genuine national agreement. The bituminous coal operators continued to argue that the mining of coal under diverse conditions made a national agreement unwieldy. After the war, anti-union operators used this position to attack the CCF and demanded that bargaining be reduced to the narrowest possible unit, preferably with temporary grievance committees in nonunion mines. In March 1922, *Coal Age*, a trade publication, reported that this policy is based on ample precedents of which the public apparently already approves. The United States Steel Corporation through Judge Gary, refused to negotiate with other than its own employees, . . . nor could there be any clearer evidence than the recent demonstration of railroad labor of the futility of such massive and country-wide effort on the part of organized labor attempting to force the continuance of an unnatural wage level through sheer strength and an alleged ability to paralyze all industry through so-called "economic power." (*Coal Age*, March 2, 1922: 381)

The second negative feature was the failure of union leaders to develop a postwar strategy for action. Believing that cooperation with management would continue into the postwar era, the union sacrificed the miner's strike weapon for the duration of the war, and the union's policy committee focused on drawing up contract proposals and disciplining workers who refused to obey the contract. A signal of the unreality of the union's position appeared in a May 1919 issue of the *UMWA Journal*. "If the miners cannot accept the promises of a department of the government and rely upon it to live up to those promises, then there is not much good in accepting the promise of anyone on the subject." The business unionists, increasingly dependent on a continuation of the wartime plan for cooperation, were unprepared for armistice in 1919 (Everling, 1976: 122–29; *UMWA Journal*, May 15, 1919).

Of at least equal significance for the UMWA during the postwar period were the close ties developed between government and business. The Fuel Administrator appointed operators and their spokesmen to most key government positions. This gave the operators a direct pipeline to government decision-making, and the result was that operator views on industrial issues were given the virtual sanctity of law. In February 1918, Fuel Administrator Harry A. Garfield allowed a price rise of up to fifty cents per ton of coal in response to operator pressure and inflation, while he continued the freeze on mine wages. This decision played a crucial role in undercutting the union's postwar position in the industry. First, the higher price for coal encouraged marginal mine properties to enter production. Instead of government regulation paring down the number of mines, it increased the likelihood of peacetime overproduction. The price increase also permitted operator profits, which rose by an average of 24 percent in 1917, to skyrocket during the duration of the war. In 1918, the coal companies earned an aggregate of $149 million in profits. The Consolidation mines owned by the Rockefeller family were able to pay off 85 percent of their initial capital investment. J. P. Morgan affiliated mines used wartime profits and high market prices to purchase nonunion mine properties in Mingo County, West Virginia, as well as the Kentucky Black Mountain District. Mellon related coal companies accrued profits of $78 million during the war years, exceeding the combined value of their common and preferred stocks. These profits became the war chest that funded the postwar open-shop drives that attempted to drive the UMWA out of the industry (Everling, 1976: 125–26; U.S. Mine Bureau, 1923, vol. 2: 608–9; Brophy, 1964: 138–39; Parker, 1940: 21, 25, 63; *Federated Press*, June 4, 1921; *Illinois Miner*, April 2, 1927; Johnson, 1979: 81–92).

As the war in Europe entered its final phase, the United Mine Workers Union faced a period of crisis. Internal opposition to John L. Lewis and the business unionism of the international administration mounted. In part the unrest reflected a labor uprising against the wartime wage freeze that was spreading through mass production industries and the railroads. In the miners' union it fed on specific grievances, especially the decision of the Fuel Administrator to end the freeze on coal prices, while continuing the freeze on mine wages. It also reflected the resentment harbored by a number of influential figures within the union who felt that they had been unfairly bypassed by Lewis when he assumed control over the union's international machinery. At a UMWA International Executive Board (IEB) meeting in March 1919, District Autonomy forces presented a program that attempted to mobilize rank-and-file unrest by challenging both Lewis' role in the union and cooperation with management and government. The IEB endorsed the program and issued a call for a special UMWA convention to discuss a 60 percent wage increase, nationalization of the mines, formation of a labor political party, a drive to organize the unorganized fields, and authorization to strike in November 1919. At the convention in Cleveland, Ohio, Lewis was forced to acquiesce to the most militant program in the union's history, despite the fact that he considered its demands unreasonable and believed that they were designed by the District Autonomy forces to raise the expectations of the membership to unrealistic levels. The operators refused to take the demands seriously and during the summer of 1919 would not bargain with the union. Thomas T. Brewster, negotiator for the operators, rejected Secretary of Labor William Wilson's call for a renewal of the Washington Wage Conference. Instead, he demanded that Lewis rescind a November 1 strike deadline and accept the government and management contention that the UMWA was bound to its present contract through April 1920. When the union would not back down, formal talks ended (Dubofsky & Van Tine, 1977: 49–58).

During the spring and summer of 1919, wildcat strikes broke out in several coalfields. In Kansas (District 14), District President Alexander Howat led a walkout against the continuing wartime wage freeze. In July, a number of Illinois (District 12) locals struck without approval of either district or national officials. Lewis and Illinois District President Frank Farrington tried to force the men back to work, accusing the strikers of "dual unionism" and blaming the insurgents for creating confusion among miners by violating the union's wartime "no-strike" pledge, which Lewis argued was still in force. Tension within the union between rank-and-file militants and the business-unionist leadership was exacerbated when Belleville, Illinois strikers were severely punished. The operators, with support from District 12 and the international office, used wartime authority to impose a fine of two days' pay for every day of work missed. The union's compliance directly contradicted its own claim that the November 1918 armistice had ended the war and abrogated the wartime no-strike pledge. Throughout the summer, rank-and-file miners chaffed against the wage freeze contending that the demand that they wait for a treaty to be signed was only a delaying tactic (UMWA MA Frank Farrington File, August 18, 1919; Weinberg, 2005: 171; UMWA Proceedings, 1919: 462–559; Kopald, 1924: 32–33, 65–100, 114–18, 122; Everling, 1976: 133).

1919 Strike

The weaknesses of the UMWA at the close of World War I became apparent during the coal strike of 1919, the first nationwide strike in the industry since the days of John Mitchell. The proposed strike put John L. Lewis and the business unionists in an untenable position. On October 25, President Wilson ruled that the strike was a violation of the Lever Act and the union's no-strike pledge and Attorney General A. Mitchell Palmer moved to secure a restraining order and temporary injunction against the union. Lewis feared that an illegal strike would jeopardize the government, industry, and union coalition that he had worked to build during the war. A strike also challenged the basic business-unionist concept of rigorously enforcing all of the union's contractual obligations as a means of establishing the organization as a responsible partner in production. Lewis realized it was unlikely that the leadership could secure the 60 percent wage increase for the CCF demanded by the September 1919 UMWA convention and knew he risked being blamed for failing to achieve the inflated strike goals, whatever settlement was finally reached (Dubofsky & Van Tine, 1977: 48–50, 52–56).

On November 1, 1919, rank-and-file UMWA miners, who had suffered through prewar depression and war-related inflation, walked off their jobs. The Central Competitive Field was completely closed, and in the established outlying districts of Central Pennsylvania, Kansas, Missouri, Montana, Washington, Wyoming, and the Tri-state Southwest, the strike was overwhelmingly effective. As a harbinger of future events, the strike was only marginally successful in the less unionized fields. While nearly 90 percent of the mines in Kanawha, Fairmont, and New River, West Virginia, were shut, mines in other parts of West Virginia, particularly Pocahontas and Winding Gulf, were unaffected. In the panhandle region, bordering the CCF, the strike was only 60 percent effective. In the nonunion coke-producing region of Central Pennsylvania (Westmoreland, Somerset, Connellsville), the captive mines controlled by the steel companies, were unaffected. In newly organized Alabama, as well as Harlan County and northeastern Kentucky, stoppages ran only between 50 and 70 percent. Nationwide, 30 percent of the coal tonnage was still reaching market. One key index particularly pinpoints the vulnerability of the union; the strike only minimally affected the aggregate production of bituminous coal during the winter of 1919–1920. Preceding the strike, production peaked during the week of October 25, 1919, as companies stockpiled coal. After the strike, coal production peaked again at approximately 2.1 million tons of coal per day the week of January 3, 1920. In effect the strike inconvenienced distributors, but stockpiling and nonunion operations allowed operators to meet production quotas. In an industry marked by intermittent production under the best of circumstances, the strike shortened the productive season, but did not seriously threaten the operators (U.S. Bureau of Mines, 1927, vol. 2: 506, 455).

Once the strike started, the government-industry alliance moved quickly to defeat the union. On November 8, an injunction ordered the UMWA to end all strike activity by November 11. Lewis decided to obey the injunction on the grounds that he would not lead a strike against the government in violation of the Lever Act. For the union leadership, the abrupt cancelation of the strike served a number of purposes. It protected Lewis and the business unionists from charges that they had violated a court injunction, while it held in check powerful district leaders, seeking to upstage the international office by winning superior contracts for their districts. Though the American Federation of Labor promised to support the UMWA in a court fight against the injunction, the international office ordered the miners back to work. However, Lewis and the international office underestimated the strike sentiment among rank-and-file miners. Despite Lewis' cancelation of the strike order, the miners refused to return to work. Lewis, facing a stiff reelection fight the next year, decided to act cautiously. The strike dragged on into December, while negotiations remained at an impasse. The UMWA accepted a proposal by Secretary of Labor William Wilson for a 31 percent wage increase, but the operators preferred a proposal by former Fuel Administrator Garfield, and supported by President Wilson, for a 14 percent raise. With negotiations deadlocked, the government moved against the union. In December, the Wilson administration threatened to deploy 100,000 troops in an all-out push to reopen the mines using scab labor. Attorney General Palmer, as part of national anti-immigrant, antiradical, and antilabor actions, launched a campaign in bituminous coal camps to weed out rank-and-file activists. When a federal court issued a contempt citation and placed eighty-four union officials under five-to-ten-thousand-dollar bonds, Lewis resumed efforts to convince miners to call off the strike. The UMWA IEB voted to accept President Wilson's proposal with the additional provision that an investigatory commission further examine the wage question (Dubofsky & Van Tine, 1977: 57–60).

Though the union's IEB unanimously endorsed the proposed settlement, Lewis met spirited opposition at a reconvened UMWA convention in January 1920. The leaders of the District Autonomy forces and a number of the more militant rank-and-file leaders charged that the union was abandoning the militant program accepted by the IEB and endorsed by the Cleveland convention. However, this time Lewis had accurately judged the mood of the miners. Exhausted by the strike and anxious for a "return to normalcy," they voted to accept the accord by an overwhelming vote of 1,639 to 231. Later the federal investigatory commission raised the wage increase to 27 percent in the tonnage rate and 20 percent in the day rate. Lewis was able to augment this victory during the summer of 1920, by negotiating a $7.50 daily base wage for the CCF. Despite his duplicity during the strike, Lewis succeeded in outmaneuvering his chief opponents in the district autonomy group and emerged as the hero and winner of the $7.50 day (Dubofsky & Van Tine, 1977: 59, 61–63).

After the strike was settled, the business unionists in both the international office and the district autonomy coalition apparently hoped that the new wage agreement would set a pattern for an amicable resolution of their differences with government and management. The IEB, which had endorsed the militant spring 1919 program, sided with Lewis and rejected a proposal from District 2 (Central Pennsylvania) to launch a major organizing campaign in nonunion fields and weaker districts. A number of locals from Somerset in Central Pennsylvania had petitioned to begin an organizing drive because only 1,000 out of 11,000 miners had joined the strike in their county. While the union's Committee on Organization agreed to recommend limited support to local initiatives, it argued that "during the present period of disturbed industrial conditions, . . . our international union should not undertake greater obligations than our mature judgment and experience would indicate an ability to carry" (UMWA MA District 2 File; UMWA MA Report of the Committee on Organization, July 29, 1920).

By the fall of 1920, Lewis was in a strong enough position to defeat an opposition slate headed by Robert Harlin of Washington and Alexander Howat of Kansas. Helped by success at the negotiating table, the fear by key elements of the district autonomy coalition of unleashing a massive organizing drive, and the widespread hope for the postwar continuation of the government, management, and labor coalition, Lewis won the election decisively and appeared to have swung the union away from its militant postwar program (Dubofsky & Van Tine, 1977: 160–62).

Chapter 3

Ethnic Division in the Coalfields

Coal companies used ethnic differences among bituminous coal miners to defeat union organizing campaigns and during the open-shop drives of the 1920s to undermine worker solidarity. UMWA locals and districts recognized what the companies were doing and developed strategies to build an inclusive union.

The ethnic divisions exploited by coal operators were explored in a 1910 federal study on the impact of immigration on workers and industries. *Immigrants in Industries (In Twenty-Five Parts)*, was a report prepared for the United States Immigration Commission. Compilation of the report was directed by political economist W. Jett Lauck, who also edited a number of the volumes. Lauck started his career as an academic at Washington and Lee University and served on a series of federal commissions as a government economist. In the 1930s, after helping draft the New Deal National Recovery Act, he became an adviser to both the UMWA and the United Auto Workers (Dillingham, 1911; Zeidel, 2004: 49; Grayson, 1975).

The Immigration Commission was a joint Congressional committee chaired by Senator William Dillingham of Vermont and created to review United States Immigration policy as part of the Immigration Act of 1907. It disbanded after submitting a report that contained recommendations for restrictions on immigration that would primarily affect Southern and Eastern Europeans. The Commission endorsed a national origin quota system that became the basis for immigration restrictions in the 1920s, limits on the admission of unskilled laborers, demand for greater financial resources on arrival, and a literacy test. Part of its report was a survey of immigrants working in the bituminous coal industry with case studies of two "representative" bituminous coal mining communities in Central Pennsylvania that documented structural bias and ethnic isolation (Abstracts, 1911: 9, 47–48).

In one "representative" community, identified by historian Millie Beik as Windber in Somerset County, coal mines operated nonunion in both the pre–World War I and postwar periods. Berwind-White, the open-shop coal company that owned Windber, Pennsylvania—the name Windber was a reshuffling of the letters in Berwind—was one of the largest independent producers of bituminous coal in the United States. The company had a monopoly on jobs, land, housing, utilities, police, civil government, and services, in the town and recruited a diverse pool of immigrant workers and barred union organizers.

During the April 1922 UMWA strike wave, 2,500 Berwind-White miners walked out of work demanding a union contract. Three thousand miners from Windber and surrounding communities attended a rally organized by UMWA District 2 despite efforts by Berwind-White to prevent the meeting and threats to evict the families of strikers. District 2 arranged for speakers to address the assembly in English, Hungarian, Italian, and Polish. When the company store refused to accept cash payments and ordered strikers to pay all outstanding debts, Windber miners, with the assistance of District 2, established their own cooperative store. Berwind-White retaliated by bringing in strikebreakers and using private Coal and Iron agents to harass strikers and block county roads to keep out union organizers. John Brophy, the president of District 2, charged that Coal and Iron agents were breaking into the homes of striking miners, claiming they were searching for illegal "moonshine" operations. Once inside, they stole anything of value they could find, threatened miners with imprisonment as "moonshiners," and in at least one case, raped a miner's wife. After another mass rally in May, Berwind-White began evictions and secured an injunction limiting crowd size in Windber. Berwind-White's actions precipitated countermeasures from striking miners. The *Johnstown Tribune* reported that company housing was dynamited and people who crossed picket lines received threatening letters signed "Black Hand." "You pussy foot. If you want to see yourself on this world, this will be your last days of work for you. Do you understand. And we want you to obey it. From your enemy." District 2 tried to stabilize an escalating situation and rally strikers by organizing labor chautauquas, modeled on religious revival meetings, in July and August (Beik, 1996: 270–88; Blankenhorn, 1924: 118–20; *Johnstown Democrat*, April 6, April 10, April 13, May 26, July 31, August 23, 1922; *Johnstown Tribune*, May 7, 9, 26, 1922).

When the UMWA signed a CCF contact that abandoned newly organized miners, Windber miners, with the support of District 2 remained on strike. Because Berwind-White mines supplied coal for the New York City subway system and the president of the company was also the chairman of the Board of Directors of the city's Interborough Rapid Transit system, the Mayor of New York City appointed a commission to investigate conditions at Berwind-White's nonunion mines. The commission's report, released in January 1923, described working conditions for Berwind-White miners as "worse than the conditions of the slaves prior to the Civil War" and urged the federal government to take over and operate the coalfields. The Berwind-White Company "treated their employes [*sic*] purely as beasts of burden and sacrificed the lives and limbs of thousands of men and the happiness and future of thousands of women and children to build for themselves an industrial autocracy." The committee's report also accused Berwind-White of hindering its investigation, refusing to appear at hearings, spying on field investigators, ransacking hotel rooms, and tampering with mail. Despite this show of support, as their situation became more desperate, Windber miners gradually drifted back to work. On August 14, 1923, delegates from Somerset County local unions met in Johnstown and voted to terminate the seventeen month long strike (Hirshfield, 1922; Beik, 1996: 288–309; *New York Times*, 1923, January 2: 1; District 2 Papers Box 15: April 13, 1923).

The other community, a union town until the UMWA local was broken during 1920s open shop campaigns, was never formally identified. The proximity of these two towns, one union and the other nonunion, and their divergent and then convergent histories, illustrates the consequences of the willingness of the national union to accept nonunion operation in potentially unionized coal fields in exchange for a contract in larger bituminous coal production centers. Part of the difficulty in identifying the exact location of the unionized town is that the commission report refers to a map that does not appear in the published version. The study, however, does offer a series of clues for identifying "Community B" (Dillingham, 1911: 531).

1. "This community is only 10 miles distant from Community A, a branch line of railroad connecting the two towns."

2. Community B's "population . . . is in round numbers the same as Community A."

3. The community "consists of an urban center with small semidetached settlements of mine workmen clustered around

coal mines which are situated on the outskirts of the town proper or at a very short distance."

4. It is located "at the junction of two small rivers."

5. In 1908, the year the data was collected, the coal industry was "in the hands of four companies which employ about 1,400 men."

6. "All the laborers and miners employed by the mining companies are members of the United Mine Workers of America . . . organized labor is probably as strongly intrenched in this community as in any in Pennsylvania."

A notation on a file in the archives of Indiana University of Pennsylvania suggests Community B was South Fork, located at the confluence of the Little Conemaugh River and South Fork Creek and 11.5 miles by road from Windber (Department of Commerce and Labor, 1913: 579, 601; Pennsylvania Department of Mines, 1919: 341–44; *New York Times*, 1889: 1).

The 1900 federal census counted 2,635 people in Community B "town proper," including 587 foreign-born, or 22 percent of the population. By 1908, as a result of the expansion of the coal mining industry, the town's population had swelled to approximately 7,200 people including an estimated 1,900 immigrants or 26 percent of the population. The immigration community was actually larger, almost one-third of Community B's residents, if you include the 340 American-born children of foreign-born fathers. The largest components of the immigrant community were Italians (32%), Poles (25%), Lithuanians (15%), and Ruthenians (a Slavic group from Lithuania), and Slovaks (22%). The newer immigrants and those with less English facility were more likely to live in the satellite mining communities outside the town and borough. Immigration from Southern and Eastern Europe to this area trailed other mining patches in Central Pennsylvania, possibly because it was a strong union town, paid higher wages, attracted more experienced union miners, and held onto its workforce. When the Central Pennsylvania bituminous coal industry expanded in the first decade of the twentieth century, Community B mine operators began to hire newer immigrants. By 1907, of the 838 people employed by the Community B mine companies, 17 percent were native-born whites, 21 percent were native-born sons of foreign-born fathers, and 62 percent were foreign-born. However, the immigrant category is deceiving. Thirty-five percent of the immigrant workers were from earlier migrations, English, Irish, Welsh, Scot, and German, as well as 87 percent of the native-born sons of immigrants. A little more than 100 of the immigrant miners were from this earlier migration and had lived in the United States for over twenty years. It appears that the mining companies employed no women and only one African American, either underground or on the surface. The new immigrant group overwhelmingly occupied semiskilled and unskilled positions underground as machine operators and pick miners. This was especially true of Italians, the most recent arrivals to the area. One group however, Slovaks, did manage to move into more skilled jobs. The study speculated that this was because Slovakian miners had lived in the community longer than miners from the other new immigrant groups (Dillingham, 1911: 533–34, 537, 540).

The Dillingham study found that different ethnicities tended to congregate in different mines, but it did not discuss whether this was a result of choice by the workers, a product of immigrants helping fellow countrymen find jobs, or a segregation policy by the mining companies (see Table 3.1). Whatever the initial reasons, ethnic isolation proved to be a serious hindrance to UMWA locals in the 1920s, when it combated open-shop drives. In Mine I, the largest of the mines surveyed, there is ethnic data for 386 of the 576 underground hand-picked coal miners. Forty-one percent were either American or English-born and another 22.5 percent were either Scot, Irish, or Welsh. There were 9 Italians, 16, Poles, and 56 Slovaks, or 21 percent of the identified miners. At Mine II, where 178 hand-pick coal miners were surveyed, 38 percent were either American or English-born. The next largest group, Southern Italians, was 26 percent. Scot, Irish, or Welsh made up only 12 percent. At Mine III, where 107 hand-picked coal miners were surveyed, 40 percent were Southern Italian, 24 percent were either American or English-born, and no other group had significant representation. At Mine IV, where 132 out of 204 hand-picked coal miners were surveyed,

Table 3.1. Ethnicity of Community B Miners

	American or British Isle	Southern Italian or Eastern European	Scattered or Unidentified
Mine I	63.5%	21%	15.5%
Mine II	50%	26%	14%
Mine III	24%	40% (largely Italian)	36%
Mine IV	46%	33% (largely Slovak)	21%

Source: Created by the author.

27 percent were either American or English-born, 19 percent were Scot, Irish, or Welsh, a third of the miners were Slovak, and only two miners were listed as from Southern Italy. These percentages may be distorted by the number of miners who did not respond (Dillingham, 1911: 537–39).

The Dillingham report found a significant wage differential between native-born and native-born sons of immigrant miners (Group A) and immigrant miners (Group B), however immigrants who were in the United States longer, primarily British Isles miners, did have higher earnings. The 255 Group A miners earned on an average $2.36 a day. The 495 Group B miners earned an average of $2.19 a day, but 43 Southern Italian miners earned an average of only $1.97 a day and 34 Lithuanian miners earned even less, $1.82 a day. Over 40 percent of Group A miners earned over $2.50 a day, compared to fewer than 30 percent of the Group B miners. Approximately 20 percent of the Group A miners were paid over $3.00 a day, compared to 10 percent of the Group B miners. There were 73 teenage boys between the ages of 14 and 18 working in the Community B mines, but data for their pay rates was very incomplete. The borough post office reported that large numbers of Southern Italian miners were sending wages home to Italy, almost $40,000 between August 1907 and August 1908, over 70 percent of the total wages sent abroad. This suggests that a large number of Southern Italian miners were men whose families had remained home when the men traveled to the United States seeking work and were migrants rather than immigrants, a factor that had the potential to undermine union solidarity, especially during times of crisis (Dillingham, 1911: 539–42).

Group A miners were much more likely than many of the immigrants in Group B to be literate. Among native-born miners and those who were sons of immigrants 97 percent claimed to be able to read and write. British Isle immigrants also reported literacy rates well above 90 percent. There was a wide range of reported literacy among the Eastern and Southern European immigrants. Poles claimed a literacy rate of approximately 80 percent compared to Southern Italians, where more than half of the miners could not read or write. The reported literacy rate for Lithuanian miners was also about 50 percent. Roughly half of Southern Italian, Slavic, and Polish immigrant miners could not speak English. The Group A British Isle and American miners frequently blamed the newer Group B immigrants for making the mines more dangerous because they are "ignorant of the language" and do not "grasp the meaning of danger signs and regulations." However, there were no serious accidents in Community B mines in the year of the study (Dillingham, 1911: 543, 561, 567). Dillingham reported that sanitary conditions in the Community B mining communities were generally "good." The mine was well ventilated and operated, however what was diagnosed at the time as "asthma" was prevalent among the miners. Today it would probably be labeled as black lung disease (pneumoconiosis). The nearest medical facility was ten miles away by rail, probably in Windber. Miners had to pay for their own medical care and any treatment for family members. The county covered some costs for an indigent family but there was no general welfare policy. In some cases, the company provided a physician, but then charged the miner. Some of the local companies paid for the funeral expenses of a miner killed in a mine accident, but others did not. Because of the cost of medical care and the marginal economic status of most miners, but especially more recent immigrants, infectious diseases were serious problems. Not surprisingly in communities where a large number of young men are detached from familial relationships with women, venereal diseases, especially syphilis, were becoming a health problem (Dillingham, 1911: 543, 563).

Pennsylvania law in 1908 prohibited mining companies from operating company stores, but each of the mines in the Community B area evaded the law, either openly or through the use of a separate corporate entity under nominally independent ownership. Purchase from company stores was not a condition of employment, but in the outlying mine patches where the majority of new immigrant families lived, they had no other option and generally purchased goods on credit. The coal companies paid employees in cash, not script, with the "company store" bill deducted directly from wages. Housing was rented to company employees and the costs were also deducted from wages. Rent typically varied from $7.50 to $9 a month, depending on the size of the unit. Most units housed two families. There were no facilities for single men, so they generally boarded with families, who used the payments to supplement their income. When a unit was electrified, the cost of electric power, approximately $1 a month, was also deducted. The Dillingham report concluded that providing rental housing was quite profitable for the mining companies. An average two-unit house that cost about $500 to build brought in almost $200 a year in rent (Dillingham, 1911: 544–45).

Italian and Slavic workers first arrived in Central Pennsylvania to work on railroad and street construction and gradually entered the coalmines as the industry expanded in the region. The companies did not actively recruit the new immigrant workforce, but relied on immigrants already in their employ to enlist their countrymen when there were vacancies. The Dillingham report estimated that 75 percent of the Slavic workforce and about half of the Southern Italian miners were already in the United States before gaining employment in Community B's mining industry. That means that half of the Southern Italian and about one-fourth of the Slavic coal miners in Community B were recruited to come to the United States from their home countries by friends and family members. Almost all of these new arrivals were single men or married men who came to the United States without their families. Southern Italian miners, as a rule, did not buy property or build homes even when it was possible. They lived inexpensively, "drink comparatively little," saved what money they could, all with the intent of someday returning home (Dillingham, 1911: 545, 552, 555).

Religious differences and fraternal organizations contributed to the segregation of the different ethnic and immigrant groups, a pattern Beik also reported for Windber. In Community B town proper, there were four English-speaking Protestant churches and an English-speaking Roman Catholic Church. Just outside town was a Roman Catholic Church that catered to the various Slavic nationalities. Nearby was a Greek Orthodox Church that served a broader geographic area. At this time there was no Roman Catholic Church serving the newest Southern Italian population. In town there was a branch of the Ancient Order of Hibernians, an Irish fraternal association, and there were Polish, Lithuanian, and Ruthenian "benefit societies" that provided impoverished or sick members and their families with some welfare and funeral assistance. Again, the Southern Italian community, as the newest arrivals, were underserved; however, they were also the most energetic entrepreneurs, operating two grocery stores in town that sold traditional food items to immigrant families, a fruit store, and businesses that provided hair and shoe repair services. The largest of the Italian-operated groceries was connected to an employment agency and steamship company that brought many of the Southern Italians to Central Pennsylvania (Beik, 1996: 124–30; Dillingham, 1911: 553–54).

The isolation of the newer immigrants was reflected in public school attendance. There were 875 children enrolled in Community B town schools but only 60, or 7 percent, were foreign-born, and only 25 of the foreign-born, or 3 percent, were from Italy. The foreign- and American-born children of the recent immigrants were almost all in the lower grades, as secondary school–aged children were withdrawn from school to go to work. There was only one school in the outlying mining communities, making it difficult for children to attend school even when families wanted them to be educated. Some Polish children attended a one-room school operated by the

Roman Catholic Church where instruction was in Polish, and English was not taught—a violation of Pennsylvania law. To save the cost of building new facilities, local authorities, including the superintendent of schools for Community B, ignored state compulsory state school attendance laws, even to the point of discouraging school attendance. The Dillingham report concluded that the "[a]loofness and indifference of Americans toward the immigrant population," the absence of schools and the lack of other public facilities, and segregation in housing and at work, inhibited the "Americanization" and assimilation of Community B's newer immigrants from Southern and Eastern Europe (Dillingham, 1911: 569, 571).

Mine operators were interviewed about the "relative efficiency of immigrants and natives." There was unanimity that the "American, English, Welsh, Scotch, Irish, and Germans" were "better miners and more efficient workmen than are recent immigrants," but disagreement in evaluations of the new immigrants. Slavs were considered the better workers, but there were complaints that they "drink excessively." Lithuanians were considered the more intelligent immigrant group, and the Southern Italians "more adaptable," the most "industrious," and the "most sober race." Other comments were that the Slavic miners were more "docile" and that the Southern Italians required "constant supervision," a complaint that seems to contradict the view that they were more industrious. The companies denied that they discriminated when hiring, however, administrative and "responsible positions" such as fire bosses, engineers, foremen, stablemen, and blacksmiths were almost always assigned to the American and British Isle miners. According to the Dillingham report, "The foreign population supplies very much more than its share of cases to the justice courts," however, most of their infractions were minor, "assault, drunkenness, and larceny." The tone of the report suggests that its writers shared some of the same biases as the coal operators (Dillingham, 1911: 549–50, 557).

In the outlying mine patches the different immigrant nationalities tended to form separate minicolonies. While the coal companies denied housing discrimination, the Dillingham report noted that the miners did not actually choose where they would rent, although they could select their own boarders. Southern Italians tended to live separately, but the various Slavic nationalities were grouped together. Dillingham reported that inside the mines the "different races are separated at their own request, because they naturally seek places among their own countrymen," with the exception of the Southern Italians "because they are inferior miners as compared with the other races, and for that reason are grouped together by the mine foreman." One coal company ran three mines with sharply different worker demographics. All Polish miners were congregated in Mine II while all the Southern Italian and most of the other Slavic miners worked in Mines I and III. There were almost no English-speaking workers in Mine III, but over half of the miners in Mine II spoke English. A possible explanation is the reported preference of the older group of English-speaking miners for hand-picked work over machine mining that exposed workers to greater supervision and regulation (Dillingham, 1911: 545–47, 563).

While all the new immigrants, and all 1,400 coal miners in Community B, were members of the United Mine Workers of America, Central Pennsylvania District 2, and their union locals, the new immigrants played a minimal role in locals whose leadership positions were dominated by American and British Isle miners. Whether it is accurate that the miners chose self-segregation in the workplace, it certainly benefited the coal companies by weakening contacts between the new arrivals and the native-born and British Isles miners with strong union traditions. In Community A, Windber, a nonunion town, the coal companies used a different strategy to divide workers. They systematically intermixed nationalities at the workplace, which allowed them to use the "barrier of language" and "traditional enmities and prejudices" to undermine union organizing drives (Dillingham, 1911: 546–47; 550).

The demographic trends reported by the Dillingham Commission played a major role in weakening union organizing efforts in Windber and Community B by UMWA District 2. In April 1906, nonunion Windber miners joined unionized District 2 miners in a national strike. Their particular grievances centered on charges that they were being short-weighted at the tipple where loaded coal cars were weighed because they did not have a union checkweightman to ensure that miners were credited for the full tonnage of the coal that they mined. According to the Dillingham report, the local union leaders were Slovak (from modern-day Czech Republic). Magyar (Hungarian) and Slavic miners (probably Polish) were among the most active participants. Windber operators used threats of violence against the mines to demand intervention by state troopers and the workers' movement was suppressed. When violence did break out, the national media printed the Berwind-White Company's version of events. According to the *New York Times*, a mob of 5,000 men, armed with rifles, attacked 100 Deputy Sheriffs, who drove the mob back with the help of the Windber Fire Department. Four members of the armed "mob" were killed, but none of the company's defenders, although some company employees fighting alongside the deputies were reported as injured. The article blamed the frustration of the mob on "heavy accessions" as local miners abandoned the strike and returned to work. Leaders of the mob included a man identified as a Polish miner named Paul Zills, who was murdered by the deputies. Two of the other dead strikers were identified as "foreigners." Twenty rioters were arrested. The next day the *Times* reported the arrival of State Constabulary, the transfer of the arrested strikers to the county lockup, and that the miners were "awed by bayonets." Other battles erupted at the end of April following a court injunction against the strikers and evictions from company housing. Deputies continued to arrest strikers until the strike, and the union, was finally broken. Based on local press reports and parish records, it appears that many of the new immigrant miners in the Windber region left the area, some seeking work in other parts of the United States, and some returning to Europe. In her history of Windber miners, Mildred Beik argues that the coal companies used nativist propaganda blaming violent immigrant radicals for the strike and the violence, and to rally anti-union forces in the area. After the strike, the Berwind-White company shifted from a strategy of mixing ethnicities on the job and in company housing to segregating them in the pattern used by coal companies in Community B (Dillingham, 1911: 500; Beik, 1996: 212–18, 221, 228; *New York Times*, April 17: 1, April 18: 1, April 30, 1906: 1).

Chapter 4

Coal-Patch Community

In isolated coal-patch communities, bituminous coal miners depended on community and family support for strikes and organizing drives to succeed. Women, who were barred from working in the mines in most United States coalfields, were crucial to building and sustaining community as wives, mothers, daughters, cousins, aunts, girlfriends, and neighbors, during the intense labor conflicts of the post–World War I era.

George Korson's *Coal Dust on the Fiddle, Songs and Stories of the Bituminous Industry* (1943), gives some insight into the difficult experience of women in isolated mountain coal patches and the crucial roles they played in building class-conscious communities. According to Korson, courting usually began when a boy reached sixteen, he had already spent a number of years working underground, and the girl was as young as fourteen and just out of school. With few work opportunities for women in the rural areas and little privacy for young couples in their parents' small company houses, pregnancy and marriage often came quickly, and with them, the need to set up one's own household (87).

In this passage, Korson describes the "lot of the miner's wife."

She was the first member of her family to get up in the morning and the last to go to bed. Long before daybreak she crawled out of bed to kindle a fire, and by the time she waked her husband the fatback was frying and the biscuits were baking for his breakfast. While he was eating, she was making up his dinner pail. As he shuffled off to work, she stood at the back door following his footsteps until he was swallowed up in the mine. The children were awakened, dressed, and given their breakfast. When they left for school she tackled the dishes. At noon came another meal for the children and more dishes. The afternoon was taken up with washing and ironing and with the preparation of the evening meal. Upon her husband's return from the mine, she hauled several buckets of water from the hydrant or water barrel and heated it on the cook stove for his daily bath. After supper her husband lit his smutty corncob and was off to the company-store porch or saloon to relax among his fellow workers. But for the wife the day was not yet over. After she disposed of the dishes, she put the children to bed. Long after her family had retired she sat up sewing, mending, and darning. The lack of household conveniences, especially running water, made her work all the harder. (88)

Coal-patch life for a miner's wife was marked by frequent pregnancies and "child-bearing, poverty, insecurity, her children often hungry and ragged, the constant battle against dirt and coal dust, and the numerous household chores"; it took a heavy toll on these women and "hard middle age and a shrewish old age came soon" (88). There were "No books or papers for a young mind hungry for mental nourishment, never a note of music to awaken the sleeping vibrations of her spirit—not a particle of beauty left within her to respond to the austere beauty that mornings and evenings brought to the mountains which circumscribed her daily existence" (89).

Other sources support Korson's description of the "lot of the miner's wife." A 1989 public history project interviewed women who lived in West Virginia company-owned housing between 1900 and 1950. These women reported gardening on available plots, cleaning outdoor privies, preserving food, earning cash by taking in laundry, bringing boarders into their homes, and sewing underwear for children out of flour sacks. They scavenged for dislodged coal along the train tracks and sold butter and eggs. Some were active as bootleggers or turned to prostitution to help support their families during especially lean times. Coal dust and smoke from burning slag heaps was everywhere in the coal camps. The ground and streams turned black. It was a constant battle to keep people, clothing, and homes clean. Water had to be hauled from outdoor pumps. A 1923 survey of coal-company owned housing in over 400 West Virginia communities found that out of almost 40,000 family dwellings, only 11.2 percent of the houses had running water (Greene, 1990: 37–54)

Korson's book is primarily a collection of bituminous coal miner songs. *The Miner's Wife* calls on men to appreciate the "little woman," because "When it comes to handing bouquets, for suffering, grief and strife, / You've simply got to hand it to the humble miner's wife; / It's a mystery how she does it on the meager pay she gets, / And through it all keeps smiling, never grouches, never frets" (95–96). "A Scab's Wife," composed by a miner's wife from West Virginia, calls on her husband to return to the fold and once again become a union man. "My husband he is scabbing, / Oh I wish that he was dead" (330). Miner's wives were often on the front lines during strikes, especially when court injunctions prevented the men from picketing. Fannie Sellers, a UMWA organizer, murdered in 1919 by coal company thugs, was not a miner's wife, but a former garment worker. She is celebrated in a song composed by the wives of two Pennsylvania coal miners. "We're union women, / We're fighting for our cause; / We're union women, / We're fighting for our cause; / Just like the one who lies here before us, / We're fighting for our cause" (352).

The role of coal-patch women in militant labor actions are well documented, largely because of the inspirational actions of Mary Harris "Mother" Jones, the "Miner's Angel." Women sustained striking miners in Trinidad, Colorado in 1913–1914, and in the Southern Illinois coalfields after World War I and during the Great Depression. In 1932, Southern Illinois women organized the Women's Auxiliary of the Progressive Miners of America. The Auxiliary solicited food from local businesses; raised money to support strikers in other coalfields; joined picket lines; organized soup kitchens, parades, and rallies; and attended funerals en mass. Speaking at the Auxiliary's founding convention, Mary McKeever demanded that women "support their husbands and sweethearts and that if their menfolk did not have enough gumption to stand staunchly for their union that they should take over the task themselves and refuse to pack their dinner buckets or to keep house for them." Katie DeRorre, an Auxiliary's Executive Board member, and her husband Joe opened their home to Progressive Miners of America organizers, and she drove "cross-dressed" union organizers through hostile territory. Because of Kate's active role, Joe often stayed home with their kids while she attended meetings (Parton, 1925; Moore 346–60; 371–92; Merithew, 2006: 82–83).

On September 9, 1932, the Springfield Illinois *State Journal* reported on one of the Auxiliary's rallies: "545 women from several central Illinois cities, dressed in the immaculate white uniforms of auxiliaries to the Progressive miners' union paraded through the streets . . . in protest against the new wage scale for miners in the Illinois district." The parade was led by the local chief of Police followed by "the Gillespie band, several hundred women and a hundred automobiles filled with men, women and children. Each unit carried an American flag." The Auxiliary also used song at its rallies to encourage women and men to resist class oppression. This song went to the tune of the "Battle Hymn of the Republic." "Arise! Arise! Brave Woman! / There is work for you to do. / Show the world that love is wisdom and love's promises are true; / Break the bonds that held you captive for the world has need of you, / And we'll go marching on" (Booth, 1996: 381, 388).

Grace Jackson and Willie Helton, interviewed in the 1970s, explained how women would help defend the jobs of their fathers, husbands, and brothers during coal-mine strikes in southern West Virginia. Squads of women would tear out train tracks to prevent the shipping of coal and block scabs from entering the mines. Jackson described how women and the men with high-powered rifles "got on their bellies and laid on each side of the track, . . . and when that train went through . . . they let one shot fire." Willie Helton remembered, "I slipped one gun down into my dress on this side. I had one gun on either side of me, and I had a pocket full of shells" (*American Experience*, n.d.).

In a 1976 interview, Katherine Welsh Martin, the daughter of a District 2 Central Pennsylvania union official, described her experiences as a young girl in the 1920s. Her father, the brother-in-law of John Brophy, started out in the union as a checkweightman at the Nanty Glo Pennsylvania Springfield Mine and was elected a District 2 board member and organizer. At the age of eight, Katherine was put to work sorting clothing donated for the 1922 Somerset strikers. During a later strike, she picked up relief checks from the District office and brought them to the local bank for deposit. Her father would write checks for the different mining families and she would use a rubber stamp to add his signature. On Saturday mornings, she would help her father distribute the checks as miners came by their house. Once, at the age of ten, because her father was worried the coal companies had hid a taping device under their house, she had to crawl in the space under the house with a flashlight to search for a "black box" screwed to the dining room floor (Singer, 1982: 211–24).

Because her father was frequently out of town on union business, during strikes a clothesline with flat iron weights on each end was stretched from her grandfather's bedroom to the room where she slept with her sister. In case of trouble, the girls could pull down on the rope causing the iron weights to drop and waken him. He would get out of bed and load his shotgun. Katherine and her brother made homemade "Billy Clubs" out of broken posts from the stairwell. They bored a six-inch hole in one end using a hot poker from the fireplace and put melted lead into the hole. Katherine reported, "We never used it but we slept with it under the pillow. That was our protection because company men could have gotten into our house easily. They went into some, but not ours."

Fact-based fiction also offers insight into the lives of coal-patch women and mining communities. Myra Page is the pen name of Dorothy Page Gary Markey, a union organizer, writer, and teacher who was active in the American Communist Party from the 1920s until 1953. *With Sun in Our Blood* is a fact-based novel first published in 1950. It told the story of Dolly Hawkins Cooper, a friend Page met in 1936, while they helped organize the Southern Tenant Farmers Union in Arkansas. Cooper was originally from Toewad, Tennessee, a small coal patch on the western slope of the Appalachian Mountains about fifty miles east of Nashville. She moved to Commonwealth, Arkansas, after her husband, a coal miner, died as the result of a mine cave-in. In Arkansas, Cooper became a local celebrity after writing a letter to Eleanor Roosevelt complaining about conditions in a local work program that prompted Roosevelt to visit Commonwealth and meet with her. In the novel, we encounter Dolly running a mine camp household, caring for her children, as well as caring for her men. With the other women, she planted her garden, nursed the sick and injured, and assisted with birthing; the women were banned from working in the mines by deeply imbedded superstition. We see and hear Dolly praying at the mine face after a cave-in, hoping her younger brother and future husband are brought to the surface safely. Dolly describes how in their coal-patch community, women played an active role, sometimes a leading role, pushing the company to retimber the drift shaft and underground tunnels to protect miners from cave-ins, to install a water pipe connecting company housing to a nearby river so families no longer had to depend on a polluted local stream, and to provide medical personnel at the mine to rapidly treat anyone injured by one of the constantly occurring accidents (Page, 1986; Baker & Page, 1996: 152–55).

In the novel, Page graphically described a coal-patch woman's fears.

When the popular trees shadow crossed her doorway, Dolly knew it was time to meet her husband John on his trek home from the mine. "I had him [John] above ground and to myself for the night—before I must see him off, giving back sass to down the fear a mine woman lives with. Since a child I had known its stillness. Ma's face gone stiff in midafternoon. Not even the smallest of us dared let out a breath, waiting for the mine to shout its message. A short friendly blast and Ma turned back to her ironing and we children too our play, knowing our Dad had work tomorrow. Risking his neck and us thankful. For there came weeks when the monster's screech failed us and our bellies grew big with hunger gas. Ma might grow worn out, praying for the whistle to find its voice. Finding it, scarce a fortnight passed but somebody's Dad was hurt down the mine. And with us now it was the same. Mishaps that cost a man his arm or leg the whistle passed over, being all in the day's work. Let a pocket of gas explode and the blast gave forth its yell of doom. Often I had seen Ma drop her work and run with other women for the pit, we young'uns after them. In time the whistle mingled in my child thoughts with the Voice of God, coming from beyond High Top to herald life or death. (Page, 1986: 143)

Denise Giardina has two fictionalized accounts of West Virginia and Eastern Kentucky coal wars in the first two decades of the twentieth century where women play a major role. The characters are composites based on historical figures and people from the region that Giardina knew. In *Storming Heaven* (1987), Carrie Bishop is a rural nurse, wife of a coal miner, and community organizer who chronicles the story. Many of the incidents in the book are based on actual events, including the Matawan Massacre; the assassination of Sid Hatfield, a local police chief, by Baldwin-Felts gunmen because he supported the miners; and the Battle of Blair Mountain. One episode, which captures the spirit of the times but is largely fictional, has a march of miner's wives overwhelming company guards and looting a company store (216–20).

Part 2

Rank-and-File Miners

Chapter 5

Rank-and-File Miners
Challenge Business Unionism

Rank-and-file rebellion in a number of the UMWA districts started with opposition to the World War I wage freeze and the no-strike pledge agreed to by the international office. It was a direct challenge to the consolidation of power by John L. Lewis as the autocratic leader of the business unionists and president of the UMWA.

During World War I, bituminous coal miners were squeezed between skyrocketing inflation, the Consumer Price Index doubled from 1915 to 1920, and a wage freeze enforced by a coalition of the federal government, the bituminous coal industry, and the UMWA. The miners' frustrations were further exacerbated as mine wages trailed those paid to workers in the defense related industries and coal operators were guaranteed exorbitant profits by the United States Fuel Administration (Kopald, 1924: 53–57; Brophy, 1964: 138–40; U.S. Department of Commerce, 1975: 211).

Over 280,000 bituminous coalminers struck during the first six months after U.S. entry into the war in April 1917, with some miners walking out on multiple occasions. These strikes were unauthorized by UMWA districts and international union officials who supported the wartime no-strike pledge. In Illinois, where 25,000 miners joined the strike wave, district officials worked with federal authorities to force miners to return to work. Local miners were infuriated by inflation, profiteering, and record profits for coal companies, as well as rumors of corporate profiteering and rising accident rates in the mines as a result of speed-up to meet wartime demand. In one southern Illinois mine, the nonfatal accident rate increased by 42 percent (Weinberg, 2005: 63–73).

In the post–war era, scattered rank-and-file discontent coalesced into organized rebellion against union leadership. While the most dramatic event was the refusal of miners to obey a directive from union president John L. Lewis to end a 1919 strike and return to work, there were other challenges to the international office's authority. Remnants of the district autonomy coalition regrouped around a more militant program. Rank-and-file groups challenged corrupt or incompetent district officials allied with the international leadership. Scattered rank-and-file wildcat strikes represented a challenge to the Lever Act and the national union's no-strike pledge.

The November 1919, strike was condemned in the media and by coal operators and the federal government. A spokesman for the operators denounced the strike as Bolshevism, charged that it was being financed from Moscow, and claimed miners were influenced by Lenin and Trotsky. A front-page *New York Times* article dismissed the strike as "embittered revolutionary radicalism" and a statement issued by President Wilson called the strike "unjustifiable" and "unlawful." Wilson placed federal troops on alert and Attorney General Mitchell Palmer obtained a restraining order and an injunction against strikers from a federal judge. When the injunction went into effect, Lewis issued a statement that "We will comply with the mandate of the court. We do this under protest. We are Americans. We cannot fight our government." However, in most fields the miners remained on strike until the first weeks of December, when with the onset of winter, and after receiving a compromise offer from President Wilson, they agreed to return to work (Weinberg, 2005: 181–89; *New York Times*, November 8, 1919: 1).

Much of the rank-and-file discontent was temporarily defused by the settlement of the 1919 strike and the achievement of the seven dollar and fifty cents base daily wage for Central Competitive Field miners. Lewis was also able to outmaneuver his opposition at the union's international conventions, playing factions off against each other, channeling opposition into areas that were less threatening to the international office, and mobilizing some of his opponents to support his challenge to Samuel Gompers's leadership of the AFL. However, by 1922 the continued overproduction of bituminous coal and the concomitant saturation of the coal market had re-created the crisis conditions that existed in the industry prior to the war. In West Virginia over 60 percent of the state's 115 thousand miners were out of work. Many of the trends obscured during the unusually high consumer demand of World War I resurfaced. From 1920 to 1930 the value of overall bituminous coal production declined by 60 percent from 2 billion dollars in 1920 to 795 million dollars in 1930. Even with increased exports during the British coal strike in 1926, the Brookings Institute estimated that capacity was twice as large as demand (Tryon & McKinney, March 25, 1922: 1009–13; *The Survey*, April 8, 1922: 40–41; Bernstein, 1966: 127; Hamilton and Wright, 1926: 263–65; Wickersham, 1951: 19).

The unionized fields, primarily in the North, suffered the most from the imbalance of capacity and demand. The southern nonunion mines were able to take advantage of favorable long-haul shipping rates and the lower nonunion wage scale to hold onto the traditionally northern coal markets they had entered during the war. Many of the larger southern operations were owned by the same companies that operated union mines in the North. These companies were increasingly meeting their contracts by using the cheaper southern coal. Other elements contributed to the problems of the union miner. Demand declined as industrial consumers used coal more efficiently and new sources of fuel were developed. From 1920 to 1929, the price of coal charged the railroads dropped from $4.20 per ton to $2.40 per ton. Meanwhile, increased mechanization boosted productivity in the coalfields from 3.84 tons to 5.06 tons per man-day (Bernstein, 1966: 128; Wickersham, 1951: 24).

The position of miners continued to deteriorate as operators worked to improve their competitive position and the trend toward mechanization increased overcapacity. In the outlying fields operator associations saw open-shop drives as their only remedy. They believed the elimination of the UMWA would free them to change traditional work patterns, lower prices, and recapture lost markets. Meanwhile John L. Lewis and the international office concentrated on securing their hold on the union machinery by combating militancy and silencing opposition. They appeared to accept the renewed crisis in the industry as unavoidable. Union spokesman, Ellis Searles, editor of the *UMWA Journal*, defined the problem as "too many mines and too many miners." He proposed a "big step in the direction of stabilization would be taken if 30% of the mines and 30% of the miners were eliminated." However, Searles did not suggest how the UMWA would survive this debacle (Searles, 1922: 639–42; Bernstein, 1966: 211–12; Zieger, 1969: 116–27, 219–27).

In opposition to the leadership's accommodationist position, a new tide of rank-and-file militancy pressed the business unionists in the international office to lead a nationwide strike in April 1922. Because of demands by Districts 2 and 5, the strike also included the long-promised effort to organize nonunion miners outside the Central Competitive Field. The 1922 strike was a key point in the conversion of the rank-and-file opposition from militant insurgency to a class-conscious working-class movement. During this period the rank-and-file opposition developed an ideology that combined the traditional values of the miner with a political program for improving the miner's position in society. The program coupled a defense of the miners' traditional work freedom with the UMWA's 1919 Cleveland program. When Lewis signed an agreement for the Central Competitive Field in August 1922 that abandoned the outlying and newly organized fields, miners in Districts 2 and 5 continued to strike. Lacking an organizational center or unified program, the miners were unable to win the strike against both the open-shop forces and the undermining tactics of Lewis and the business unionists. However, as a result of their efforts during the strike, rank-and-file miners developed a new corps of leaders, and by 1923 this leadership group was attempting to organize a permanent opposition structure within the UMWA. They were supported by leftwing and radical organizations that saw the miners' movement as a force for progressive change in America (Brophy, 1964: 176–99).

Rank-and-File Rebellion

Rank-and-file unrest reached a climax in the UMWA at the end of World War I. During the next three years union activists tried to capitalize on the postwar resentments of bituminous coalminers to build a vigorous class-conscious challenge to the business unionism that dominated the UMWA. John L. Lewis initially tried to take advantage of localized insurgencies to consolidate his hold on the union, however as the rank-and-file movement developed into a significant political force, it threatened both business unionists in the district autonomy coalition and the union's international office. In 1919 rank-and-file bituminous coal miners were upset by several developments: the relative deterioration of their standard of living compared to workers with similar levels of skill in other industries; a growing sense among miners that the union's leadership lacked a coherent vision for the future; and the international office's preoccupation with the Central Competitive Field at the expense of the outlying districts. From December 1915 through 1919, the cost of living for American workers rose by 99.3 percent. With the lure of higher paying jobs in munitions plants, many miners left the coalfields, and in April 1917, operators were forced to pay a "voluntary" wage increase to hold their workforce. However, by 1919 the average bituminous coal miner was earning only $1,583 per year, equivalent to about $28,000 in 2023 dollars. This was below the minimum subsistence level of $1,600 set by the Bureau of Labor Statistics (Kopald, 1924: 53–57).

Hard-pressed coal miners believed that the suspension of the wartime coal price freeze on February 1, 1919, signaled a long overdue wage increase. This was especially true in the areas outside the Central Competitive Field. In the western fields of Washington, Montana, and Wyoming union miners were earning between seventy-five cents and a dollar a day less than miners in Illinois in the CCF, and they were demanding wage equalization. In the UMWA district in British Columbia, disgruntled miners toyed with the idea of seceding from the UMWA and joining an Industrial Workers of the World type group, the One Big Union. In District 14 (Kansas) District President Alexander Howat led a walkout against the wage freeze in April 1919 (Kopald, 1924: 64–70; Everling, 1976: 133).

By July 1919, the restiveness among the coal miners had spread to the established Central Competitive Field. A number of Illinois District 12 locals struck without the approval of either the District or national offices. Theoretically, they were participating in a four-day nationwide strike set for July 4–8 to protest the arrest of San Francisco labor organizer Tom Mooney. However, the key demand of the strike was an end to the wartime wage freeze. Though the striking coal miners were only scheduled to work on Monday, July 7, and Tuesday, July 8, the operators used the penalty clause established under the Lever Act to fine the men a dollar a day for four days. This particularly rattled the miners because work was slack, and the mines were operating only one or two days a week. When the miners received their docked paychecks on August 1, a general walkout was launched in Illinois Subdistrict 7 located around Belleville. Under the leadership of local union officers Freeman Thompson and Luke Coffey, the strike quickly spread into the adjacent Peoria subdistrict (Kopald, 1924: 33, 64–70, 122).

The Illinois wildcat strikes were a direct challenge to the authority of the District and international offices and drove a wedge between District 12 President Frank Farrington and Alexander Howat, key leaders of the district autonomy–based coalition. Initially the wildcat strikers appealed to Farrington requesting a special District Policy Committee meeting to explain the issues in the strike. When Farrington and the District office refused to call the meeting, the insurgents bypassed the district structure and made a direct appeal to the miners of District 12. An insurgent district convention was scheduled for August 19, 1919. The insurgents claimed support for the convention from 141 locals representing 57,703 Illinois miners. Faced with open rebellion, Farrington put aside his differences with John L. Lewis and the international office. After consulting with Lewis, Farrington declared the insurgents dual unionists and directed Illinois miners to scab against the strikers. In a circular addressed to the miners of District 12, Farrington presented a business-unionist view of rank-and-file activism. He argued, "Our union is facing a crisis. The elements of destruction are at work. The issue is: 'Shall the forces of defiance and rebellion prevail and stab our union to death, or shall reason and orderly procedure dominate the affairs of the United Mine Workers of America?'" (Kopald, 1924: 32, 88–100; Everling, 1976: 149–50; Wickersham, 1951: 35–86).

In a circular issued by the international office, Lewis accused the insurgents of creating confusion among miners by violating the no-strike pledge in the wartime Washington agreement. Lewis argued that the agreement was still in force and charged that the leaders of the strike were dual unionists committed to destroying the UMWA. Lewis empowered Farrington to spend $27,000 to suppress the strike and authorized him to revoke the charters of striking locals. Under pressure from Farrington and Lewis, and with a slow summer production schedule diluting the impact of the strike, many of the miners started to drift back to work. However, twenty-four locals, centered around Locals 238 and 99 in the Belleville subdistrict, continued the walkout. When Farrington revoked their local charters, they carried their fight to the September 1919 UMWA convention (Kopald, 1924: 118; UMWA MA, Circular, August 18, 1919).

At the convention, Alexander Howat, who led District 14 (Kansas) miners on a similar wildcat strike in April, 1919, sided with the insurgents and introduced a motion to seat delegates from the suspended locals. The convention debated whether the insurgents intended to set up a new and dual miner's union when they issued their call for a District 12 convention. Spokesmen for the insurgents denied any dualistic intentions. They insisted that their strike was legal and cited the withdrawal of the penalties by some companies because the men had not actually missed any work during the July protest. They also argued for the legality of the insurgent convention. The locals had followed the district bylaws and circulated valid petitions demanding a district convention. They accused Farrington of violating union procedures by refusing to honor the petitions. John L. Lewis, as chairman of the UMWA convention, sided with Farrington and the District 12 office. To silence debate on the wildcat and the no-strike pledge, he made a procedural ruling that Howat's motion to seat the delegates was out of order because it violated UMWA bylaws forbidding the seating of locals that were not in good standing. The convention sustained the ruling by a vote of 1,704 to 288 (UMWA Proceedings, 1919: 462–559).

The insurgents continued their struggle at the Illinois District Convention where debate centered on the validity of independent political action inside the miners' union. District President Farrington condemned all political factions and independent committees and demanded a constitutional amendment outlawing any political or union activities outside the established district channels. His supporters tried to discredit the rank-and-file strike movement, charging that it was instigated by the Socialist Labor Party. Farrington's views on political activism, which carried the district convention, later emerged as the official stance of the business unionists in the international office. A UMWA constitutional amendment was never needed however, as insurgency eventually became proof of dual unionism and grounds for expulsion from the union (UMWA District 12 Proceedings, 1920: 14–17).

Despite the concerted efforts of Lewis and Farrington, the rising tide of rank-and-file unrest was not easily quashed. Pockets of discontent emerged in other districts in the union paralleling the growth of insurgent forces in Illinois. District President Alexander Howat led an insurgent struggle in District 14 Kansas, an outlying district only marginally related to the national coal market. During the fall 1919 strike, the state of Kansas, heavily dependent on locally mined coal for home heating fuel, pressed Howat to negotiate an independent settlement for the district. When Howat refused to break ranks with the rest of the union, the Kansas State Supreme Court authorized the governor to seize and operate the mines. Eventually the governor assigned 1,500 state troopers to reopen the mines using scab labor. The battle between the militant Kansas district and the Kansas state government continued for the next four years. It finally ended when UMWA president John L. Lewis, in an effort to break the insurgent movement in the union, declared District 14 in violation of a legal contract. Lewis created a "new" district office and barred Howat from holding any position in the union; the miners were ordered back to work by their new officers, and scabs from neighboring unionized fields were used to undermine any continued resistance (Gagliardo, 1941: 16–20, 135–40; Wickersham, 1951: 68–71; UMWA MA Circular, December 19, 1921; Vorse, 1922: 359–60).

In District 5, the western Pennsylvania region that included the Pittsburgh area, rank-and-file opposition to the district office and the international union stemmed from an unpopular 1916 district contract signed by Van Bittner, an international union agent and an important Lewis ally. A caucus of dissatisfied miners emerged in Charleroi, Pennsylvania, with a program that included opposition to penalty clauses, a demand for honest district elections, accident compensation, and a drive to organize nonunion miners in the neighboring coke fields south of the district. An important feature of the Charleroi group was its conscious attempt to appeal to the increasing number of non-English-speaking Slavic, Hungarian, and southern Italian miners in the district. The group demanded that contracts and district notices be printed in a number of different languages. It carefully avoided political dogma in its releases and urged the district's leadership to join in involving the miners of District 5 in active political struggle (Everling, 1976: 153).

In 1920, the Charleroi miners circulated a petition calling for a special district convention to discuss their program. Fifty locals were required to endorse the call to make it official and the insurgents received the backing of seventy. The district office's response was to ignore the call for a convention. When the insurgents bypassed the district office and scheduled the convention for November 1920, they were denounced as dual unionists. Even without the endorsement by District 5, 100 delegates representing 81 locals attended the convention. At the conference, the most pressing call was to organize nonunion miners in the coke fields in neighboring Districts 2 and 6. The insurgents' also challenged District 5 leadership loyal to John L. Lewis and the international office. Michael Halapy, a longtime associate of the district autonomy group, editor of the *UMWA Journal* under union President White from 1910 to 1911, and candidate for District 5 president in 1911, chaired the convention. Frank Farrington, Robert Harlin, and Alexander Howat wired pledges of support. The most influential member of the convention was its secretary, Thomas Myerscough. Myerscough was an officer of Local 1198, a founder of the Charleroi group and a member of the Workers' (Communist) Party. Under Myerscough's direction the convention attacked the legitimacy of the incumbent District 5 office. It set up a new district organization and requested insurgent locals to send dues to the new District office (Everling, 154–55).

District 2 (Central Pennsylvania) also emerged as a center of rank-and-file activism during and after World War I. In 1916, John Brophy was elected district president on an insurgent slate when incumbent district officials alienated miners by ignoring local issues. As district president, Brophy pressed the national union for a drive to organize nonunion miners in District 2 and near-by nonunion fields. District 2's support for an organizing drive was stimulated by the local impact of the nationwide 1919 steel strike. On September 22, 1919, Cambria Steel in Johnstown, Pennsylvania, locked out its employees. The company fired the leaders of the local AFL affiliate, requested federal immigration officials deport "alien" dissidents among the local union leaders, and demanded that the steelworkers agree to return to work on a nonunion basis. District 2 miners saw the steel strike as an opportunity to organize steel-company–owned bituminous coal mines in the southern end of the district. Dominick Gelotte, a former checkweightman from nearby Nanty Glo, Pennsylvania, and a District 2 mine organizer, was dispatched to Johnstown to aid the striking steelworkers. While armed vigilantes succeeded in closing Johnstown to Gelotte and other "agitators," the miners continued with a push to organize nonunion mines in Somerset County. The fall 1919 organizing drive in District 2 was ultimately stymied by confusion over the legality of the November strike because of the wartime wage freeeze, but District 2 applied to the international union for support for an independent drive in 1920. When Lewis denied the district's request, Brophy and the District 2 miners primed for a new organizing drive scheduled for spring 1922 (Brophy, 1964: 121–22; Soule, 1920: 10, 23–26, 40–43; UMWA MA, Committee on Organization, July 29, 1920).

Lewis' Counterstrategy

John L. Lewis was sensitive to the new political balance in the UMWA created by the rank-and-file insurgents. While keeping a cautious eye on the development of the rank-and-file movement, he tried to use this new force to enhance his political position. When it suited his purposes, Lewis adopted parts of their program or supported local struggles against his union opponents. On other occasions Lewis hammered away at the illegality of rank-and-file wildcat strikes in an effort to drive a wedge between district autonomy coalition leaders. Lewis used the militant program adopted by the UMWA in 1919 in an unsuccessful drive in 1921 to unseat Samuel Gompers as president of the American Federation of Labor. Lewis had remained silent at the UMWA convention when the district autonomy forces pressed for the adoption of a program endorsing nationalization of the coalmines, formation of a labor party, and a drive to organize the nonunion coalfields. He remained silent on the program during the next two years as Lewis and the international office focused on the 1919 strike, periodic wildcats, the prolonged wage negotiations that followed, and the 1920 UMWA elections (UMWA Proceedings, 1919: 841–49; Dubofsky & Van Tine, 1977: 71–75).

The cornerstone of the Lewis candidacy for AFL president was the UMWA three-point program, coupled with the nationalization of the railroads and unemployment and old-age compensation. Lewis calculated that his endorsement of the militant miners' program would solidify the UMWA dissidents behind his candidacy and attract support from other progressive union leaders. However, while Lewis was able to secure active support from Adolph Germer and John Brophy, district autonomy coalition opponents Walker, Howat, Harlin, and Farrington worked to help Gompers turn back the Lewis challenge. By the September 1921, UMWA convention, Lewis' support for the program had dissolved. He told the UMWA convention that "eminent authorities" had declared nationalization unpractical in the American federal system of government. To remove the issue from the convention floor, he proposed that a Nationalization Research Committee be formed to "translate our declaration into the realm of practical accomplishment" (Dubofsky & Van Tine, 1977: 73–75; Brophy Papers, June 1921; Brophy, 1964: 157–60; UMWA Proceedings, 1921: 92).

Lewis also supported rank-and-file insurgent groups that threatened to undercut his opponents. He backed rank-and-file activists in District 10 (Washington) in an attack on his 1920 election opponent, Robert Harlin. In February 1921 operators in the state of Washington announced a wage cut and locked out union miners. The state government appointed District 10 President Harlin as a member of a fact-finding commission to investigate the issues and make recommendations to solve the impasse. When the commission reported in favor of a wage cut, Lewis supported district miners who accused Harlin of selling out. Lewis supporters also spread rumors that Harlin had diverted district funds toward his 1920 candidacy for UMWA president (Everling, 1976: 167–68).

In a major political setback for the district autonomy coalition, Lewis took advantage of the Illinois rank-and-file movement's attack on Frank Farrington to drive a wedge between Farrington and Alexander Howat. Howat, president of District 14 (Kansas), was an outspoken advocate of rank-and-file activism. He viewed the district autonomy coalition as a way of defending union democracy and local initiative. Howat rejected the business unionist's concept of the contract and argued that the willingness to strike was the miner's principle weapon. From 1919 to 1922, Howat led strikes in Kansas and supported wildcats in other fields over grievance issues and in violation of state laws and court injunctions. Farrington epitomized the business-unionist conception of the UMWA. He supported the district autonomy–based coalition to protect the independence of District 12 against the encroachments of Lewis and the international office and as a vehicle to challenge Lewis for the UMWA presidency. The differences between Howat and Farrington came to a head in 1919, when Howat supported wildcat strikers in Illinois.

Lewis, who authorized Farrington to suppress the wildcats, worked to keep this division fresh to split his opposition. At the union's September 1921 convention and the reconvened sessions in February 1922, Lewis used the conflict between Farrington and Howat to eliminate Howat as a force in the union. Howat was in a vulnerable position, despite his popularity among rank-and-file union militants. Lewis suspended Howat from district office when District 14 struck against a Kansas state law requiring compulsory arbitration in all labor disputes involving "public utilities." Lewis argued that the strike was in violation of a valid contract. When Farrington and other district autonomy advocates opposed the removal of a district president from office as a threat to the union's district structure, Lewis turned on Farrington. In a series of acrimonious letters, Lewis demanded an official accounting of a $27,000 fund Farrington was charged with diverting from the fall 1919 war chest to defeat dissidents (UMWA MA Frank Farrington File; Gagliardo, 1941: 135, 140; UMWA Proceedings, 1921, vol. 2: 606–7, 614–28).

At the 1921 convention Lewis presented the international union's explanation for its suspension of Howat from office and cited testimony by UMWA representatives before a Senate Investigatory Committee to support his position. "They asked whether the United Mine Workers was an honorable institution and believed in carrying out its pledges and contracts, and they said: 'Yes.' And then Mr. Olmstead, Secretary of the Labor Committee of the Williamson Coal Operators' Association read into the record that session a list of 705 unauthorized strikes in District 14 in 45 months." Lewis then quoted John Mitchell, "I attribute the success of the United Mine Workers of America to the fact that its officers have been men who, in season and out of season, and even though heavens may fall, urged upon their members to comply with their moral and legal obligations under their wage agreements." John Walker of Illinois presented the district autonomy coalition's response to Lewis. Walker argued that "any district has a right to fight for the things it believes it should have that are right without consulting the international union or even getting the consent of the international if they do not want to, providing they do not ask the international to finance their strike." Despite Walker's argument, Lewis carried the convention in a surprising show of strength by a vote of 2,925 to 1,510 (UMWA Proceedings, 1921, vol. 2: 628, 630, 684, 953).

At the close of the convention Lewis moved to consolidate his victory, setting up a parallel district structure in Kansas to bypass officials loyal to Howat. Van Bittner, a Lewis representative, and George L. Beck, a District 14 representative on the International Executive Board headed the new pro-Lewis district office. Lewis was supported by local coal operators who refused to hire miners loyal to Howat and federal officials who used prohibition violations as an excuse to raid pro-Howat mine camps. District coal miners who refused allegiance to the new district office were denied transfer cards that would permit them to work in neighboring districts. By December 2021, the international office claimed most Kansas miners had accepted the authority of the new district office and returned to work. While Lewis acted in Kansas, the district autonomy forces mobilized to reraise the issue at the reconvened UMWA convention in February 1922. At the convention they succeeded in pressuring Lewis to permit Howat to speak and cut sharply into the Lewis majority. However, Lewis marshaling all the powers of office, including a solidly pro-Lewis delegation from the new Kansas district office and the votes of international appointees to sustain the Howat suspension (Gagliardo, 1941: 140–45; Wickersham, 1951: 71–75; Dubofsky & Van Tine: 118–21).

One of Lewis' most effective devices against rank-and-file insurgency was a spy network of organizers on the international payroll. These organizers were used to keep track of potentially dangerous rank-and-file militants, to report on dissident meetings, to spread dissension in districts and locals hostile to Lewis, to locate loyal miners willing to oppose insurgents in their locals, and to collect potentially damaging information that could be stored for future use. The reports from the spy network were extensive and carefully collected in files at UMWA headquarters. When the network proved inadequate, private security police and informers were hired to supplement the data. One example of the Lewis network in operation was the careful compilation of information on John Brophy. Brophy was a relative political unknown when he was elected District 2 president as a reform candidate in 1916. International organizer David Irvine began submitting reports on Brophy and District 2 political affairs soon after Brophy took office (UMWA MA Anti-Communism File; UMWA MA District 2 File).

During World War I, Brophy supported a controversial call for a national convention to discuss an end to the wage freeze. The international office viewed this as a direct challenge and international organizers Irvine and Fred Thomas were assigned to work against Brophy in the 1918 district elections. Thomas openly supported an opposition slate headed by a district board member, traveling the district to attack Brophy for "knifing the national." In an open violation of the UMWA by-laws, Thomas refused to report to the district office. After Brophy was reelected, Thomas tried to undermine Brophy's reputation, accusing him of stealing the election. Thomas operated in District 2 as long as Brophy was perceived as a threat to Lewis. During the 1922 Somerset strike, Thomas worked with Charles O'Neill, Secretary of the Central Pennsylvania Coal Producers' Association and a district organizer accused of financial malfeasance, to torpedo efforts to organize unorganized miners because they upstaged the limited efforts by the international union (UMWA MA District 2 File; Brophy, 1964: 127; Blankenhorn, 1924, passim; UMWA District 2 Proceedings, 1923).

Open-Shop Drive

Lewis and the international office's preoccupation with stifling dissent and cementing control over the UMWA combined with their philosophical commitment to continued accommodation with the bituminous coal industry blinded them to the increasing open-shop sentiment among the large operators. The union's failure to secure a nationwide contract during the war and to expand membership in the outlying and nonunion fields after the 1919 strike left the UMWA vulnerable to an open-shop campaign in the 1920s as conditions in the industry deteriorated. Lewis believed that the union could build on its wartime relationship to government and the industry to find an equitable solution to the problems of mining bituminous coal. He counted on Secretary of Commerce Herbert Hoover to mediate the differences between the union and the coal operators, however, Lewis and the business unionists in the international office overestimated the willingness of both government and capital to grant labor a voice in the management of the industry.

The first successful open-shop drive against the UMWA was launched in Mingo and McDowell counties, West Virginia, in 1921. Nestled in the southwest corner of the state, these counties were isolated from the stronger union fields and made poor showings during the 1919 strike. The open-shop drive was instigated by two of the country's leading corporate empires, U.S. Steel and the J. P. Morgan financial interests. Morgan interests were represented in the field by the Norwalk and Western Railroad, part of the Pennsylvania system, that held an interlocking directorship with the Morgan-dominated Girard and Guaranty Trust banks. The U.S. Steel Corporation owned 150,000 acres of coal land in the region, much of it purchased during World War I. The open-shop drive, headed by Tom Lewis, a former president of the UMWA and secretary of the New River Operators Association, was well organized and financed. The companies provoked a strike by lowering the wage scale below the union rate. Private Baldwin guards were used to evict striking miners and protect strikebreakers. When miners attempted to interrupt operation of the mines, state troopers reinforced the private police force and UMWA organizers were driven out of the counties. The companies also secured court injunctions in West Virginia and neighboring Kentucky outlawing any UMWA activity in the area. Despite John L. Lewis' protests to President Harding that the state courts had effectively outlawed unionism, the federal government did not intercede. By 1922, wartime membership gains in Kentucky, Tennessee, and West Virginia were lost; the unionized portion of the West Virginia mine workforce declined from a high of 29 percent to 22.4 percent; and southern West Virginia was totally nonunion (*Federated Press*, June 4, July 31, 1921; January 1, 1924; Warne, 1922: 1246–49; Lauck, 1922: 2207–307; Dubofsky & Van Tine, 1977: 76–79; UMWA Archive Lewis Misc. File, August 26, 1921).

The threat by bituminous coal operators to either lower the wage rate or operate nonunion spread to other fields. In Central Pennsylvania, Thomas Watkins, president of the Pennsylvania Coal and Coke Company and of the Central Pennsylvania Coal Producers' Association, demanded that District 2 miners break with the national agreement and mine coal on the 1917 wage scale. Central Competitive Field operators, anxious to improve their declining competitive position, pressed the union to accept a lower wage rate and permit the mechanization and reorganization of production without interference. Increasingly, nonunion tonnage played a dominant role in mining affairs. By 1922 the nonunion fields were capable of supplying the nation's coal needs for a sustained period in event of a strike. The operators in the union fields believed that the UMWA could not risk a nationwide strike, and in February 1922, the *New York Times* accused Lewis of bluffing when he issued a strike threat. UMWA Secretary-Treasurer William Green commented on the crumbling of the fragile remnants of the wartime coalition of business unionists, government regulators, and union operators in his report to the 1921 UMWA convention: "The idealism which seemed to inspire all classes of people during the World War had disappeared. . . . The forces of opposition have become arrogant and aggressive until now organized labor is forced to defend itself against hostile legislation, open-shop attacks, and destructive enemies" (Dubofsky & Van Tine, 1977:

80–82; Lesher, 1022: 1040–41; UMWA District 2 Proceedings, 1922: 29; Central Pennsylvania Coal Producers' Association, 1923: 5–108; Response to the Brief of the Central Pennsylvania Coal Producers' Association and the Association of Bituminous Coal Operators of Central Pennsylvania, August 4, 1923, Hapgood Papers; Tryon & McKenney, March 25, 1922: 1009–12; Hamilton & Wright, 1926: 276–77; *New York Times*, February 2, 1922: 17; February 3, 13; February 23: 1; April 4: 11; UMWA Proceedings, 1921: 3).

In spring 1922, the major operators refused to renew the Central Competitive Field Agreement. Lewis, elected UMWA president in 1920 on the strength of the $7.50 daily base wage for the CCF, could not accept a wage reduction or the abandonment of the CCF as a bargaining unit and was forced to support a nationwide strike under the banner of "No Backward Step." With a strike unavoidable, the union sought a strategy to inhibit nonunion production. Eventually the international office acquiesced to pressure from the rank-and-file movement and the beleaguered outlying districts and issued a call inviting nonunion miners to join the walkout. Though the international office officially sought a uniform $7.50 base daily rate in the coalfields, Lewis viewed the broader strike as a tactical move to prevent the CCF operators from meeting their contracts during a strike with coal mined in nonunion southern fields. His real goal was to draw operators representing sufficient bituminous coal tonnage to the negotiating table so the union could renew the CCF pact.

Lewis believed the federal government would intervene in the conflict to produce a settlement that would help stabilize the bituminous coal industry. However, he completely misjudged the willingness of the Republican administration to support the kind of tripartite operation of the industry that existed during the war. President Warren G. Harding and Secretary of Commerce Hoover insisted that the government had to protect the public interest and encouraged the nonunion production of coal. As the strike dragged on into the summer, Harding telegrammed twenty-eight governors of coal-producing states urging state militia protection for nonunion operation of the mines. The Harding administration's concept of the public good was decidedly pro-business. In the bituminous coal industry, it was based on the false premise that the union and nonunion operators were competing groups. It assumed that if nonunion production threatened traditionally union markets, the union operators and union miners would recognize their common interests and compromise. The plan failed to take account of the expansion of the large operators into the nonunion fields during the war. If they were able to run their nonunion mines with government protection, they would starve the UMWA into submission. Meanwhile, internal bickering between Lewis and Farrington threatened to undermine the strike. Farrington, in an effort to upstage Lewis, threatened to sign an independent agreement with the Illinois operators. UMWA Secretary-Treasurer William Green ordered him not to sign a district pact as long as the international union had a chance to set up a CCF Conference (Dubofsky & Van Tine, 1977: 83–84, 86; Zieger, 1969: 116, 127; Wickersham, 1951: 40–44).

Throughout all this, the men in both the union and nonunion fields held on doggedly. They received a boost when a July 1 railroad shopmen's strike interfered with the shipment of nonunion southern coal, and by the end of July the operators were prepared to negotiate. In August, Michael Gallagher, president of the Pittsburgh Vein Operators' Association, and Lewis arranged a deal that set up a Central Competitive Field Conference. Gallagher provided sufficient tonnage for Lewis to claim a national agreement, and in return Lewis agreed to sacrifice the nonunion and outlying fields, permitting operators to sign contracts for selective operations. The deal, engineered by Al Hamilton, Lewis' longtime associate among District 5 operators, also included a two-hundred-thousand-dollar loan from the Harriman National Bank of New York to guarantee the union's solvency. To ensure compliance with the agreement, Lewis withdrew strike benefits from miners in the nonunion fields, claiming the need to consolidate funds (Dubofsky & Van Tine, 1977: 87–88; *New York Times*, August 8: 1, 2; August 10: 1, 3, August 13, 1922: 3).

The CCF conference hit a temporary snag when, at Farrington's prompting, Illinois operators refused to attend. Instead, Lewis substituted some Northern West Virginia operations traditionally excluded from the CCF settlement. With approximately 100 million tons of coal from outlying districts, and 70 percent of the CCF tonnage, Lewis declared that a CCF agreement had been reached. On August 15, Lewis signed a contract that covered Ohio, Indiana, and Western Pennsylvania. Farrington, outmaneuvered by Lewis, signed the same agreement for Illinois on August 22 (*New York Times*, August 8: 1, August 10: 1, August 13, 1922: 3; Wickersham, 1951: 44; Brophy, 1964: 192–99).

The operators viewed the final settlement as a major victory and announced that the CCF had been repudiated. At the conclusion of the conference, Thomas H. Watkins, president of the Pennsylvania Coal and Coke Company declared, "The Central Competitive Field, to which we attribute most of our past difficulties, was definitely broken up and abandoned yesterday and the meeting thrown open to the operators and miners from every district in the United States." Major companies like U.S. Steel were able to operate union mines in Illinois and Indiana, while operating nonunion at Frick Coal in Pennsylvania. Consolidation Coal, a Rockefeller company, signed union agreements for its northern West Virginia mines, but continued to operate nonunion in Maryland and Central Pennsylvania. Peabody Coal, whose officials maintained close ties with District 12 and the international office, ran union in Illinois and nonunion in Pennsylvania (*New York Times*, August 16, 1922: 3; Brophy, 1964: 190–91).

Whether the contract was a victory for the operators or not, Lewis had traded on the future of the UMWA to secure a short-term contract and temporary advantage over his opposition in the union. The business unionists in the international office were betting the solvency of the UMWA on cooperation with management and a Republican administration that had demonstrated its unwillingness to cooperate with labor. The thousands of miners in the outlying districts and nonunion fields who joined the strike to win a national contract and union recognition were closed out of the agreement. Lewis miscalculated if he expected the activism and spirit of unionism generated by the strike to easily defuse. Many coalfields were racked by wildcats as union miners refused to return to work while their neighbors remained on strike. During the long summer months, the ideas of group solidarity and of organizing the unorganized spread deep roots. Instead of collapsing, the rank-and-file movement in the UMWA continued to grow.

Chapter 6

John Brophy and the "Miners' Program"

The 1922 nationwide bituminous coal strike presented UMWA insurgents with an opportunity to develop the class-conscious understanding of rank-and-file miners in the union and nonunion fields while organizing against the business unionist practices of Lewis and the UMWA international office and the open-shop drive mounted by the operators. During the strike, two groups emerged committed to integrating trade union organization and political struggle in a battle to defend the "Miner's Freedom" and achieve the political goals of the 1919 Cleveland convention. Each group had a distinct base of support that contributed to its organizing efforts during and after the strike. One group was located in District 2 (Central Pennsylvania) and centered on its district president, John Brophy. District 2 provided a political subdivision inside the UMWA where programs could be implemented and ideas tested. The second group was organized by the Charleroi Committee in District 5 (Western Pennsylvania). This group maintained close ties to William Z. Foster, and many of its leaders were affiliated with the Trade Union Educational League (TUEL) and the Workers' (Communist) Party. This relationship gave the group national connections and ideological and organizational support. However, it also opened it to charges by the international office of taking direction and funds from the Soviet Union. The effectiveness of these groups was circumscribed by their differences. By the time the groups coalesced in 1926, the open shop drive had already defeated the miners and the union in the nonunion and outlying fields and much of the Central Competitive Field (Brophy, 1964: 149–75; Progressive International Conference, 1923).

A number of factors contributed to the emergence of District 2 as a key locus of opposition to the business unionism of the UMWA international office. They included John Brophy's leadership as district president, the district's workers education activities and commitment to the Miners' Program, and the mineralogical, topographical, and ethnic geography of the Central Pennsylvania region. UMWA District 2 included fourteen Central Pennsylvania counties, but its core was Cambria, Clearfield, Indiana, Jefferson, and Blair counties. For the UMWA, it served as a buffer between the Central Competitive Field and nonunion southern Pennsylvania and West Virginia coalfields. It also included the steel-company–owned captive coking mines of Westmoreland-Connellsville and open-shop Somerset County. Its narrow coal seams prevented the District from being included in the CCF accord and District 2 contracts traditionally had slightly modified work rules and wage scales. Because of the expense of widening shafts to install mechanized equipment, manual car-pushing and hand-picking of coal continued to predominate in the district after they were disappearing in other union fields (Blankenhorn, 1924; Goodrich, 1925).

Prior to World War I, District 2 bituminous coal was an important source of fuel for the Pennsylvania Railroad system, the New York City Transit System, and the eastern shipping ports. However, during World War I, many of its markets were taken over by nonunion mines that paid lower wages. A 1922 study prepared by the district showed that a union pick miner in Central Pennsylvania was paid $1.1431 per net ton of bituminous coal, compared to $.9031 per net ton paid to nonunion miners. In neighboring nonunion fields, the differential was even greater. Connellsville miners earned $.626 per net ton; Westmoreland wages ran as low as $.55 per net ton; and in Somerset county wages varied between $.67 and $.98 per net ton. The wage rates in other job categories fluctuated correspondingly (Tyron & Sydney, 1924: 445–662; Brophy, 1964: 193; *New York Times*, January 2, 1923: 1; Fritz & Venstra, 1935: 44, 50, 54, 71–76, 89).

For District 2 miners, the shift in bituminous coal production to the nonunion fields exacerbated the impact of the postwar industrial slump. From 1918 to 1921, production in Cambria County declined from 20.5 million tons to 12.9 million tons per annum. In Clearfield and Indiana counties, production dropped about 60 percent. Overall, in 1921 Central Pennsylvania produced its lowest bituminous coal tonnage since 1908. An open-shop drive in neighboring West Virginia and Maryland fields contributed to the decline. In Maryland, wages dropped to between eighty and ninety cents per net ton. Partly as a result, the Leigh Valley Coal Company completely stopped production at its union mines in District 2. These mines remained closed until an attempt was made to operate nonunion in 1923. In December 1921, the Central Pennsylvania Coal Producers' Association demanded that the wage scale in District 2 be lowered to the prewar 1917 level. In 1923, John Brophy reported on these developments in testimony submitted to the United States Coal Commission (U.S. Mine Bureau, 1921: 650; Central Pennsylvania Coal Producers' Association, 1921, District 2 Papers; Central Pennsylvania Coal Producers' Association, 1923; Brophy, 1964: 170).

The threat of the open-shop drive pressed District 2 officials to develop an imaginative program for stimulating rank-and-file activism and strengthening the district. Organizing in District 2 was difficult. Coal miners lived in isolated coal towns in sparsely settled counties scattered across the Allegheny Mountains. Johnstown, home of Bethlehem Steel, was the only medium-sized city in the region. The situation was also complicated by the large number of Eastern and Southern European immigrants working in District 2 mines. British Isle and native-born miners had to teach this group trade unionism and the traditional notions of the Miner's Freedom while they were learning job skills and the English language. The multiethnic character of these coal towns required the development of a class-conscious rank-and-file movement in Central Pennsylvania, simply so the union could survive—a goal made more difficult when coal operators used a reemergent Klan in the region as a tool to divide miners.

A 1920 ethnic census of Clearfield County in the district revealed that 41 percent of its population of 103,236 was foreign-born or the children of immigrants. The foreign-born population included 2,049 Austrians, 1,063 Czechs, 1,463 Englishmen, 655 Germans, 334 Hungarians, 334 Irish, 2,196 Italians, 1,028 Poles, and 666 Russians; a fair sampling of the late-nineteenth and early-twentieth-century Eastern and Southern European influx into the coal mining region. As early as 1902, records from a gas explosion in a Johnstown coal mine show that among the 114 dead miners, 58 were Poles, 26 Slovaks, 11 Croats, and 4 were Hungarians. Nanty Glo, typical of the larger mining towns in the district in 1920, listed the following organizations among its list of religious institutions and voluntary associations; the St. Nicholas Byzantine Church, the St. John Vianey Church, a Ukrainian Orthodox Church, St. Mary's Roman Catholic Church, a Slovak Hall, and a Sons of Italy. The district office had to win the trust of the non-English-speaking miners to effectively combat operator efforts to undermine the union contract, run open shop, and violate state labor laws (*Pennsylvania Manual*, 1929: 448–49, 456; Storey, 1907: 573–79; *Nanty-Glo Journal*, 1968; Bussel, 1999: 33–34; Hapgood, 1921).

A key element in the development of the District 2 program was the leadership of District President John Brophy. Brophy was elected president of District 2 in 1916 as a dissident candidate opposed to an unresponsive district office. His campaign challenged nepotism and the unwillingness of district officers to contest the operators on payment for car-pushing and unpaid "dead-work" widening tunnels in the narrow-seamed mines. In office, Brophy's ideas matured. In 1919 and 1922, he endorsed a UMWA organizing drive in the nonunion coalfields and supported rank-and-file democratic participation in the union. He also recognized the need for a clear political program rooted in the traditional values and job concerns of the miners to unify the diverse groups in the district and the national union (Brophy, 1964: 121–22).

As District 2 president, Brophy developed an educationally oriented philosophy for stimulating rank-and-file understanding of broader political issues and participation in the daily affairs of the union. A key to his approach was integrating the defense of the traditional concept of the Miner's Freedom on the job and trade union practice, with active organizing for the political program of the 1919 UMWA Cleveland convention. Brophy publicized the 1919 program of nationalization of the mines, organization of the unorganized, and formation of a labor party, as the "Miners' Program," and propagated it through a series of pamphlets and labor education workshops across the district. During the 1922 strike, District 2 utilized Brophy's educational concepts for developing working-class consciousness in its efforts to organize the neighboring nonunion Somerset coalfields. Brophy and the district recognized that the success of the strike, and ultimately of the UMWA, depended on the maturation of the consciousness of union and nonunion miners and the development of a rank-and-file movement. Organizers and educators in the district, some of whom came from outside the union movement, continually worked to develop indigenous leaders among the strikers (*Illinois Miner*, February 3, 1923; Brophy, 1928: 186–91; Hapgood, 1923; Brophy, Mitch, & Golden, 1922b).

A brief look at Brophy's background offers insight into his development as a leader and the growth of political activism among miners in District 2. Brophy, who was born in England and migrated to the United States with his parents in 1892, entered the coal mines in 1895, at the age of twelve. Initially he worked as his father's apprentice, loading coal that his father cut. His interest in unionism was kindled when District 2 was reorganized in spring 1899. Self-educated, Brophy developed his facility in reading and writing and was elected secretary of his Greenwich, Pennsylvania local in 1904, at the age of twenty-one. In this position he earned the trust of his local, and in 1905 he was elected checkweightman. In 1906, he was chosen local president after uncovering a plan by a committeeman to steal strike relief funds. As local president, Brophy helped organize an Independent Labor Party in the Greenwich area. Brophy's activities in Greenwich were short-circuited when the local was defeated in the 1906 strike, which resulted in Brophy being fired and blacklisted in the area (Brophy, 1964: 36–37, 49–50, 80–83, 89–92; Albertson, 1955: 215–38).

Brophy blamed the defeat of the Greenwich local on the international union's decision to accept piecemeal district and local contracts rather than holding out for a national agreement. In 1908, he campaigned against William Wilson's candidacy to succeed John Mitchell as union president because Wilson had endorsed the 1906 decision. The successful candidate, T. L. Lewis, offered Brophy a position as an international organizer, however, Brophy was involved in rebuilding Local 1386 in Nanty Glo, Pennsylvania, and declined. Brophy was elected to a number of local positions in Nanty Glo, and in 1908 was chosen a representative to the UMWA's international convention (Brophy, 1964: 98–100).

Brophy did not emerge as a significant figure in the national union until his 1916 election to the District 2 presidency. He was propelled to a narrow victory by the general rank-and-file dissatisfaction with the failure of wages to keep up with the rising cost of living. Once in office Brophy tried to channel the unrest that led to his election into an organizing drive in the neighboring nonunion Somerset field. The international union, suspicious of Brophy as an outsider, refused to assist the campaign. John L. Lewis responded to an appeal for help by rejecting what he considered guerrilla warfare against two of the largest operators in Somerset County— Consolidation and Berwind-White—as folly (UMWA MA District 2 File; Dubofsky & Van Tine, 1977: 77–78; Brophy, 1964: 121–22, 136).

When the district continued the drive independently, Lewis dispatched international organizer Fred Thomas to the field to undercut Brophy and his supporters. In 1918, Thomas and former District Vice President O'Neill, now a district administrator for the United States Fuel Administration, launched a campaign accusing Brophy of failing to win a closed shop in the district because he would not cooperate with the operators. They also sponsored Frank Waite for district president in an effort to oust Brophy, but misjudged the depth of support for Brophy in the district. Waite, who was easily defeated, was then placed on the international office payroll (UMWA MA District 2 File; Brophy 1964: 120–28).

Organization of Somerset County bituminous coal miners remained a priority for Brophy and District 2. At the 1919 UMWA convention, the district appealed for international support in an organizing drive. After funds were denied, the District 2 delegates decided to press their position again at the 1921 UMWA convention where representatives of Somerset miners pleaded with the convention to support a drive to organize 90,000 nonunion miners and to prevent their being used to undercut union wages in neighboring fields (Brophy, 1964: 176–99).

Brophy's concept of trade unionism made his ideas a significant challenge to the business unionism of Lewis and the international office. His philosophy, which he described in the pamphlet, *The Miners' Program* (1921), coupled the idea of trade union responsibility with the democratic participation of the rank-and-file, and included the expansion of the union through organization of unorganized workers, respect for education and ideas, a willingness to form coalitions to achieve mutual goals with groups outside the labor movement, and a commitment to long-term goals and struggles. Brophy believed that responsible and disciplined militancy was the strength of the union movement and rejected the idea that cooperation with the operators would protect the worker (Brophy, 1964: 154–56; Brophy, 1922: 1026–29; Brophy, 1928: 186–91).

Brophy's strong belief in organizational responsibility and union discipline made him somewhat of an enigma to some union militants and members of the district autonomy coalition. During World War I, he opposed unauthorized wildcat strikes, declaring that strikes "in violation of the Agreement cannot be justified and should not occur. Union men should not, and if they understand the principles of our union, they will not be a party to, or promote or approve such strikes." In November 1919, Brophy decided not to openly challenge Lewis' efforts to torpedo the nationwide strike. At both the 1921 and 1924 UMWA conventions, Brophy broke ranks with militant rank-and-file activists when he felt the issues they were raising, a challenge to Alexander Howat's suspension and the election of international organizers, threatened the integrity of the union (UMWA MA District 2 File; UMWA Proceedings, 1919, vol. 1: 462–559; UMWA Proceedings, 1921, vol. 2: 953; UMWA Proceedings, 1924, 622).

Typical of Brophy's concept of responsible unionism was his contin-ued effort to win the support of the international union for a campaign to organize nonunion miners in Somerset County. After repeated rejection, the

District 2 Executive Board met with Vice President Philip Murray in August 1921 to "clear up misunderstandings," and Brophy agreed to postpone a campaign until the CCF contract expired in April 1922 (Brophy, 1964: 176–80; UMWA MA District 2 File).

One of the key qualities that made Brophy an effective leader was his open and curious mind. Though he had no formal education, Brophy respected ideas and learning. As a young man he read many socialist books and periodicals and became an admirer of Eugene Debs and an independent labor or progressive political party. Brophy was also a labor representative to the Brookwood Labor College and was active on their Labor Cooperating Committee. He frequently spoke at the Brookwood campus in Katonah, New York, and he helped establish a scholarship program for miners from his district (Brophy, 1964: passim; *Brookwood Review*, March 20, 1923; April 5, 1925).

As part of Brophy's commitment to rank-and-file participation in union decisions, District 2 and the Pennsylvania Federation of Labor jointly sponsored a Worker's Education Bureau. District 2 arranged for an itinerant teacher, Paul Fuller, to tour the coal towns, teaching classes, and organizing labor "chautauquas." The labor "chautauqua" utilized techniques developed by religious revivalists to spiritualize the faithful in scattered rural communities. The District used the chautauqua to organize unorganized communities, to educate workers in the unionized areas, and to reinforce the spirits of miners engaged in prolonged strikes. They brought entertainment and a sense of social togetherness, and helped miners see the relationship between their local struggles and the broader union movement. Generally, public meetings were held every night for four days. Each evening a different speaker, sandwiched between performances by local bands, addressed a different facet of unionism and the district's program. Fuller followed up each chautauqua by organizing continuing study classes in the town. Women's auxiliaries involved local women in understanding the issues impacting on the coal industry and providing strike support and picketing. To spread ideas as widely as possible, District 2 published its own newspaper, the *Penn-Central News*. When the paper failed in 1924, the district continued to publish an irregular bulletin (*Brookwood Review*, March 20, 1923; January 1, 1924; April 5, 1925; UMWA MA District 2 File; Golden, 1925; Brophy, 1964: 181–82, 201–2; Brophy, 1922: 20–21; Brophy, 1924).

Through its educational programs District 2 succeeded in bringing the 1919 Cleveland program alive for Central Pennsylvania miners. The programs also served as models for the Nationalization Research Committee's proposals to educate the entire UMWA membership. It succeeded in influencing many miners, expanding their visions beyond the boney piles towering over the company towns. Many District 2 miners and new locals that were organized through these activities became active in the opposition to business unionism. In 1923, some of them sent representatives to an opposition Progressive Miners Convention while others asked speakers to visit them. Agents from the UMWA international office reporting to UMWA Vice President Philip Murray kept track of all of these activities (UMWA MA District 2 File; Bussel, 1999: 57–58).

Brophy's commitment to the education of the working class was reflected in his devotion to free expression and open debate. He explained his philosophy in an address to the 1927 District 2 convention.

> If our organization is democratic in aims and purposes, there must be necessarily a wide range of discussion. You can't get conclusions in a democratic organization, in a mass movement, without a lot of discussion, in Local Unions, in District conventions, and in National gatherings. All of these are part and parcel of a mass movement such as the United Mine Workers, and of course there will be differences of opinion as to the wisdom or lack of wisdom of certain actions or certain conclusions. That is the book of life. It is inescapable because all men don't see eye to eye or all men are not in possession of the same set of facts, and all men don't have the same mental make-up, and consequently there are differences of opinion, sharp differences of opinion but the aim and purpose of these gatherings where opinion is expressed and conclusions are reached, is that somehow through the avenue of free discussion there will be reached a conclusion, unanimous conclusion if that is possible, but if not, that at least a majority conclusion as far as determining issues for the time being. (UMWA District 2 Proceedings, 1927: 281–82)

Brophy rejected the idea that debate was a product of factionalism and argued that factionalism developed when debate was cut off, a position that put him in direct opposition to John L. Lewis and the international office.

Following this principle, District 2 conventions were very different from UMWA conventions. Chaired by Brophy, they were marked by their openness and the leadership's commitment to having issues aired on the floor. Agents of the international office who were openly maneuvering to oust Brophy, including Fred Thomas, Sam Nunnamaker, and T. D. Stiles, were allowed to address the convention at length without attempts to harass them or using parliamentary procedures to silence disagreements. Generally, the leadership held its statements until rank-and-file delegates had opportunities to respond to issues. Rather than pack conventions with allies, Brophy instructed District 2 organizers to remain in the field instead of attending a 1923 Special District convention (Brophy, 1964: 200–5; Singer, 1982: 46).

John Brophy was a product of a social background similar to that which produced the ties between the British Trade Union movement and England's Labor Party. He believed that American political democracy would not be complete unless it included economic democracy as well. A crucial element of this view of democracy was public ownership of the society's natural resources and utilities. While most of the district autonomy coalition was content with a symbolic victory over Lewis with the adoption of its program at the 1919 UMWA Cleveland Convention, Brophy promoted the program as the key element for organizing and educating coal miners. He was convinced that trade union economic demands and business unionism were insufficient for resolving the problems of the bituminous coal industry and saw political organization as the only effective basis for preserving the miners' economic gains and traditional job freedom. At the 1921 UMWA convention, when John L. Lewis attempted to bury the 1919 program by proposing a committee to study "the problems at issue and translate our declarations into the realm of practical accomplishment," he appointed Brophy chair of the Nationalization Research Committee (NRC). However, Brophy's appointment had an impact opposite of Lewis' strategy. Brophy used his position as committee chairman to bring the 1919 Cleveland platform to the forefront of debate in the union and to develop relationships with a broad range of groups that believed in nationalization and were committed to working-class educational programs. Collaboration between District 2, the Nationalization Research Committee, and Heber Blankenhorn and Arthur Gleason of the Bureau of Industrial Research, helped Brophy to better organize his own ideas and present the case for nationalization more effectively (UMWA Proceedings, 1921: 91–92; Brophy, 1964: 160–64; Brophy, 1922a, 1922b).

The Miners' Program

UMWA conventions repeatedly endorsed the idea of nationalization of the mines starting in 1908, but the union never seriously campaigned for it. In

1919, radical and opposition groups in the union insisted that the demand be included as part of the preliminary preparations for a nationwide strike challenging the federal government's continued wartime wage freeze and no-strike decree. The strike and subsequent negotiations were directed by John L. Lewis and his supporters in the UMWA international office who ignored broader issues and focused entirely on wage rates. Following the 1919 strike, John Brophy seized on the union's Cleveland platform as the best way to improve conditions for miners, redirect the leadership of the union, and reorganize the bituminous coal industry. In 1921, he supported John L. Lewis' candidacy for president of the American Federation of Labor, when Lewis endorsed the program and Brophy was appointed chairman of the UMWA's Nationalization Research Committee. While the international office attempted to stymie Brophy by denying the NRC access to the *UMWA Journal* to present its findings to the membership, the committee published its reports independently through District 2 and sympathetic journals. Brophy chaired the committee until 1923, when increasing philosophical and political conflicts with Lewis forced him to resign (Everling, 1976: 1–30, 129–40; Brophy, 1964: 151–75; Singer, 1982: 147–48).

The main conclusions of the Nationalization Research Committee were codified in a pamphlet, *How to Run Coal*. Initially published by District 2, the pamphlet was accepted as the second report of the NRC and Lewis authorized its publication and payment of the printing bill. Coal, according to Brophy, had to be treated as a public utility, because it was a necessity in industrial production and home heating. In another pamphlet, *The Government of Coal*, Brophy wrote, "It is a necessity which cannot advantageously be sold for profit. The use of it, the service in it, are killed by competition. Business enterprise, pivoted on profits, mismanages a public utility." The coal industry was compared to the Post Office and National Forest Reserves. The reports proposed a government fact-finding body to investigate the industry and ease the transition to public control. They also offered a plan for administration of the industry after nationalization. In *How to Run Coal* and *The Government of Coal*, the NRC proposed a tripartite administration of the mines by government, representing the public interest, the miners' union, and industrial technicians and managers. The plan included a cabinet-level Secretary of the Mines, a permanent federal fact-finding commission to control budget and policy, and a permanent joint conference to protect collective bargaining and separate the management and production of bituminous coal from issues of wages and coal prices (Brophy,

1964: 169; Brophy, 1921; Brophy, 1922; Brophy, Mitch, & Golden, 1922a; 1922b; Brophy Papers, Box 10).

While Brophy accepted Lewis' claim that nationalization of the mines was unlikely under the existing political organization of the United States, he believed the campaign for nationalization would be the basis for achieving total unionization of the industry and the creation of a Labor Party. In a speech to the 1922 District 2 convention Brophy insisted that "If labor and other forward looking groups want to accomplish anything substantial in the way of enacting progressive laws, it must provide either sufficient opposition to compel the dominant party to action or vote them out and fill their places with Labor's own representatives." As part of this strategy, Brophy was active in organizing the Farmer-Labor Party convention in 1923, although he later withdrew, and in 1924 was a Pennsylvania elector for Robert LaFollette on the Farmer-Labor ticket (Brophy, 1964: 210; Albertson, 1955: 311; District 2 Proceedings, 1922: 26; Ebensburg *Mountaineer-Herald*, October 23, 1924; Singer, 1988b: 54–55).

One gauge of the impact of Brophy's program was the international office's recognition that it was a threat to the business-unionist faction's control over the union. When Brophy used the NRC to publicize the Miners' Program beyond District 2 and to unite with groups outside the union, Lewis responded with a vicious campaign against the committee. On December 29, 1922, Chris Golden of the NRC presented the outline of *How to Run Coal* at the annual meeting of the League for Industrial Democracy in New York City. A month later, Lewis met with the NRC and accused its members of violating the committee's mandate from the international union. The charges were made public in a press release issued by *UMWA Journal* editor Ellis Searles on January 29, 1923. According to Searles, "newspapers and public have been misled with reference to the proposed plan for the nationalization of the coal industry. The United Mine Workers as an organization has not approved, endorsed or adopted any plan for nationalization." The release claimed the committee had no authority to commit the union to any specific plan and charged that the report actually was prepared by the group of "Greenwich Village radicals" where it was presented (Brophy, 1964: 170–75; Dubofsky & Van Tine, 1977: 92–94; Singer, 1982: 149; L.I.D., February–March 1923: 3).

Chris Golden and John Brophy argued in a series of letters that they were within the committee's province as they understood it. They cited Lewis' original letter of appointment that authorized the NRC "to aid in the dissemination of information among our members and the public and the crystallization of sentiment for the attainment of such end." However, when Lewis continued to press the attack, Brophy and Golden resigned from the committee. While Brophy claimed in his letter of resignation that the committee had already achieved the goals he had hoped to accomplish, Lewis' attacks succeeded in driving a wedge between Brophy and a number of the nonunion organizations that had aided the Nationalization Research Committee, and despite Brophy's resignation, the Lewis machine in the international office continued its campaign to discredit him. The April 1, 1923 issue of the *UMWA Journal* ran an article claiming "President Brophy's Representative Suggests a 20 Per Cent Cut in the Wages of Mine Workers" and an editorial repeating the charges (Singer, 1982: 149; Beik, 1996: 304–5; *UMWA Journal*, April 1, 1923: 3, 6; Brophy Papers, Box 10).

For John Brophy, the "Miners' Program" offered a solution for conditions faced by bituminous coal miners and for the chaotic nature of the industry. It valued democratic decision-making and was based on a concept of social justice and the miner's image of himself as an independent artisan victimized by impersonal forces and economic giants. It was a program that miners could examine and endorse as the basis for struggle. Using the "Miners' Program," workers' education in District 2 became the "intelligent guide to a new social order" envisioned by Pennsylvania State Federation of Labor President James Maurer, an ally of Brophy, as the goal of workers' education. The nationalization campaign required 100 percent unionization in the bituminous coal industry. It necessitated a labor political party, to defend civil liberties and democratic rights in mining towns, to elect pro-nationalization representatives, and to defend the interests of workers after nationalization of the mines. Most importantly, it required educated miners, who understood the world, their place in it as workers, and who were willing to fight for their rights as Americans (Hardman, 1928: 186–91; Brophy, 1921; Brophy 1922: 1026–29; Singer, 1988b: 50–64).

The Miners' Program was first formally presented as part of John Brophy's presidential address to a special District 2 Convention in Du Bois, Pennsylvania, on February 22, 1921. After a three-hour debate, it passed unanimously. In his speech Brophy charged that the UMWA's "old policy" of fighting individual grievances and pressing small demands could never achieve a "good American life" for the miner. Miners had to fight for nationalization of the coal industry, with a six-hour workday and a five-day workweek. "Every strike to correct a grievance after this must mean an improvement in our status. We must never fight a grievance again except by heading it up into the larger program" (UMWA District 2 Proceedings, 1921).

Brophy believed that the key to winning nationalization and a new life for miners was education; education of the general public and workers' education. He argued that the "private ownership of the great natural resource of coal is morally indefensible and economically unsound." The union had to convince coal consumers that their complaints about erratic coal supplies and high prices, and the miners' grievances about substandard pay and dangerous working conditions, had the same source, "the greed of the owner." Workers' education was required so that the "Miners' Program" could work its way "down into their consciousness." Classes and discussion groups had to be established. Miners had to research, write, publish, and distribute the facts about bituminous coal mining. A statewide labor newspaper was needed to overcome the isolation of scattered mining communities. This type of education campaign would "make the district acquainted with itself" and "spread the movement to other districts." An expanded version of the "Miners' Program," with a forceful introduction titled "Why the Miners' Program," was distributed to District 2 locals and at the October 1921 UMWA international convention. The pamphlet stressed that "A labor movement can never rise higher or go further than its rank-and-file. . . . What you do with this pamphlet and this Program will make your history for the next ten years. It will determine the life of your son. . . . Without this Program, we shall go on with low pay, slack work, meagre [sic] life." It urged miners to "Speed up your local." "Get the 15 Old Timers talking Nationalization. Shake up the Regulars, the Standbys, who turn up at every meeting. Find out what they think of the Miners' Program. If they don't think, shock them into forming the habit. Tell them this Program beats booze fighting. There is more hot stuff in freeing the miners than in following the racy divorce news of our captains of industry" (UMWA District 2 Proceedings, 1921; Brophy, 1922a; Brophy, 1964: 165–75).

Strategies for promoting the Miners' Program were difficult to implement. The Pennsylvania State Federation of Labor ran workers' education classes in the state's larger cities, but high cost prevented them from helping the district organize classes in small mining towns. A statewide daily labor newspaper proved to be too expensive, so District 2 established its own weekly, the *Penn-Central News*. While the goals and general outline of District 2's education program were spelled out at its 1921 and 1922 District conventions, its structure and organizational details emerged during

UMWA national strikes in 1922 and 1924. In both strikes, the district's educational programs helped mobilize miner and public support and made possible short-term local organizing success, highlighting its potential for promoting working-class consciousness. Unfortunately, given the depressed state of the bituminous coal industry, both campaigns ultimately failed, exposing the limitations of workers' education (Brophy, 1964: 157–75; UMWA District 2 Proceedings, 1922: 18–24).

Strike for Union

The expiration of the CCF contract in spring 1922 brought the Miners' Program and business unionism into direct and open conflict. District 2's efforts during the strike to expand into the non-union Somerset Field was a test of the Miners' Program's ability to mobilize coal miners with a conscious ideological alternative and vision for the future rooted in the "Miner's Freedom." Lewis and the business unionists in the international office saw efforts to expand the strike into the nonunion coalfields as a challenge to their authority and instead focused on protecting the CCF agreement. Brophy believed that the organization of Somerset County was crucial to the survival of both District 2 and the UMWA. He saw no alternative than to launch a massive organizing drive among nonunion miners as a part of the struggle to implement and develop the Miners' Program and transform the UMWA. During the strike, Lewis also had to contend with attempts by Frank Farrington and business unionist elements of the old District Autonomy coalition to maneuver the strike to improve their own personal political position in the union (Brophy, 1964: 169–75).

Somerset County in Central Pennsylvania was a pivotal area for a number of reasons. Its location nestled near the CCF made it possible to send in organizers, while success in the field was a direct rebuff to many of the industry's major nonunion operators. The companies in the Somerset field were tied through their boards of directors to the Mellon National Bank, the Girard Trust Company, the Guaranty Trust, and the Reading, Interborough, and Erie Railroads. They were also affiliated with the National Coal Association and the Anthracite Operators' Association. The staunchly open shop Consolidation mines in the county were controlled by Rockefeller interests who claimed "the relations with our labor were pleasant; the miners have been working regularly; there was never any trouble of any kind" (Blankenhorn, May 24, 1922: 360; Blankenhorn, 1924: 3–12).

If the UMWA could organize Somerset County it would break a major open shop stronghold, stymie the open shop forces, and lay the basis for a genuine national contract, while a nonunion Somerset remained an Achilles heel for District 2 and the CCF. On January 9, 1922, the officers and membership of District 2 sent a letter to President Warren G. Harding outlining their views on the situation. The previous year intermittent employment, they averaged only one to three days a week of work, left thousands of District 2 miners and their families with depleted resources and in serious want. The industry, the District 2 office argued, provided no relief and the District and local unions were forced to care for the indigent out of the dues of those lucky enough to find work. The District accused the operators of hoarding unconscionable wartime profits and using hard times as an excuse to cut wage rates, with no promise of increased work. It demanded that the government investigate their plight, asking, "Is the only noticeable motion of Government to be measures taken when desperate miners rebel in strikes?" Not surprisingly, given ties between corporate interests and the Harding administration, the appeal fell on deaf ears (Brophy, 1964: 179; District 2 Papers, January 9, 1922).

In March, Brophy addressed the District 2 convention and argued for an all-out organizing effort against the nonunion operators in Somerset in the event of a nationwide bituminous coal strike. Brophy reported that nonunion operators were reducing wages to the 1917 scale on a massive level. This was placing pressure on unionized operations, and operators were beginning to openly violate the existing contract in an effort to force wage reductions. Union miners were responding by walking off the job, and the district treasury was being depleted by piecemeal strike efforts. In his address, Brophy accused the district's operators' association of actively supporting the wage cuts. Its president, Thomas Watkins of Pennsylvania Coal and Coke, was pressuring miners at the mines he controlled to sign petitions to the union demanding a lower wage settlement. Somerset operators were preparing to combat any union initiative by circulating yellow-dog contracts. Brophy concluded that the district had to organize Somerset simply to defend its position in the rest of Central Pennsylvania (UMWA District 2 Proceedings, 1922: 28–29).

When the UMWA launched a nationwide coal strike in defense of the CCF contract and the $7.50 day on April 1, 1922, the ideas and activities developed in District 2 as part of the Miners' Program were put to the test. Using reports on the nonunion mines prepared by Powers Hapgood for the Bureau of Industrial Research as a guide, the District flooded Somerset

County with copies of its newspaper, the *Penn-Central News*, and dispatched organizers to Somerset to build support for the strike (Hapgood, 1921).

Powers Hapgood was a protégé of Brophy and a major ally and friend during the 1920s. Hapgood was a Harvard University graduate, who as a young man dedicated his life to the labor and socialist movements. Brophy and Hapgood were introduced in 1921 through ties to the Bureau of Industrial Research. Hapgood was instrumental as a District 2 organizer during the 1922 strike and played major roles in Brophy's campaign for UMWA President in 1926 and efforts to rebuild the UMWA in 1928 as part of the "Save the Union" campaign (Bussel, 1999).

On April 3, Brophy announced that the strike was 100 percent effective in the unionized fields of District 2. However, in the nonunion fields the organizers were meeting stiff resistance from the operators. The Berwind-White Coal Company closed the company town of Windber to organizers and hired 150 extra Coal and Iron police to arrest anyone carrying strike literature. Despite these efforts, 229 miners from St. Michael's marched to neighboring South Fork and joined the union on April 5. South Fork was the likely Community B in the 1911 Dillingham report discussed in chapter 3. In other major union victories, 2,500 men walked out of the Berwind-White operation in Windber to sign up with the union, and 200 Revloc miners paraded to Nanty Glo to join the strike (UMWA District 2 Proceedings, 1922: 20–21; Brophy, 1964: 181, 184–85; *Johnstown Democrat*, April 5–13, 1922; Blankenhorn, 1924: 41–84).

Berwind-White and Revloc counterattacked by evicting miners and their families from company-owned houses. Miners were also evicted in the traditionally strong union towns of Nanty Glo and Twin Rocks. In other actions designed to break the strike, coal companies stopped credit in the company stores as soon as the men walked off the job, Coal and Iron police terrorized strikers, and in Colver mounted police ran down union organizers. In Windber, seventeen women and children were arrested for parading in support of the strike. The Coal and Iron police also used phony searches for illegal moonshine to ransack the homes of miners. The companies tried to stir up ethnic conflicts to divide the miners. On May 26, a company house was bombed in Windber. Police claimed they discovered a letter signed by the Black Hand at the house and the company charged local Italian miners with terrorizing nonunion miners (Blankenhorn, 1924: 85–108; Beik, 1996: 268–88; *Johnstown Democrat*, April 10, 1922, 13; *Nanty-Glo Journal*, May 5, 1922; *Johnstown Tribune*, May 26, 1922; *Federated Press*, June 5, 1922: 2).

District 2 moved in court to protect the legal rights of the miners and place constraints on the Coal and Iron police. It obtained an injunction against Berwind-White guards for violating legal and human rights and convinced a judge to throw the company's charges against local Italian miners out of court. With the help of the American Civil Liberties Union, District 2 pressed the local courts to enforce freedom of speech and assembly in company towns. A major legal victory occurred when a Somerset judge ruled that union meetings were not in violation of an injunction that prevented interference with nonunion miners going to work. In another legal success, two Berwind-White security guards were arrested after raping a miner's wife (Bussel, 1999: 43–63; Blankenhorn, 1924: 97, 118–20; *Johnstown Democrat*, May 6, 1922; *Johnstown Tribune*, May 27, 1922; Beik, 1996: 278–79; Hapgood Papers, May 27, June 3, 1922).

From April through August, the strike in the nonunion fields continued to grow. In Fayetteville, Pennsylvania, 2,000 miners walked out from a mine that had not been on strike since 1888. By May 25, the only mines working in the entire District 2 region were in four localities—Colver, Hooverville, Vintondale, and Heilwood. However, the July 13 issue of the *Nanty-Glo Journal* reported organizers William Welsh, John Maholtz, and John Madoni pulled the Colver mine, signing up 500 members. The following week the paper announced that 170 men walked out of the captive Bethlehem Steel mine at Heilwood. By any analysis, the strike effort in District 2 and Somerset pointed toward success. It was well organized, the miners remained peaceful even when provoked, and the District had mobilized outside aid and dispatched legal experts and foreign language organizers across the fields to open the nonunion mines.

As early as April 8, international organizer Fred Thomas wrote Lewis that the strike was going well, and he recommended cooperation with Brophy, even though District 2 had not requested help from the international. By August, after four months, the strike was still growing, and funds were coming into the District from local civic groups. For the first time in its history, the legal rights of miners had been established in Somerset County, basic rights like freedom of speech, assembly, and protection from illegal search and seizure. Berwind-White, which had confidently declared its intention to continue nonunion operation throughout the strike, was paying scabs to load coal cars with boney and waste in an attempt to convince strikers that the mine was in operation (*Johnstown Tribune*, May 7, 1922; *Nanty-Glo Journal*, May 25; July 13; 20; August 3, 1922; UMWA MA District 2 File; *Federated Press*, June 17, 1922: 2).

District 2's activities during the strike stimulated the growth of community support from local civic organizations. In Nanty Glo, the Businessmen's Association and Volunteer Fire Department joined the UMWA local in sponsoring a July 4 celebration to raise money for the strikers and the Ex-Servicemen's Fund, a group of World War I veterans, turned its treasury over to the union. The town bordered on Somerset County and the home of UMWA District Board member William Welsh became a center of strike activities and a jumping off point for organizers headed into the nonunion field. Momentum, however, was undermined when Lewis announced the settlement of the strike in the CCF. The agreement allowed companies to sign contracts in the Central Competitive Field or for previously unionized operations, while maintaining nonunion mines in other fields. Essentially, the agreement allowed the companies to resume selected production while continuing the open-shop assault in the outlying fields.

In District 2, Brophy demanded that operators sign for all their mines. Many operators were initially prepared to unionize all their operations until they learned that Lewis had allowed the Consolidation Coal Company to enter the CCF agreement with its Northern West Virginia mines while remaining nonunion in Somerset. On August 17, the *Nanty-Glo Journal* reported a shift in the position of the District operators. They now demanded the right to resume nonunion operation in mines that were nonunion before the strike. They received a big boost when Lewis sent Brophy a telegram ordering the resumption of work at University Clearfield Bituminous Corporation and at the Pennsylvania Coal and Coke Company, despite the fact that they refused to sign for their Somerset mines (Brophy, 1964: 176–99; Dubofsky & Van Tine, 1977: 86–90; Bussel, 1999: 43–63; *Johnstown Tribune*, July 3, 1922; *Nanty-Glo Journal*, August 3, 1922; August 17; UMWA MA District 2 File; Katherine Welsh Martin Interview, 1976; Hapgood Papers, August 19, 1922).

Brophy recognized that Lewis' actions would undermine the Somerset strike and resisted implementing them. At an August 23 meeting of the Central Pennsylvania Coal Producers' Association, Brophy announced that the district intended to continue its policy of refusing to sign contracts with companies that operated nonunion mines. A telegram was sent to the Somerset operators calling them to a conference to accept the CCF accord. Thirty-nine new Somerset County locals were represented at the August 28 meeting, but it was boycotted by the operators and their representatives. Nevertheless, the representatives of the 20,000 striking Somerset miners resolved to remain firm in their fight for union recognition (Blankenhorn, 1924: 151–53, 160; Brophy, 1964: 192; UMWA MA District 2 Papers; *Nanty-Glo Journal*, September 7, 1922; Hapgood Papers, September 3, 1922).

The resolve of the Somerset strikers and the district were quickly tested by Lewis and the international office. The Monroe Coal and Mining Company in Revloc and the Heisley Mines in Nanty Glo were both tied to J. H. Weaver mining interests. Though they were located only four miles apart, Heisley was traditionally a union mine, while Revloc operated nonunion. At the start of the strike Heisley Local 1347 helped organize the Revloc miners. Revloc's Local 4209 pressed the Nanty Glo miners and the district not to return to work until Weaver signed for both mines. The Nanty Glo men accepted the appeal and refused to return to work. L. G. Ball, president of the Heisley Coal Company wrote Lewis and Brophy on August 24, 1922, protesting the decision. The company claimed that it was a party to the previous CCF contract for its mines in District 17 (West Virginia) and at Nanty Glo, and that this contract had automatically been renewed when they signed the Cleveland CFF accord (*Penn-Central News*, September 30, 1922: 4; Brophy, 1964: 194; Brophy Papers, Box 10, August 16, August 24, 1922; *Nanty-Glo Journal*, September 21, 1922).

On September 5, 1922, Charles O'Neill, the secretary of the District Producers' Association wrote Lewis supporting the Heisley Coal Company and complaining that Brophy was misapplying the CCF agreement by insisting on a clause in the district pact binding operators to sign contracts for all their mining operations. The proposed clause read, "The signing of this scale agreement will include all mines under the management and control of each member of the two associations whose mines are now organized and on strike. Where individual operators do not accept this agreement we will consider the contract null and void with such operator or operators." O'Neill demanded that Lewis force the district to rescind this policy. Lewis accepted Ball and O'Neill's position. He personally signed a contract for the Heisley operation in Nanty Glo and forwarded it to Brophy. When the District 2 Executive Board refused to honor the contract, Lewis bypassed the district office and ordered the men to return to work. In an exchange of letters, the District Executive Board requested a meeting with Lewis to discuss their differences, but Lewis responded with a threat to suspend the board unless Brophy forced the Heisley miners to abandon their support of the Revloc miners (Singer, 1982; 158–60; Brophy, 1964: 194; UMWA MA District 2 File; Brophy Papers, Box 10, September 11, 1922).

The contractual dispute over Revloc represented in miniature the conflict between the two conceptions of unionism. Lewis' decision to protect the CCF and his personal hold on the international office by sacrificing the outlying and nonunion coalfields undermined UMWA efforts in these fields for more than a decade with many areas abandoned to open-shop operators. Because of this strategy, mines in the nonunion fields remained permanent threats to the stability of the CCF agreement and the UMWA. When Lewis forced Brophy to back down or face expulsion from the UMWA, he undermined the Miners' Program at a point when it had mobilized record numbers of nonunion miners and had the potential to spark a national rank-and-file movement that could challenge the open-shop intentions of the operators. Despite the continued maturation of the leadership and ideology of the Miners' Program, the 1922 defeat permanently alienated large groups of miners and weakened the ability of the union to resist open-shop drives Lewis' decision did not alter Brophy's belief that the Somerset strike was the key to defeating the open-shop campaign and preserving the UMWA in District 2. Despite the termination of the national strike, District 2 continued the struggle in Somerset through August 1923. During this year, the district developed new tactics to press its demand for union and achieved a number of its educational goals. It also challenged Lewis' position that these fields could not be organized and that a national contract encompassing all bituminous coal production was impossible (Brophy, 1964: 193–94, 197–99; Blankenhorn, 1924: 155–60).

The Somerset "Strike for Union" was a model large-scale organizing drive—the culmination of five years of organizing in the county—that demonstrated the Miner's Freedom could be politicized through a class-conscious working-class program. Organizers had crisscrossed the district since 1917 and prior to the strike, Powers Hapgood prepared a detailed report on conditions and sentiments in Somerset. During the strike, District 2 kept running accounts of the number of striking mines, people on relief, coal cars loaded before the strike, coal cars being loaded by scab labor during the strike, men in the locals, and scabs in the fields. Because of prior preparation, the district was able to effectively utilize its limited resources and to marshal organizers when and where they were needed most (Hapgood, 1921; Bussel, 1999: 43–63; Blankenhorn, 1924: 38–39; 65, 80, 134–35, 174; District 2 Papers, 1922, November 18; Hapgood Papers, July 20, August 14, 1923).

The Somerset strike taught rank-and-file miners how to organize and broke the local omnipotence of the operators. Cooperative stores and strike relief centers were set up. In a 1976 interview Katherine Welsh Martin, daughter of district board member William Welsh, described a strike center in Nanty Glo.

A train load of tents came into our town. They were put on a local coal miner's truck and he took them up and tossed them off in our yard. . . . Then men and women would come and they'd get in line and the clothes would be doled out to them. . . . The salt pork and salt side came in wooden barrels. The mob would line up at our house and my Dad would whack off a chunk for this family, and a smaller chunk for a smaller family. (Katherine Welsh Martin Interview, 1976)

The strike also underscored the importance of political action in labor struggles. In Nanty Glo the miners dominated the local government and were protected from arbitrary police action. During the strike District 2 miners challenged the operator's control over other towns. In one significant battle, they ousted operator D. B. Zimmerman as Republican county boss in Somerset, breaking the operator's iron grip on politics in the county (*Johnstown Democrat*, April 13, 1922; Hapgood Papers, May 21, May 27, 1922).

The Somerset strike demonstrated miners could bridge religious and language differences operators used to undermine unionization. One important strategy by the district was pairing foreign language and English-speaking organizers. Powers Hapgood and George Boyton, a Slavish-speaking miner, worked to pull the Meyersdale mines, and Mike Fazio helped Hapgood organize Italian mines at Consolidation Mines in Acosta. At Ralphton, Kustac Murawsky addressed the miners in the five languages he had learned while working in the pits. It was not unusual for meetings to bring together Slavic, Italian, Hungarian, Black, and "American" miners (Blankenhorn, May 17, 1922; Blankenhorn 1924: 23–26; *Johnstown Democrat*, April 10, 1922).

The strike also illustrated the value of coalition with nonlabor civil rights and political groups and using the media to shape public opinion and garner support. With the assistance of the American Civil Liberties Union the district pressed local courts to enforce first amendment rights of freedom of speech and assembly. ACLU Executive Director Arthur Garfield Hayes personally toured the district and helped secure the right of organizers to enter the previously closed company town of Vintondale. Working through the courts they broke an injunction forbidding them to organize miners who had signed yellow-dog contracts and secured the right to hold meetings off of company property. They also secured injunctions against brutal sheriffs and company guards (*Johnstown Tribune*, May 27, June 6, June 9, 1922;

Blankenhorn, May 24, 1922: 360; Hayes, June 14, 1922; Blankenhorn, 1924: 80–82; *Penn-Central News*, May 6, 1922).

Perhaps the most outstanding innovation of the Somerset strike was the miners' lobby in New York City at the offices of companies directing the national open-shop drive. This enabled the district to keep the strike in the public eye after the national settlement was reached. The union pressed the city government to intervene against the Berwind-White Company, which held the coal contract for the New York City subways. Berwind-White was part of the Morgan financial group and E. J. Berwind was a director of the Interborough subway. They wanted New York City to insist that Berwind-White meet its contractual obligations and to send investigators to the coalfields to witness the operation of the coal company. The committee also picketed the Rockefeller New York offices to demand an explanation why Consolidation Coal had signed with the UMWA for its West Virginia operations, but insisted on working nonunion in Somerset County. Consolidation dominated the operators' association in Somerset, and the Rockefeller interests feared the adverse publicity that would follow any violence in the region (Blankenhorn, 1924: 176–89; Bussel, 1999: 54; Brophy, 1964: 193–94).

High-handed behavior by the companies, particularly Berwind-White, won the union favorable public support that helped to keep the strike alive. The Bureau of Industrial Research, the League for Industrial Democracy, and the ACLU all sponsored meetings that collected funds for strike relief. A representative of the Polish National Allied Societies toured Somerset and promised money to help the families of strikers. A New York City mayoral commission issued a blistering report condemning the operators. The report charged Berwind-White miners were forced to live in conditions "worse than . . . slaves prior to the Civil War." It also accused the president of Berwind-White of manipulating the city as a director of the IRT "to purchase from his own company coal mined under unfair and heartbreaking conditions and reap enormous profits amounting in 1921 to over $1.6 million with corresponding financial detriment to the tax and rent payers of New York City." It recommended that the city take over full operation of the subway system (*New York Times*, January 2, 1923: 1; *Penn-Central News*, September 30, 1922; Blankenhorn, 1924: 190–97).

Although the strike was ultimately defeated, the threat of unionization led to improved living and working conditions for miners who remained in Somerset after the strike. Prevailing wages became comparable with the union scale and men were paid for tasks like widening tunnels and coal shafts. Public roads and towns were now open to union organizers. The ability of District 2 and the Somerset miners to sustain the strike shows the importance of a broader working-class community, including shopkeepers and religious institutions, for building local workers' movements (Walkowitz, 1978; Beik, 196; Bussel, 1999: 58; District 2 Papers, August 14, 1923; Brophy, 1964: 197–98).

The Somerset strike also had a broader impact on the spirit of the rank-and-file movement in the union. In June 1923 rank-and-file militants at the Tri-District Anthracite Conference forced their Scales Committee to accept contract demands of a 10–20 percent wage increase, check-off, pay for dead work, an eight-hour day, and a two-year contract. A group of District 2 organizers, led by Powers Hapgood, joined rank-and-file militants from Kansas, Illinois, and Western Pennsylvania in Pittsburgh at the Progressive Miner's International Conference of the United Mine Workers of America. The conference tried to establish a permanent relationship between the various rank-and-file groups developing inside the miners' union (*New York Times*, June 27, 1923: 1, 29: 3, 30, 1923: 1; *Penn-Central News*, July 24, 1923; Brophy 1964: 205–6; Dubofsky & Van Tine, 1977: 123–24).

Somerset Defeat

Despite imaginative efforts to sustain the Somerset strikers after the August 1922, CCF settlement, a localized strike had only marginal impact on bloated coal markets and little chance of success. Operators either imported scabs from other nonunion fields or shifted production to working mines, while waiting for the rebellion to fold. The national union, suspicious of the motives of District 2, and with its own treasury depleted, offered little more than verbal praise of a "gallant" effort. On October 20, 1922 the UMWA Committee on Organization promised to support the 17,000 strikers "as circumstances permit," but little aid was forthcoming. Lewis also refused to underwrite a relief loan to the district from the American Fund for Public Service. Brophy charged that the international union actually pulled more money out of the district in assessments than it provided in strike relief. Meanwhile, the operators worked to break the strike. The Consolidation Coal Company imported hundreds of scabs from their West Virginia mines and the operators placed expensive advertisements in foreign language newspapers to interrupt the flow of aid to the strikers. In October, Berwind-White and Consolidation welcomed the coming winter months with a new round of evictions from company housing (Dubofsky & Van Tine, 1977: 99; Brophy, 1964: 195; Blankenhorn, 1924: 97; *Penn-Central News*, September 30, 1922; *Johnstown Democrat*, October 13, 1922; UMWA MA District 2 File; Hapgood Papers, September 3, September 14, 1922).

The Somerset strikers were kept going during the hard winter by the hope that the strike would be joined by the rest of the union when the CCF pact expired in April 1923. This dream died when the international and the operators agreed to a one-year extension of the pact for Ohio, Indiana, and Illinois on January 4, 1923. The International Executive Board followed the contract extension by calling off a companion strike in neighboring Connellsville, Fayette, and Westmoreland in District 5. Despite these developments, the District 2 Executive Board voted on January 30, 1923, to continue the strike. A district-wide referendum voted 32,402 to 8,193½ to assess working District 2 miners a dollar per day to raise a new strike fund for an April offensive against Somerset operators. Unfortunately, the District's plans were not based on a realistic evaluation of conditions in the field. Slack work made it impossible for miners to pay into the strike fund. Meanwhile Somerset County was becoming depopulated as strikers migrated away looking for work. As early as December 1922, Powers Hapgood wrote that "all of the men with the most initiative and pride have migrated to the union fields." In Grey, Pennsylvania, the number of strikers had dwindled from 225 to 34. One hundred and seventy-six men had left town and fifteen others had returned to work. Finally, on August 14, 1923, the district office issued a statement ending the Somerset strike and the district-wide strike assessment. A more realistic appraisal showed that while production in the county had never climbed above 30 percent of capacity, the non-union operators had diverted orders to other fields and were ready to hold out indefinitely (Dubofsky & Van Tine, 1977: 91; Brophy, 1964: 195–99; Hapgood Papers, December 10, 1922; UMWA MA District 2 File).

While a number of District 2's goals were achieved during the year-long Somerset strike, there was a fundamental problem that was beyond the ability of Brophy or other rank-and-file leaders to alter. Conditions in the postwar bituminous industry, particularly slack work, overcapacity, the commitment of the international office to cooperate with the operators, and the anti-union sentiments of leading segments of the industry, forced rank-and-file miners into limited strikes and localized organizing drives that they could not win. Their actions were undermined by business unionists who controlled the international office and viewed the insurgents as the antithesis of their concept of the union and as a threat to their personal positions. The opposition of the international union made it possible for the operators to shift production to alternative coalfields and starve out the insurgent miners. The rank-and-file movement did not have the strength to both defeat Lewis and effectively challenge the open-shop operators.

Lewis, after years of bureaucratic infighting and battling with the elements of the district autonomy coalition for control of the international office, was sensitive to any sign of opposition, potential or actual. He viewed the Miners' Program as a direct assault on his vision of trade unionism and Brophy's motives through his own ambitions. From the start of the strike, agents reporting to Lewis worked to subvert the District 2 organizing drive. In a report dated April 15, 1922, international organizer Fred Thomas wrote Lewis, "My idea is to coach these men to issue circulars setting forth all those things that have transpired, . . . and send out broadcasts among the local unions of Territory 5 . . . and throughout the district." A typical written "broadcast" accused Brophy of failing to defeat car-pushing and highly praised a Lewis supporter in the district. In September 1922, Lewis agent James Kelly organized a slate to oppose Brophy in district elections and continuation of support for the Somerset strike (UMWA MA District 2 File).

Lewis secured a valuable supporter when Tom Stiles, editor of the *Penn-Central News* and head of the District Co-operative Store program broke with Brophy over the conduct of the Somerset strike. Stiles refused to surrender the editorship of the paper and began to use it to attack Brophy. After the strike was over, Lewis appointed Stiles to the international staff. Lewis agents also negotiated with District 2 Secretary-Treasurer Richard Gilbert to disrupt relief payments to striking Somerset miners. The Lewis forces seized on District 2 mistakes to embarrass Brophy and weaken the strike effort. On March 2, 1923, District 2 lawyer J. J. Kinter testified on car-pushing before an Interstate Commerce Commission hearing. Kinter offered his personal judgment that the miners would accept a reduced hourly wage rate if car-pushing was outlawed and they received a guarantee of steady work. Though the District Executive Board disclaimed the statement and fired Kinter, Lewis used the testimony to charge that Brophy supported a pay cut. UMWA Vice President Philip Murray circulated a flyer in the district insinuating that Kinter was representing Brophy when he spoke. Meanwhile Lewis agents in Subdistrict 5 used the Kinter statement to claim that Brophy supported a wage reduction while Lewis stood firm for the $7.50 day. Lewis agents also used Brophy's commitment to union democracy to throw the 1923 District 2 convention into turmoil. Brophy and the District 2 Executive Board accepted back wages withheld during the 1922 strike, even though the walkout continued in Somerset. At the convention, Lewis supporters launched a campaign to have Brophy censured. Brophy was so exasperated by the continuous attacks in the District and by *UMWA Journal* editor Ellis Searles that in July 1923 he wrote Arthur Gleason that he planned to resign from District office (Brophy, 1964: 200–6; Blankenhorn, 1924: 164–68; Everling, 1976: 180; UMWA MA District 2 File; UMWA District 2 Proceedings, 1924: 21–27; Illinois Miner, April 7, 1923; Brophy Papers, Series 1, Box 1).

Worker's Education

District 2's workers' education program was originally intended as a supplement to traditional trade union activity and as a guide to political action, the same function education and publicity had played during the 1922 strike. However, with the district besieged by an open-shop drive, workers' education developed a new and expanded role. As strikes dragged on or coal companies locked out miners, workers' education became the union's primary defensive weapon to mobilize communities, rally miners against the open shop, and to revitalize their commitment to collective action. In April 1924, a number of UMWA districts went on strike in an effort to preserve gains achieved in the 1922 CCF contract. In conjunction with the strike, District 2 started its first formal workers' education activities in the Pennsylvania town of Broad Top and its surrounding mining communities. Broad Top, located in an isolated area without passenger train service, had 3,500 miners out on strike. Many of the miners were immigrants from Southern and Eastern Europe and had little formal education. Paul Fuller met with Broad Top union officials and toured the mining communities, trying to organize classes. On his first go-around, most miners were not interested when they realized the amount of time and effort the classes would require. During a second round of meetings, Fuller convinced a few striking miners to try workers' education as a vehicle to better conditions in the coalfields for themselves and their children. He set up small classes and arranged to meet the miners at regular intervals in their local union halls. Once the classes started, interest grew until they involved approximately 150 people in seven communities. Meanwhile the strike was going badly and miners were returning to work. The men in the workers' education classes discussed ways of resurrecting the strike, eventually deciding to invite outside speakers to the region to talk with larger groups of miners and their families at labor chautauquas modeled on traditional rural religious revivalist tent meetings (Fuller, 1925: 10. Fuller, 1926: 324–26; *Illinois Miner*, April 26, May 17, July 12, July 19, August 16, August 30, December 13, 1924).

The labor chautauquas were designed to revive the collective spirits of isolated mining communities, stimulate interest in the workers' education program, and lay the basis for continued struggle against the open-shop drive. They also provided the district with a forum for presenting rank-and-file miners with the "Miners' Program" as a long-term solution to the problems of the bituminous coal industry and as a vision of the future that beleaguered miners and their families could grasp onto. The first labor chautauqua in this series was held in a local park in Six Mile Run, near Broad Top. The camp meetings began on Tuesday, August 12, and they ran through Sunday, August 17. Each evening brought a different speaker to address a new topic. District 2 Vice President James Mark opened with a personal talk on his experience in the labor movement. Other speakers included Dr. Harry Laidler of the League for Industrial Democracy, the director of the Pennsylvania State Federation of Labor's Workers' Education Department, a representative of the Co-Operative League of America, and Paul Fuller. On the last day, John Brophy discussed conditions confronting the union as it battled the open shop, the mismanagement of coal by private industry, and the ideas of the "Miners' Program." The Six Mile Run Labor Chautauqua produced immediate and significant results. Most of the men who had returned to work, rejoined the strike and the union. Local workers' education classes tripled their enrollment. A group of thirty boys and girls raised money for instruments and organized a "Workers' Education Band" to perform at other union activities and a neighboring town asked the District and Broad Top miners to help them sponsor a labor chautauqua. At the conclusion of the second chautauqua, 52 Broad Top women established a Women Workers' Education League with their own class. Eventually the labor chautauqua expanded to include more than lectures and discussions. Students from the workers' education classes entertained, played music, sang, danced, and produced one-act plays. Ladies' Auxiliaries recruited other local entertainers and arranged for food. Miners from the surrounding area, their families, and local supporters, gathered for three days of picnicking, singing, speech-making by district officials, and classes. At the labor chautauquas speakers discussed the formation of Labor Parties to challenge operator control of local government and defend the civil liberties of the miners. They promoted nationalization of the mines as the way to protect the right of the miner and his family to a decent life and the public's right to an inexpensive and adequate fuel supply. Speakers also combated a resurgent Ku Klux Klan and its ideas (Singer, 1988b: 61–64; Fuller, 1925: 10; Fuller, 1926: 324–26; *American Labor Yearbook*, 1926, VII: 305–10; *Illinois Miner*, September 6, 1924; Golden, 1925).

Ten chautauquas were organized during the summer of 1925, and the District 2 Education Department organized follow-up classes. Generally, classes met weekly, using Nationalization Research Committee pamphlets, a book about the Somerset strike published by the Bureau of Industrial Research, and materials from the Workers' Education Bureau, as texts. Curriculum included nationalization of coal, the uses of coal, its waste under private ownership, the history of the American labor movement, women and the trade union movement, and the social and political history of United States. The Ladies' Auxiliaries sponsored classes for women and picket support committees and some groups studied elementary English. An important aspect of the labor chautauqua was its ability to unify divided and bickering miners. Following a lockout, miners in Nanty Glo were divided along ethnic lines by operator-supported Klan activity and a battle for control of their local. A labor chautauqua was organized in Nanty Glo for August 1924. In September, Paul Fuller returned to address a large Labor Party rally. Nanty Glo miners responded by electing the local Labor Party candidates to the Court of Common Pleas, to the Pennsylvania State Legislature, to the Municipal Council, as town Burgess (Mayor), and as Justices of the Peace. A second Nanty Glo labor chautauqua was held in May 1925, to rally the entire region against the operators' efforts to force skilled men to sign "yellow-dog" contracts and reopen the mines nonunion. Bands and entertainers flocked to Nanty Glo from neighboring South Fork, Gallitzin, Portage, and Broad Top. Speakers included UMWA Vice President Philip Murray, James Maurer, International Ladies Garment Workers' Union organizer Kate O'Hare, Paul Fuller, John Brophy, and local foreign language speakers (Fuller, 1926: 324–26; *American Labor Yearbook*, 1926, VII: 305–10; Golden, 1925; *Nanty-Glo Journal*, July 17; September 18; October 30; December 11, 1924; January 8; May 21; May 28, 1925; *Illinois Miner*, October 31, 1925).

The District 2 workers' education program, especially the labor chautauqua movement, helped hold remnants of District 2 together during the 1925 and 1926 open-shop drive. It cemented the social bonds between miners, made the "Miners' Program" an active part of their consciousness, and gave miners a vision of the world they could fight for. The educational programs were most successful when union leadership used them to give a broader perspective to the struggles of the miners and direction to their day-to-day trade union activities and community political involvement. Classes, pamphlets, and lobbying campaigns made sense to workers when they pointed to long-term solutions to their problems, while at the same time helping them win strikes and elect local government officials. However, despite its educational successes, the labor chautauqua movement suffered from an inherent flaw. When trade union organizing failed under the weight of a massive open-shop campaign, even the most ingenious and elaborate workers' education program, the labor chautauqua, could only temporarily sustain union miners. It couldn't win strikes or provide miners and their families with permanent relief from hardship. Economic deprivation remained, demoralization set in again, and eventually the strongest locals in the district succumbed (Singer, 1988a: 59–63; *Nanty-Glo Journal*, May 21; May 28; June 11; July 2; September 17; November 5, 1925; *Illinois Miner*, October 31, 1925).

Charleroi and the Progressive Miners

Paralleling efforts in District 2 to develop a working-class conscious movement based on the Miners' Program, miners from the Charleroi group in Western Pennsylvania, with support from William Z. Foster and the Trade Union Educational League (TUEL) and the Workers (Communist) Party, organized the Progressive Miner's International Committee of the UMWA. The Progressive Committee sought to unify the rank-and-file opposition based on the Spring 1919 program adopted by the UMWA international convention. The Progressive Committee was handicapped because it lacked a district base of support similar to John Brophy's role in District 2, however, it did generate a major challenge to Lewis at the 1924 UMWA convention and trained many of the organizers active in the struggles of the union during the decade.

William Z. Foster emerged as a major figure in the American labor movement after leading successful union organizing drives among Chicago stockyard workers in 1917, and steel workers in 1919. In 1920, he founded the Trade Union Educational League (TUEL) to promote his idea of working for radical change from inside established American Federation of Labor unions. Foster opposed revolutionary independent or "dual" unions like the Industrial Workers of the World, because he believed that they left radicals isolated from the bulk of the working class. Initially the American communists supported the formation of independent unions, but in 1921 the Workers (Communist) Party endorsed the TUEL's "boring-from-within" program and William Z. Foster became its chief labor spokesperson (Foster, 1947, 9–87; Draper, 1957, 61–79).

Conditions in the coalfields and the conflicts within the UMWA created avenues for Foster and the TUEL to establish ties with the union's militants. Alexander Howat, suspended from the miners' union by Lewis, joined the TUEL, which took up the campaign to win his reinstatement as president of UMWA District 14 (Kansas). While the Kansas District was very small and had limited influence on union affairs, Howat had developed a close relationship with District 12 dissidents as a result of his support of wildcat strikes in Illinois in 1919. The connection with Howat helped Foster and the communists win the confidence of the Illinois militants. Meanwhile, Foster's work during the 1919 steel strike brought him into contact with Pittsburgh area miners in UMWA District 5 and the Charleroi group (Gagliardo, 1941, 16–20, 135–40; Wickersham, 1951, 68–71; Foster, 1947, 145; Schneider, 1928, 40–52).

The most influential member of the Charleroi group was Thomas Myerscough, an officer of Local 1198 in Lawrence, Pennsylvania near Pittsburgh. Myerscough was born in Lancashire, England, emigrated to the United States with his family while a teenager, and was recruited as a miner by the Pittsburgh Coal Company because management wanted him to play on its soccer team. After the UMWA international office called off the November 1919 nationwide strike, Myerscough and other the Charleroi miners circulated a petition calling for a special District 5 convention to plan an organizing drive in neighboring nonunion fields. When the District office ignored their petitions, the Charleroi group issued an independent call for a convention. Although UMWA District 5 officials charged the group with dual unionism, the convention was attended by 100 miners representing eighty-one union locals. Myerscough later became an active member of the Workers' (Communist) Party (Shields, 1986, 78–80; Everling, 1976, 154–55; UMWA AC 1924b).

In February 1923 the TUEL, working with Alexander Howat, Freeman Thompson, a socialist who was a leader of southern Illinois strikes by miners during World War I, and Myerscough, organized the Progressive International Committee of the UMWA in an attempt to unite local rank-and-file opposition groups in the miners' union. The Progressive Committee announced a June conference, set up an organizing committee to promote the conference, and published a platform, consistent with the TUEL philosophy and based on the Spring 1919 UMWA program and District 2's Miners' Program. The organizing committee also proposed a committee structure with local, subdistrict, and district chapters. The conference call emphatically rejected dual unionism and insisted that the opposition forces were determined to fight for change within the UMWA. The platform avoided inflammatory rhetoric, emphasized local and national issues affecting coal miners, sharply condemned dual unionism, and urged militant miners to organize inside the UMWA. It endorsed a nationalized coal industry with mines operated by committees of union miners, a shorter workweek to address unemployment, the election of union organizers, an alliance with the railway workers against the coal operators, the reinstatement of suspended UMWA radicals, a drive to reorganize the miners who had left the union since the end of World War I, industrial unionism, the formation of a broad-based labor party, and affiliation with the international labor movement. It also condemned electoral corruption in the union and charged Lewis and the international's officers with illegally ignoring votes taken at the UMWA's international conventions (Kopald, 1924; 264; Bussel, 1999: 57; UMWA MA Anti-Communism File; Progressive International Committee of the UMWA Program, Hapgood Papers).

While approximately 200 delegates from twelve UMWA districts attended the June 2–3 conference in Pittsburgh, William Z. Foster and miners related to the TUEL and the Workers' Party clearly played the leading role. Alex McKay of UMWA District 26 (Nova Scotia), who was suspended from the miners' union when his district affiliated with the communist Red International of Trade Unions, was chosen chairman of the conference. Myerscough of the Charleroi group and the Workers' Party, was elected secretary of the conference and secretary-treasurer of the Progressive Committee. The Workers' Party also provided organizational assistance and speakers, including Joseph Manley, William Z. Foster, and Ella "Mother" Bloor. The influence of the Workers' Party was also apparent when conference participants enlarged the Progressive Committee's platform to include two new planks; a demand for United States recognition of the Soviet Union and support for an expanded Farmer-Labor Party that the Workers' Party was trying to build with the help of James Fitzpatrick, president of the Chicago Federation of Labor (Progressive International Conference Minutes, Hapgood Papers; UMWA MA Anti-Communism File; Foster, July 1923: 3–6; *Federated Press* June 27, 1923).

While nonminers gave important leadership to the Progressive Committee, most of the people who attended the conference were rank-and-file coal miners, and the conference was clearly an effort to build a coalition that included noncommunist union militants. The organizing committee was careful to run an open and democratic conference; nominations to committee assignments were made directly from the floor and delegates from District 2 and other independent miners were selected for responsible positions. In sharp contrast to UMWA conventions where international officers and staff dominated debates, a rule was established that no speaker could address an issue a second time until everyone who desired had a chance to speak. Subcommittees set up to report to the conference included a broad spectrum of the delegates. Active in the conference from the Charleroi group were Anthony Minerich of North Bessemer Local 4238 and Patrick Toohey of Local 1724. Other significant participants were Alexander Howat and August Dorchy, the ousted vice president of District 14 (Kansas), Dan Slinger, president of Marissa, Illinois Local 4701, who represented Illinois militants, and a number of representatives from District 2, including Powers Hapgood (Progressive International Conference Minutes, Hapgood Papers; UMWA MA Anti-Communism File; Foster, July 1923: 3–6; *Federated Press*, June 27, 1923).

The Progressive Conference was subject to the same divisions that plagued the rest of the American left during this period, and it was unable to create the measure of unity among rank-and-file forces that Foster and the TUEL had hoped to achieve. Hapgood and the District 2 delegation failed to convince John Brophy to support the new coalition. While Brophy generally approved of the conference's platform, he was suspicious of communist influence in the Progressive Committee. Brophy disagreed with communist tactics in the Farmer-Labor movement and felt that they reflected the party's inflated evaluation of the revolutionary potential of the American working class. As president of District 2, Brophy wanted to avoid open warfare with Lewis and the UMWA international office. He feared that Lewis would brand anyone related to the TUEL and the communists as dual unionists and purge them from the union (Brophy, 1964: 205, 210).

Brophy's fears were well founded. John L. Lewis and his supporters in the UMWA international office recognized the seriousness of the Progressive Committee's challenge to their control over the union and launched a comprehensive campaign to destroy it. They used the Progressive Committee's ties to the Workers' Party to claim that it was a front organization dominated by William Z. Foster. Prior to the Pittsburgh gathering, international organizers assigned to District 5 were instructed to tail Thomas Myerscough and Alexander Howat and interfere with their efforts to organize the Progressive

Conference. Agents were also assigned to infiltrate the conference and its Workers' Party caucus. At the conclusion of the conference, Lewis issued an official union circular declaring the Progressive International Committee a "dual" organization, instructing all Districts and locals to expel members who participated. In a sweeping statement, Lewis charged that association with known communists was proof of "dual" intentions and that the Workers' Party/TUEL strategy of "boring-from-within" was sufficient grounds for expulsion from the UMWA (Dubofsky & Van Tine, 1977: 122–25; UMWA MA Anti-Communism File).

The Progressive Committee responded to the expulsion order by challenging Lewis' control of the union at the January 1924 UMWA convention. Freeman Thompson, who did not attend the Progressive Conference and was therefore not expelled from the union, headed the effort. He mobilized considerable support from UMWA District officials for an ultimately unsuccessful resolution that called for the election of union organizers. However other motions supported by the Progressives, including the reinstatement of Myerscough, Howat, and the leadership of the Nova Scotia District, were roundly defeated. By the end of the 1924 convention, the isolated Progressive forces were engaging in futile shouting matches with Lewis from the floor (UMWA Proceedings, 1924: 588–94, 617–22, 697, 709, 759–61, 793–95, 800, 845).

Unfortunately for the unity of the rank-and-file movement, basic philosophical disagreements about the vitality of American capitalism and the value of democratic procedures prevented the communist-supported Progressive Miners and District 2 from developing an effective coalition. John Brophy, while not a member of the Socialist Party, was a student of early-twentieth-century reform American Socialism. Brophy believed that the profit motive was an inefficient means of organizing production; however, he did not reject private ownership or challenge existing property rights. Brophy viewed the Miners' Program as a way of extending American political democracy into the economic sphere and believed a Labor Party could win a large following within the American electoral system by advocating a public service government that would rationalize essential industries in the public interest. Brophy and his supporters were prepared to work with a broad spectrum of society in a long-term movement for democratic change, while the communist miners in the Progressive Committee believed that the United States was on the verge of a cataclysmic class conflict between workers and capitalists. Anticipating this conflict, they rejected the American electoral system and gradual political reform and envisioned the rank-and-file miners' movement as the class-conscious vanguard of a revolutionary working-class movement that would seize state power and transform American society. A programmatic difference between the groups that illustrates a more fundamental disagreement was their positions on the nationalization of the mines. Brophy endorsed a tripartite body to administer the mines, including government representatives for the public interest, mine technicians and managers, and the UMWA. The Progressive Committee program rejected any role in the management of the industry for any group but the miners. While Brophy respected the communists' seriousness and organizing ability, he was suspicious of the Progressive Committee, and doubted its commitment to the Miners' Program. In July 1923 Brophy withdrew from the Farmer-Labor Party Convention in Chicago because he believed the communists were using the labor movement for their own ends and were determined to impose transplanted "Russian Methods" on the Party. On July 12, 1923, he wrote Arthur Gleason that the communists in the Progressive Committee were pursuing a path that would lead to their expulsion from the UMWA by the International Executive Board as "dual unionists" (Brophy et al., n.d.; Brophy, 1964: 116–117, 205, 210; Foster, July 1923: 3–6; Brophy Papers, Series 1, Box 1).

At this point in his struggle for the Miners' Program, Brophy still believed that a rapprochement with Lewis was possible and he was not prepared to risk expulsion from the UMWA for allying with the communists in the Progressive Committee. Brophy hoped that reconciliation would allow District 2 to salvage the struggle for union in Somerset and permit Brophy to percolate the Miners' Program throughout the UMWA. It was not until 1926 that Brophy abandoned his efforts to work with Lewis and agreed to coalesce with the communist miners from the Charleroi group and remnants of the Progressive Committee. In the Save the Union committee, communist miners agreed to work for the District 2 version of the Miners' Program and Brophy declared, "Nothing can take the place of working-class solidarity." Unfortunately for the rank-and-file movement in the UMWA, the three-year delay from 1923 to 1926 proved too costly. By the time District 2 and the communists put aside their differences, the rank-and-file miners' movement was seriously weakened by the open-shop drive and its ability to challenge Lewis for control of the UMWA was sharply reduced (Brophy, 1964: 214–18; Save the Union, September 24, 1926, Brophy Papers, Series 1, Box 3).

Chapter 7

Combating the Open-Shop Drive

From 1923 through 1925, John L. Lewis and the business unionists in the United Mine Workers Union's international office worked to consolidate their hold on the union by purging rank-and-file insurgents and securing a solid majority at the union's international convention. Lewis' activities maintained his control over the union machinery by undercutting the rank-and-file groups that were battling the open-shop drive in the coalfields and fighting to preserve the Miner's Freedom. Increasingly, the international office depended on cooperation with friendly Central Competitive Field operators and the federal government to maintain the union's position in the industry. Lewis' decision to sign the limited bituminous coal agreement in August 1922 ended the international union's efforts to organize the nonunion fields and win a national contract. Instead, the union attempted to negotiate a long-term CCF contract that would stabilize bituminous coal production and protect the unionized areas from nonunion competition. However, neither the Republican administration nor the unionized operators were committed to the survival of the UMWA. The open-shop drive expanded and by 1926 threatened to engulf the CCF and eliminate the union as a force in the industry (Dubofsky & Van Tine, 1977: 105–8).

During this period, Lewis invested considerable time and resources in a systematic campaign against his opponents in the union. He used the precedent established when Alexander Howat was removed from district office by the International Executive Board to seize control of what he considered to be insubordinate districts and districts and union locals decimated by the open-shop drive. In 1923, Lewis removed the leadership of District 26 (Nova Scotia) on the grounds that they had illegally affiliated with the "dualistic" Red International, and in February 1924 he rooted out their supporters, joining with operators to crush a sympathy strike (Dubofsky & Van Tine, 1977: 102; *Illinois Miner*, February 2, 1924; *UMWA Journal*, August 1, 1923).

In June 1924, District 17 (West Virginia), bankrupted by a sustained open-shop drive, petitioned Lewis and the International Executive Board to assume the administration of the district office. Lewis appointed Percy Tetlow and Van Bittner to run District 17 as a pocket borough of the international office. The newly appointed officials in other districts were usually international organizers loyal to the Lewis machine. They represented these districts and phantom locals at the union's international conventions where they formed a sizable pro-Lewis voting bloc. The "payroll" votes often held the balance on closely contested issues before the convention. At the February 1922 reconvened UMWA convention, votes from "blue-sky" Southern Appalachian locals with little if any membership gave Lewis sufficient votes to uphold Alexander Howat's expulsion from the union. Locals without working members were called "blue-sky" locals because working miners rarely saw blue skies (Dubofsky & Van Tine, 1977: 102, 121; *Illinois Miner*, March 1, March 29, 1924; UMWA MA Anti-Communism file).

Lewis' Anticommunism

Lewis recognized the seriousness of the Progressive International Committee's challenge to business unionism and launched a comprehensive campaign to discredit the committee. International organizers in District 5 were assigned to follow Thomas Myerscough and Alexander Howat and interfere with efforts to organize the Progressive Committee's June 1923 Convention. Hired agents infiltrated both the convention and a Workers' Party caucus. They provided the international office with transcripts of the proceedings and a list of all participants and their affiliations. On June 20, 1923, Lewis issued an official circular declaring the Progressive International Committee a dual organization, despite the committee's repeated opposition to dual unionism. In a sweeping statement Lewis charged that association with known communists was sufficient proof of dual intentions and banned the Workers' Party strategy of "boring-from-within" established unions. Lewis claimed the authority to expel any UMWA member who associated with left-wing organizations or challenged the union's leadership. He instructed all districts and locals to expel any union member who participated in the Progressive Conference.

Lewis picked up key support for his position identifying left-wing political activism with dual unionism from Frank Farrington. Despite his hatred of Lewis, Farrington endorsed the statement because he feared attack from Illinois militants holding elective office in District 12 Subdistricts 4 and 7 (Dubofsky & Van Tine, 1977: 122–25; Foster, July 1923: 3–6; UMWA MA Anti-Communist file; Laslett, 1996: 111–12).

Lewis also used the campaign against the Progressive Committee to present himself as a national leader in the crusade against the international communist conspiracy. He issued a report titled *Attempt by Communists to Seize the American Labor Movement* that was serialized in a number of newspapers and published in the *Congressional Record*. The report charged that liberal and communist groups were working in the labor movement as agents of Moscow to subvert American workers in an effort to destroy the American way of life. The report, without evidence, claimed Moscow provided American communists with a million-dollar fund for fomenting armed insurrection among coal miners during the 1922 strike. It blamed the communists for pressing the 1922 strike to bankrupt the UMWA, for raising the divisive issue of nationalization of the mines, for sabotage in Southwestern Pennsylvania, and for planning the massacre of scabs in a bloody battle at Herron, Illinois, during the strike (Lewis, 1924; Angle, 1992).

The conflict between Lewis and the Progressive Committee came to a head at the January 1924 UMWA convention, the first international convention since February 1922. Lewis' strategy was to take credit for the $7.50 day in the CCF, while Vice President Philip Murray accused the Progressive Committee of supporting wage reductions. Lewis and Murray counted on an alliance with Farrington against the insurgents to silence the opposition. Preceding the convention, Lewis announced that a joint wage conference had been scheduled for Jacksonville, Florida, with the assistance of Secretary of Commerce Herbert Hoover. This enabled Lewis to enter the convention claiming the success of a business unionist strategy based on collaboration with government and coal companies. In the presidential address to the convention, Lewis praised his role in the 1922 Cleveland CCF settlement for breaking the resistance of open-shop operators and "ending the most memorable struggle in the annals of the United Mine Workers, from which we have emerged with outstanding success, having maintained our position against concentrated opposition involving all equations of industry, finance, and politics." Murray, who followed Lewis at the convention, accused the leaders of the Progressive Committee of supporting operator efforts to lower the District 5 wage scale to the 1917 level. Murray concluded his speech with a patriotic appeal to the convention calling for vigilance against "sovietism and fascism" (UMWA Proceedings, 1924: 9–14, 20–34; Dubofsky & Van Tine, 1977: 124–25).

The Progressive Committee's convention strategy was to undermine the union bureaucracy by demanding the direct election of international organizers. Opposition delegates also tried to attract district autonomy advocates and disaffected representatives from the outlying districts to block the "payroll" vote at the convention and to prevent the use of blue-sky locals to steal the 1924 union elections. Initially Lewis underestimated the level of support for the proposal to elect union organizers. The resolution's committee rejected the motion but was reversed by a hand vote of the convention—760 to 734. Lewis quickly ordered a roll-call ballot and both sides mobilized their supporters. In the final tally the motion to elect international organizers was narrowly defeated by a vote of 2,263 to 2,166 (see table 7.1). An analysis of the vote shows the depth of dissatisfaction with Lewis' conduct of union affairs. Lewis' narrow victory margin depended on solid support from the Anthracite field and the payroll vote representing blue-sky Kentucky, Tennessee, Alabama, and West Virginia locals. Farrington was unable to control the Illinois delegation that supported the resolution—856 to 97. Ohio was the only organized bituminous coalfield to solidly support the union leadership. For reasons not completely clear, Brophy broke with his supporters from District 2 and voted against the election of international organizers (UMWA Proceedings, 1924: 594, 617, 618, 622).

The vote on the election of international organizers was not a general endorsement of the insurgent program. The Progressive Committee also proposed a motion to eliminate the international president's authority to remove elected officials and appoint provisional officers. This was defeated by a vote of 905 to 468. Later in the convention, a frustrated Freeman Thompson antagonized a number of delegates during an emotional debate on the Ku Klux Klan by comparing the Klan to the Democratic and Republican Parties. This probably contributed to the Progressive Committee's defeat by a voice vote when it appealed a Lewis ruling that barred Thomas Myerscough from participation in the convention (UMWA Proceedings, 1924: 588, 795, 845).

Jacksonville Agreement

Following the international office's narrow victory at the January UMWA convention, Lewis turned his attention to the approaching Jacksonville,

Table 7.1. Vote on the Election of International Organizers

Pro-Lewis Districts	Vote on Election of International Organizers Against/Favor	Divided Districts	Vote on Election of International Organizers Against/Favor	Anti-Lewis Districts	Vote on Election of International Organizers Against/Favor
Anthracite 1, 7, 9	748–138	2 Cent. Penn	159–128	5 West Penn	191–213
4 SW Penn	9–0	10 Wash.	6–4	11 Indiana	88–154
6 Ohio	284–125	17 WV central	154–92	12 Illinois	97–856
8 Indiana	12–0	21 Arkansas	66–62	14 Kansas	29–62
13 Missouri	93–36	22 Wyoming	38–30	18 Brit. Col.	4–47
15 Colorado	15–6			24 Michigan	0–18
16 Maryland	26–0			26 Nova Sc.	0–55
19 Kentucky	88–0			27 Montana	6–38
20 Alabama	4–1				
23 Kentucky	82–34				
25 Missouri	52–20				
30 WV north	10–0				

Source. Created by the author.

Florida, CCF negotiations. The union leadership wanted a long-term contract to stabilize production and protect the CCF. They were assisted in achieving this goal by the Republican administration's desire to avoid a bituminous coal strike in a presidential election year. Secretary of Commerce Herbert Hoover pressed open-shop Mellon interests to participate in the talks and encouraged a settlement. With Hoover's assistance, the union and the operators negotiated a three-year extension of the $7.50 day. The miners covered by the extension welcomed the Jacksonville pact, voting to accept the contract by a six-to-one majority. Lewis also took advantage of the Jacksonville meetings to improve his personal contacts with powerful operators. One group of Illinois operators offered Lewis a position as head of the Illinois Operators Association and of a projected National Union Operators' Association. Following the conference, Ellis Searles continued a cryptic correspondence with this group as Lewis' representative, but negotiations fell through in November 1924. The Jacksonville agreement had additional subsidiary benefits for Lewis. It enhanced his reputation as a national labor statesman, and Lewis used it as a platform to offer himself as a potential Republican vice presidential candidate (Dubofsky & Van Tine, 1977: 107—9; *Illinois Miner*, April 1924, 5:1; *New York Times*, April 20, 1924: sec XX 10; UMWA MA K. C. Adams, Pursglove, and A. D. Lewis Files).

The long-term peace promised by the Jacksonville CCF settlement proved to be exceedingly short-lived. Companies in the outlying Oklahoma and Kentucky fields rejected the pact and lowered the wage scale to the 1917 level and Colorado operators lowered the wage scale by 15 percent. To stem the open-shop shift, Lewis offered Western Kentucky operators a twenty cents a ton wage differential to sign with the union, but was turned down and the largest union mine in that area of the state announced it would resume work on a nonunion basis. In District 2, the Central Pennsylvania Coal Producers' Association reluctantly signed the pact but threatened to lay off 2,500 miners and close 50 percent of the mines in the district. Meanwhile neighboring nonunion Somerset County mines operated on the 1917 scale. By the end of April, the *Illinois Miner* reported that 75,000 miners were striking against wage reductions. In May, the open-shop drive spilled over into the CCF. On May 1, 150 District 12 (Illinois) mines closed and the district's remaining 374 shipping mines were working less than half time and producing less than 50 percent of the previous year's tonnage. In an effort to maintain the competitive position of the working mines, the district office waved certain work rules and discouraged unemployed miners from running the closed mines cooperatively (*Illinois Miner*, April 12, April 26, May 10, May 17, 1924; UMWA MA Farrington File).

The situation in the union fields continued to deteriorate during the summer and fall, and the UMWA appeared helpless to combat it. In July, Kanawha, West Virginia companies owning forty-nine mines locked out union miners and after depleting stockpiled coal they returned to operation on the 1917 scale. By the end of the year the UMWA West Virginia membership had decreased to 10,000 members with 75 percent of those miners on strike. In August 1924, the United States Bureau of the Mines reported that the union fields were operating at between 25 and 43 percent of capacity, compared to between 50 and 70 percent in the nonunion fields. Ninety percent of the coal received at the Great Lakes ports was nonunion. In December, the *Illinois Miner* reported that during the peak November bituminous season, nonunion fields in Illinois produced at 75 percent capacity compared to 43 percent for Illinois's union mines, 37 percent for unionized mines in Indiana, and 42 percent for unionized mines in Western Pennsylvania. At the start of 1925, CCF operators demanded a wage conference to set a lower scale for the field. The UMWA refused to participate and the conference collapsed. This set off a new round of mine closings and wage reductions in Western Pennsylvania, Somerset County, and Western Kentucky (Dubofsky & Van Tine, 1977: 136; *Illinois Miner*, July 12, July 19, August 16, August 30, December 13, 1924; March 21, March 28, April 4, April 25, May 2, May 9, May 30, June 13, 1925).

John L. Lewis, committed to the business-unionist strategy of cooperation with union operators and the federal government, ignored signals during the preliminary negotiations for Jacksonville that the operators intended to renew the open-shop drive in the outlying fields. While the operators reluctantly accepted the Jacksonville pact as a temporary truce in the CCF, they always insisted that the open shop was necessary for the mechanization and consolidation of production. In February 1924, *Federated Press* economic analyst Leland Olds predicted that the operators' plans to reorganize production and consolidate ownership in the bituminous coal industry awaited the destruction of the UMWA. He cited the call by *Black Diamond*, a leading trade publication, for a bituminous coal monopoly in a union-free industry. *Black Diamond* argued that the UMWA had to be broken to rid the industry of the tradition of the "independent miner, capable and responsible" and reorganize work using factory-style mass production techniques (Olds, February 2, 1924).

The pressure for open-shop operation was increased by the rapid introduction of bituminous coal machine loaders and conveyor belt systems from
1923 through 1925. During these two years, the use of machine loaders
increased by over 300 percent. Illinois companies produced 1.3 million tons
of machine-loaded coal in 1925, and by 1926 eighteen leading Illinois mines
were loading 25 percent of their tonnage by machine. In nonunion West
Virginia, the amount of machine-loaded coal jumped from 1,367,688 tons
in 1923 to 2,480,768 tons in 1925. The machine loaders and conveyor
systems required a number of shifts in the organization of production to
ensure steady work and maximum profitability. The companies did not want
interference from organized miners wedded to the traditional concepts of
work. U.S. Steel standardized work rules and increased supervision at its
Gary, West Virginia, mines. It assigned one "cut boss" or assistant foreman
for every twenty-five workers. The "cut boss" received a set of printed
instructions regulating all levels of work and was responsible to ensure that
loaders achieved production quotas. All miners were treated as inexperienced
unskilled laborers and no independent decisions were tolerated. When loading machines were connected to a conveyor belt system at the nonunion
West Virginia Coal and Coke mine in Norton, West Virginia, farmers were
hired instead of miners, and teams of four or five were assigned to tend
the machines in large underground workrooms (American Mining Congress,
1928: 16; Tryon & Hale, 1923; Kenny and Tyron, 1926: 847–48; Stewart,
1928: 29–36; Goodrich, 125–28, 132–36, 160).

The UMWA leadership completely misjudged the strength and determination of the open-shop forces. Open-shop companies included some of
the giants of American industry. Consolidation and Old Ben mines were
controlled by Rockefeller interests; Pittsburgh Coal was a Mellon company;
Peabody Coal was part of the Insull power-utility empire; and Pittsburgh
Terminal Coal Corporation was a subsidiary of U.S. Steel. Nonunion Western
Kentucky Coal, controlled by Morgan banking interests, used the open-shop
drive to expand rail connections into traditionally Illinois markets. These
companies were supported by anti-union advocates across the American
industrial landscape. The Ford Motor Company opened its own nonunion
mines in Kentucky. The National Association of Manufacturers and the
Metal Trades Association pressed their members to patronize non-union coal
where possible. The Interstate Commerce Commission contributed to the
problems of the union fields by reducing shipping costs to the Northwestern
market from nonunion Kentucky by fifty-four cents per ton while raising
the rate from unionized Illinois by twenty-eight cents per ton. In frustration,

District 12 President Farrington accused the ICC of being an open-shop club (Olds, May 1927, 4: 1; *Illinois Miner*, August 9, September 20, 1924; *National Labor Tribune*, August 21, 1924).

Despite losses during strikes, the large coal companies were not seriously hurt by scattered UMWA resistance. Record profits during World War I enabled companies to sustain prolonged losses while they combated the union. The Mellon-owned Pittsburgh Coal Company lost 4.5 million dollars during 1925 and 1926, while switching over to open-shop operation, closing fifteen union mines. The change over included working played out mines to publicly justify dropping the union wage scale. These losses were minimal compared to the seventy-nine-million-dollar war chest the company accumulated from wartime earnings. The company used the open-shop drive as an opportunity to purchase new machinery, modernize mines, abandon old works, and buy up outstanding shares of stock at depressed prices. The open-shop drive also fueled merger talks, increasing the value of some coal stocks. Fifty small nonunion West Virginia firms merged to form Rain Creek Coal capitalized at twenty-five million dollars and some Morgan and Rockefeller properties combined operation in West Virginia. On Wall Street, rumors spread of a possible merger between Rockefeller's Consolidation Company and Mellon's Pittsburgh Coal to create a billion-dollar coal trust. While the companies were making a mockery of the union contract, Lewis continued to affirm the UMWA's commitment to the Jacksonville CCF agreement. He refused to reopen negotiations and demanded government intervention to preserve the contract. On June 30, 1925, speaking at the Tri-District Anthracite Convention, Lewis threatened a nationwide combined Anthracite and Bituminous strike. However, the Coolidge administration refused to be drawn into negotiations and the operators recognized that the bituminous coal strike threat was a bluff. When Anthracite miners walked out alone, operators flooded markets with bituminous coal (Dubofsky & Van Tine, 1977: 140; *Illinois Miner*, April 2, 1927; August 15, August 22, October 3, November 28, 1924; *New York Times*, July 1, 1925: 1; July 22: 1; August 16: 27, November 23: 4, November 28: 3; Olds, June 10, 1925: 5; December 2: 1; July 1926, 27: 3).

The collapse of the Jacksonville CCF agreement revived the Progressive Committee after its defeats at the January 1924 UMWA convention. The committee concentrated its efforts on organizing a full slate of candidates to challenge Lewis and Farrington in the December 1924 international and District 12 union elections. Lewis and Farrington responded by suspending insurgents in Illinois and Pittsburgh from their union posts and locals. In

November 1924, Farrington suspended the Progressive Committee–endorsed candidate for president of the Illinois State Federation of Labor from his Springfield, Illinois, local. In April 1925, Farrington removed James Watt and Freeman Thompson from the District 12, Subdistrict 4, office, charging election irregularities. The charters of union locals that supported Watt and Thompson in the dispute were revoked for dual unionism. During the summer of 1925, the purge continued. The Springfield, Illinois, Miners' Educational League was declared a dual union and its head, Joe Tumilty, was suspended. In Subdistrict 7, Vice President Luke Coffey was removed from office. Thomas Myerscough, secretary of the Progressive Committee, was blacklisted in District 5, and the charter of his Lawrence, Pennsylvania local was revoked. When Myerscough tried to find work in the Anthracite fields, the District 1 office published a notice in a Wilkes-Barre, Pennsylvania, newspaper warning local unions and companies not to employ him (*Illinois Miner*, November 15, 1924; April 11, April 18, May 23, June 6, July 18, August 8, 1925; UMWA MA Anti-Communism File).

The suspensions forced the Progressive Committee to run three relatively unknown miners for the major international offices; George Voyzey of Verona, Illinois, for UMWA president; Anley Staples of Christopher, Illinois for vice president; and Joseph Nearing of Nova Scotia for secretary-treasurer. Despite the handicap of personal anonymity, the ticket received surprisingly strong support from all sectors of the union. The Progressive endorsed slate tallied 32 percent of the overall vote and 48.8 percent in Illinois. They carried Kansas, British Columbia, and Nova Scotia and scored better than 30 percent in Districts 5, 18, 22, 24, 26, and 27. Only inflated vote totals from blue-sky Appalachian locals and the Anthracite fields, and the inability of the Progressives to develop a working relationship with Brophy in District 2, prevented a closer election (*UMWA Journal*, March 1, 1925).

The Miners' Fight for American Standards

In 1925, John L. Lewis began his new term in office with a shaky hold on a besieged union in an increasingly open-shop industry. In an effort to defend his business unionist strategy for the union and to recoup his national reputation, Lewis published *The Miners' Fight for American Standards*. The book, researched and ghostwritten by K. C. Adams and W. Jett Lauck of the UMWA publicity and legal departments, spelled out Lewis' alternative to the open-shop drive supported by the operators, and the Miner's Program, endorsed by his UMWA opponents. His proposals were an attempt to justify Lewis' decision to abandon the outlying and nonunion fields during the 1922 strike, and his rejection of the slogan "organize the unorganized" (Lewis, 1925).

In *The Miners' Fight*, Lewis called for federal-government-sponsored, union-endorsed, cartelization of the bituminous coal industry as the solution to excess capacity and overproduction. The Lewis plan endorsed price fixing and the distribution of markets among the large, mechanized producers to drive the small irregular mines out of the industry. Lewis believed that the UMWA and the Central Competitive Field could survive the weeding out of the industry because of the CCF's proximity to the established markets and wider coal seams favorable to mechanization. While the industry would collapse in the nonunion and outlying fields, hardships for union miners would at least be partly offset by a relocation fund. Lewis also argued the benefits of unionization in response to open-shop critics of the UMWA. He claimed that union wages would speed up the mechanization and rationalization of mining while increasing the purchasing power of the worker. Lewis characterized the open-shop anti-union businessman as a "pre-capitalist with a feudal mind." For Lewis, "Trade unionism is a phenomenon of capitalism quite similar to the corporation. One is essentially the pooling of labor for purposes of common action in production and sales. The other is a pooling of capital for exactly the same purposes. The economic aims of both are identical—gain." Leland Olds, writing in the *Federated Press Newsletter*, described Lewis' position as a defense of the existing capitalist order (Lewis, 1925: 15, 40–41, 122–27; Dubofsky &Van Tine, 1977: 106; Olds, July 8, 1925: 5).

The Lewis plan in *The Miners' Fight* contained the same inherent weaknesses that had crippled the Jacksonville CCF agreement. These included an inaccurate appraisal of the position of the CCF operators and a misinterpretation of Secretary of Commerce Herbert Hoover's views on government's role in labor-management relations. The plan depended on support from large mechanized pro-union Central Competitive Field operators. However, by 1925, most of the large operators in the CCF had diversified their holdings into the nonunion fields. The CCF operators that depended on the union to stabilize labor costs were the smaller less efficient mines in Illinois, Ohio, and Indiana. These operators were threatened with extinction by the plan. Lewis also continued to count on Hoover's support for the union. Although Hoover accepted the government's role as a mediator between labor and capital, he rejected government-sponsored cartelization and did not advocate unionism. In fact, Hoover stood on record arguing that labor organization beyond the shop floor impinged on management's authority and created inefficient operation. While Hoover had hoped that the three years of industrial peace promised by the Jacksonville CCF accord would end inefficiency and overproduction in the industry, he was not committed to the long-term survival of either the CCF or the UMWA (Zieger, 1969: 15, 64–65, 116–27; Searles, 1922: 639–42; Coleman, 1943: 125).

Open-Shop Drive Renewed

While Lewis, Hoover, and the bituminous coal operators argued at the conference table or in the press, rank-and-file miners in local unions fought the open-shop drive in mining towns across the country. Desperate men with hungry families were pitted against local elites, national business empires, a pro-business Republican administration, the Ku Klux Klan, and an unsupportive and occasionally hostile UMWA international office. The battle in the bituminous coalfields tested the class-consciousness of the rank-and-file miner, his sense of group solidarity, his commitment to the Miner's Freedom and traditional work patterns, and his understanding of the alternative political program espoused by various segments of the rank-and-file miner's movement. Bituminous coal operators recognized the need to extirpate the class-conscious underpinnings of the UMWA before they could break the union. They attempted to undermine the roots of the miner's class-consciousness at work and employed the Ku Klux Klan to weaken the bonds that united miners in coal patch communities. Spokesman T. A. Stroup, mine superintendent of the Utah Fuel Company, argued that the UMWA was basically a craft union, its strength resting on the ability of the miner to independently choose how to organize his tasks and use his time. According to Stroup, if operators could eliminate choice and skill, they could eradicate the union. Trade periodical *Black Diamond* echoed Stroup, calling on operators to replace the tradition of the "independent miner, capable and responsible," with factory-style mass production (Goodrich, 1925: 22; Stroup, 1923: 467–68; Olds, February 2, 1924).

At the same time that the operators were negotiating contracts for the Central Competitive Field, they developed a strategy to uproot union locals in the weaker outlying fields. The union local was the miner's first and foremost line of defense against his employer. The local monitored wages and weights, and its bank committee enforced work and safety rules. To break the local, operators unilaterally lowered wage scales and introduced new work rules and procedures. If miners refused to accept the changes, they were locked out, and coal orders were shifted to nonunion fields. Operators used the lockout to introduce new machinery and further reorganize work. In an effort to demoralize the miners, unskilled farmers were recruited to take their jobs. Often companies had the farmers loading rail cars with slate and boney, discarded dirty coal that could not be utilized with existing technology, to maintain the appearance of full operation and to convince the miners that the mine could operate without them. When well-organized locals resisted the open-shop drive, operators tried to unravel the community bonds that sustained their struggle. Miners were evicted from company-owned housing and company stores suspended credit. Coal and Iron police harassed their movements and political and legal rights were ignored. The companies also used the resurgence of the Ku Klux Klan in the 1920s to divide workers along religious and ethnic lines. Despite a UMWA constitutional ban on membership in the Klan, it emerged as a key weapon in the drive to wrench apart mining communities in Alabama, Illinois, West Virginia, and Pennsylvania. In Illinois, the Klan intimidated foreign miners, using prohibition as an excuse to break into their homes. In West Virginia, it burned crosses to threaten strikers, and in District 5 it organized strikebreakers. At the 1924 UMWA convention, President James Hessler of District 11 (Indiana) declared the constitutional ban on Klan membership unenforceable and admitted thousands of Indiana miners were openly members (UMWA Proceedings, 1924: 795–813).

As the open-shop drive gathered momentum, it overwhelmed the business-unionist strategy of the international union and the trade union practices of union locals. District and local leaders sought new ways of mobilizing rank-and-file miners to save the union. Increasingly, the survival of the UMWA, first in the outlying fields, and then in the CCF, rested on the miner's class-conscious understanding of his world, and the militancy that Lewis and a generation of business unionists had worked to eliminate from the union. From 1924 through 1926, District 2 (Central Pennsylvania) was a crucial area in the battle to save the union by kindling and mobilizing the class-consciousness of the miner. District 2 pioneered in developing educational programs to increase the miner's level of understanding and willingness to struggle during the 1922–1923 strike in Somerset County. District President John Brophy retained his commitment to worker education and continued many of the district's programs after the strike was called off. District leaders also maintained contact with the rank-and-file movement in other parts of the union, despite Brophy's unwillingness to endorse the Progressive Committee or their campaign to unseat Lewis.

District 2 mines were crucial to the success of the operator's open-shop drive. For the UMWA, the district functioned as a unionized buffer between the Central Competitive Field and the nonunion Appalachian fields. District 2 was particularly vulnerable to the open-shop drive because many of its largest operators, including Consolidation Coal and Hillman Coal and Coke, operated mines in both the union and nonunion fields. The Central Pennsylvania Coal Producers' Association launched the district's open-shop drive soon after signing the Jacksonville CCF pact. On April 19, 1924, Association President B. M. Clark demanded that District 2 renegotiate a lower wage scale. Meanwhile nonunion Somerset County operators, led by Berwind-White, reverted to the 1917 pay scale. In September 1924, the Producers' Association formally voted to abandon the Jacksonville CCF contract. It unilaterally lowered the tonnage rate and authorized operators to install 1½ inch screens to sift coal before weighing it at the mine tipple. Central Pennsylvania Coal Producers' Association President Clark closed his mines until early 1925, when he reopened them nonunion (*Federated Press*, June 27, 1923; May 20, 1925; October 21, November 11, March 31, 1926; *Illinois Miner*, August 30, 1924, December 13, April 25, 1925; *National Labor Tribune*, September 11, September 25, 1924).

During the summer of 1924, District 2 bituminous coal production hovered at approximately 40 percent of capacity. Though it climbed to 53.5 percent in the fall, most of the increase was in nonunion mines. During 1925, union mining in District 2 came to a virtual halt. The Erie Railroad closed its mines indefinitely, throwing 1,300 union miners out of work. Bethlehem Steel and the Pittsburgh Coal and Consolidation Coal companies closed union mines in District 2 and shifted production to nonunion mines in Pocahontas, West Virginia. In a September 1925 report to the international office, District President Brophy reported that 100 mines had officially broken the Jacksonville CCF contract, and 216 of the district's 315 mining operations were closed. From 1923 through 1926, the District 2 dues-paying membership declined from almost forty thousand to seventeen thousand miners. Field reports to John Brophy indicated that by fall 1925, only two of the nine subdistricts continued to function, and in both territories union miners were on strike (*Illinois Miner*, August 30, 1924; December 13; March 27, 1926; *National Labor Tribune*, September 4, 1925; Brophy Papers, September 6, 1925, Series 1, Box 2; Brophy, 1964: 227).

Weakened by limited resources and the ineffectiveness of its strikes, District 2 searched for other methods to rally miners against the open-shop drive. Drawing on its labor education activities during the 1922–1923 Somerset strike, Brophy and Paul Fuller, a former miner, ordained minister, and Pennsylvania State Secretary of the Farmer-Labor Party, turned to the labor chautauqua. As noted earlier, the labor chautauqua was modeled on rural religious revivalist tent meetings. It was designed to revive the collective spirits of isolated mining communities and laid the basis for continued struggle against the open-shop drive and for reconstructing the district organization. The labor chautauqua provided the district with a forum for presenting rank-and-file miners with the Miner's Program as a long-term solution to the problems of the bituminous coal industry and as a vision of the future that beleaguered miners could clasp onto. Fuller, head of the District's Education Department, was responsible for organizing the chautauquas. Fuller met with local union leaders to draw up plans for the union "revival." He was assisted by Clara Johnson, who organized Ladies Auxiliaries to recruit local entertainers and arrange for food. At the labor chautauqua, miners from the surrounding area, their families, and local supporters, gathered for three days of picnicking, singing, speech-making by district officials, and labor education classes. At the labor chautauquas, speakers discussed the formation of Labor Parties to challenge operator control of local government and defend the civil liberties of the miners. They promoted nationalization of the mines as the way to protect the right of the miner and his family to a decent life and the public's right to an inexpensive and adequate fuel supply. Speakers also combatted the divisive influence of the Ku Klux Klan and its ideas in the district. The District 2 Education Department organized follow-ups to the tent meetings. Regular Labor Education classes were continued. Generally, they focused on local organization and used the pamphlets published by the Nationalization Research Committee and Heber Blankenhorn's account of the Somerset Strike, *Strike for Union*, as texts. The Ladies Auxiliaries also sponsored women's labor education classes and acted as picket support committees (Brophy, 1964: 212; *Illinois Miner*, September 6, 1924; Golden, 1925; District 2 Bulletin, June 29, 1926; UMWA MA District 2 File).

The labor chautauqua movement held the remnants of District 2 together during 1925 and 1926. Incomplete records reconstructed from Fuller's Travel Vouchers and reports by the district's Secretary-Treasurer list eight District 2 tent-revivals in the last six months of 1924, and six during the second half of 1926. The labor chautauquas made the Miner's Program an active part of the class-consciousness of the district's rank-and-file, giving miners a vision of the world they could fight for. A striking example of the impact of the labor chautauqua was its ability to show miners the value of class political power. Following a labor chautauqua in Nanty Glo, the Cambria County Labor Party elected a Judge to the Court of Common Pleas, a number of justices of the peace, a representative to the Pennsylvania State Legislature, the Burgess of Nanty Glo, and half of the borough's municipal council. Local miners were able to secure injunctions against companies that interfered with their right to picket, and 100 strikers were sworn in as special deputies to protect miners and their families from harassment by the Coal and Iron police. Miners had won the basic right to walk along a public road without fearing attack by operator-hired goons (Plaintiff's Bill, June 1925; *Illinois Miner*, October 31, 1925).

Despite successfully stimulating political understanding and class awareness among rank-and-file miners, the labor chautauqua provided no immediate relief from hardship during the open-shop drive. The labor chautauqua was an educational supplement, never intended to replace trade union activity and permanent local organization. As the open-shop attack in District 2 and the UMWA continued, economic deprivation remained, and demoralization set in again. Eventually the strongest local in the strongest county in the district, Nanty Glo local 1386 in Cambria County, succumbed to the open-shop drive. By 1926, Brophy and his supporters recognized that a district-wide solution was unachievable while Lewis and a business-unionist ideology dominated the international office. Brophy reversed his previous decision not to work in coalition with communists in the union and a compromise was hammered out between Brophy and the Progressive Committee. They both agreed to organize around the District 2 version of the Miner's Program. United under the banner, "Save the Union," they used the programs and techniques developed by District 2 to challenge Lewis in the 1926 UMWA elections.

Part 3

Nanty Glo

Chapter 8

Nanty Glo, Pennsylvania

While the struggle by bituminous coal miners to gain control over their lives and work meant forcing coal operators to accept a national contract governing all coalfields and defeating business unionists in contests for international and district offices, many crucial battles were fought on the local level where they were sustained by the class consciousness of coal miners and support from their communities. In the Central Pennsylvania District 2 coalfields, developments in Nanty Glo, the home base of District President John Brophy, illustrate the strengths and weaknesses of efforts to defeat a coordinated open-shop drive by coal operators during this period.

Nanty Glo History

Nanty Glo was the largest community in the Blacklick Valley of Central Pennsylvania, located about thirteen miles northwest of Johnstown in Cambria County, where it sat above an excellent grade of high-volatile coal. Bituminous coal outcroppings were first discovered in Cambria County in 1769. By 1822, coal was being mined commercially for use locally as a domestic fuel. In 1843 a rail spur connected the county with the Portage Railroad and commercial shipment began to Pittsburgh and Philadelphia. During this period there were approximately forty producing mines in Cambria County. In 1905, the county provided 3½ percent of the nation's coal tonnage. It ranked number one in Pennsylvania counties in the number of operating mines and number four in tonnage. Most of the county's coal was shipped to the Port of New York for use as steamship fuel. During World War I, Cambria mines contributed an average of 20 million tons annually to the war effort. In 1924, the county's estimated coal reserves were 4.6 billion tons. Despite its favorable location and high-quality coal, Cambria was never included in the CCF because narrow coal seams hindered the laying of underground track, increasing mining costs. The first commercial mine in the region, Dunwiddie's Nanty Glo No. 1, started operating in 1896, followed by Webster 14, Lincoln, and Ivory Hill. In 1902, the Webster mine became part of the Pennsylvania Coal and Coke Company and in 1909 Dunwiddie was purchased by the J. H. Weaver mining interests and renamed Heisley #3. In 1918, eight large and several small bank mines in Nanty Glo employed over 2,200 men and produced over 1 million tons a year of coal (Gable, 1926; Storey, 1907: 573–77; White & Law, n.d.; "*Life*, May 10, 1943b: 26–29; Pruner, 1954; Dunwiddie, 1968; *Nanty-Glo Journal*, August 14, 1968; Williams & Yates, 1976; Dropcho & Cashdollar, 2005: 1–9).

As mines opened, Nanty Glo borough's population grew from approximately 300 people in 1900 to 5,028 in 1920 and 6,217 in 1940. Irish, Welsh, Scottish, and English immigrants settled in the town, followed by Southern and Eastern Europeans. A United Methodist Church was established in 1901, St. Mary's Roman Catholic Church in 1902, a Finnish-language Lutheran church in 1903, an Italian Fraternal Society in 1903, and a Slovak society in 1919. When the borough was incorporated in 1918, it had over 1,500 working coal miners. The first labor union locals in the area were affiliated with the Knights of Labor. These locals joined the UMWA as District 2 when the miners' union was founded in 1890. The district collapsed during the mid-decade depression but was reorganized by William Wilson in 1899. Local 1386 was chartered at the Nanty Glo Mining Company's Dunwiddie mine. John Brophy moved to Nanty Glo in 1906. Along with William Welsh, Harry Carnahan, and Dominick Gelotte, he helped organize the local in the town's other mines. By 1914, 1386 was so large that a second local, 1347, was organized at the Heisley #3 mine. The UMWA locals emerged as a major force in municipal politics, working with independent merchants to prevent operator domination of the town. Local 1386 President Harry Carnahan ran third in the initial election for town burgess, the equivalent of mayor, with 25 percent of the vote. Carnahan was elected burgess in the early 1920s, and helped coordinate efforts by the local Businessmen's Association and the UMWA to organize the town's volunteer fire department (*Nanty-Glo Journal*, 1968, August 14; Williams & Yates, 1976; Martin, 1968; *Nanty-Glo Journal*, March 23, 1922).

Bituminous coalminers and other Nanty Glo area residents were members of the same civic and fraternal organizations. Prominent local groups included the Ancient Order of Hibernians, the volunteer fire department, and veterans' groups. Nanty Glo Miner's Hall was the center of the community. Many groups met there, and the *Nanty-Glo Journal* was published out of its offices. Because of this network of relationships, miners were often aided by Nanty Glo civic groups in their conflicts with the coal mine operators. In 1922, the Ex-Servicemen's Fund contributed to the local union's strike fund. In 1922 and 1924, independent merchants aided union rallies in Nanty Glo organized to raise money and support strikes against J. H. Weaver's efforts to mine coal nonunion at Heisley #3 (*Nanty-Glo Journal*, August 3, 1922; July 17, 1924; August 14, 1968; *Johnstown Tribune*, July 3, 1922).

Nanty Glo continued to grow after World War I, despite the slumping coal market. The town boasted a high school, three theaters, five company stores, a Catholic school, a band, and its volunteer fire department. Its newspaper, the *Nanty-Glo Journal*, began publishing May 5, 1921. The ethnic mix of the town was reflected in its large number of churches. They included the Pike Brethren Church, St. Nicholas Byzantine Church, Church of the Brothers, First Baptist, St. Mary's Roman Catholic, St. John Vianey, Nanty-glo Methodist, Christian and Missionary Alliance, Finn-Lutheran Church, and Ukrainian Orthodox (*Nanty-Glo Journal*, August 14, 1968).

Although the State of Pennsylvania outlawed company stores in 1874, coal companies evaded the law by independently incorporating the stores. The Springfield, Heisley, Webster, and Imperial mines each operated a company store. Under the law, coal companies could not issue script for payment at stores, but the stores could legally provide credit against future wages with repayment automatically deducted by the coal company before workers were paid. To encourage miners to patronage company stores, workers who used this check-off system received a store discount, however, they would also be charged interest if they fell behind with repayments. Companies tracked store purchases and miners who avoided the company store could face reprimand, reassignment to a less productive location in the mine, or even dismissal. Some miners preferred to remain in debt to the company store as a precaution against layoff when work was slack. Most miners and their families lived in semidetached company housing. Typically, they were wood-framed built on wood foundations, with unplastered interior walls, no running water or bathrooms, with two upstairs bedrooms. The kitchen coal stove was the only source of heat for the entire house. Many households were three-generational or extended or stepfamilies living together, including adult in-laws and adult siblings. Census records show that approximately 10 percent of the families took in boarders, usually miners who did not have families. If miners worked different shifts, they might share a bed. Nanty Glo boys generally entered the mines between the ages of ten and twelve, either working as trappers, opening and closing underground doors for coal cars being pushed through the tunnels or as a coal loader assisting a family member. Girls assisted their mothers, caring for younger children, cooking, hauling water from a well, cutting wood and gathering coal to maintain a fire, doing laundry, and endlessly cleaning coal dust off every surface. In 1924, Heisley, one of the largest coalmines in Cambria County with 564 employees, announced it was closing its operation and would reopen nonunion. On April 23, 1925, Heisley posted a notice in the *Nanty-Glo Journal* that it would resume operation on April 27, paying miners the 1917 wage scale. Nanty Glo women were at the forefront of organized opposition to the company's actions and eleven women were arrested for "appearing at the homes of Heisley employees and making insulting remarks, as well as hooting at the workmen going to and from work" (Brinton, 1914: 328; Williams & Yates, 1976; *Nanty-Glo Journal*, August 14, 1968; *Nanty-Glo Journal*, April 23, 1925).

1920 Census Snapshot

The 1920 federal census provides an in-depth look at the demographics and social organization of Nanty Glo, Pennsylvania, after the 1919 strike and prior to the 1922 Strike for Union. According to the official summary of the fourteenth census of the United States, the population of Nanty Glo was 5,028 people, including 2,768 men (55%), 2,260 women (45%), 1,553 native-born Americans with native-born parents (31%), 2,100 native-born Americans with foreign-born parents (42%), and 1,373 immigrants to the United States (27%). There were 1,382 men over age twenty-one (50% of the males), including 808 who were foreign born (29% of the males), 227 of whom had become naturalized citizens (28% of the male immigrants). The disproportionate number of men reflected single men who migrated to the area to work in the mines (U.S. Department of Commerce, 1922: 879).

There are some minor differences in the official census summaries published by the Department of Commerce and manuscript census forms. The 1920 manuscript census shows an additional eight people in Nanty Glo, bringing the total population of the borough to 5,036. These 5,036 people included 1,277 mine workers, coal miners, mine laborers, and skilled workers employed by the mining companies. Mine workers is an inclusive term describing nonsupervisory workers in all of these mine-related categories. Census categories tended to be inconsistently employed. Some tracks referred to coal loaders, others to miners, and others to mine laborers. All of these mine workers were men; 73 percent either were the head of a household or were boarders. Mine workers and their immediate families dominate the population of Nanty Glo. Over 4,400 Nanty Glo residents (88% of the population) lived in households where one or more of the people were mine workers. This represented approximately 778 of the 904 households (86%) in Nanty Glo.

In the 1920s, the United Mine Workers of America was an industrial union organizing all workers employed by the coal companies. The manuscript census lists a number of occupation titles that would have been included in the union. There are 949 men listed as miners, 249 men listed as laborers, 82 men listed by an assortment of skilled or semiskilled trades, including 13 men listed as checkweightmen—union representatives elected by the workers and paid by the coal companies to ensure the accurate weighing of coal cars. The 949 miners are tonnage workers. The 82 skilled or semiskilled tradesmen, including the checkweightmen, would be hourly employees. From the census, it is impossible to tell what percentage of the laborers worked underground (as loaders paired with miners) or above ground, the type of work they did or the nature of their wages (hourly or per ton).

Table 8.1. Ethnic/Job Category Breakdown of Nanty Glo Mine Workers by Place of Birth

Place of Birth	All Miner Workers	Miners	Other Mine Workers	Skilled/ Semiskilled	Laborers
U.S.	810 (50.2%)	302 (31.8%)	253 (76.4%)	52 (63.4%)	203 (81.5%)
Britain	118 (7.3%)	59 (6.2%)	27 (8.1%)	13 (15.8%)	19 (7.6%)
Italy	120 (7.4%)	95 (10%)	13 (3.9%)	6 (7.3%)	6 (2.4%)
Poland	119 (7.3%)	111 (11.6%)	4 (1.2%)	2 (2.4%)	2 (.8%)
Lithuania	69 (4.2%)	58 (6.1%)	7 (2.1%)	2 (2.4%)	2 (.8%)
Russia/Pol	28 (1.7%)	28 (2.9%)	0	0	0
Finland	48 (2.9%)	46 (4.8%)	1	1 (1.2%)	0
Hungary	29 (1.8%)	25 (2.6%)	2 (.6%)	1 (1.2%)	1 (.4%)
Slovakia	226 (14%)	188 (19.8%)	20 (6%)	5 (6%)	13 (5.2%)
Bel/France	19 (1%)	19 (2.0%)	0	0	0
Other	25 (1.5%)	18 (1.8%)	4 (1.2%)	0	3 (1.2%)
Non-British Immigrants	683 (42.3%)	588 (61.9%)	51 (15.4%)	17 (20.7)	27 (10.8%)
Total	1611	949 (58.9%)	331 (20.5%)	82 (5%)	249 (15.4%)

Note: Britain includes England, Scotland, Wales, and Ireland (2 of total).

Source: Created by the author.

Table 8.2. Ethnic/Job Category Breakdown of Nanty Glo Mine Workers by Father's Place of Birth

Father's Place of Birth	All Miner Workers	Miners	Other Mine Workers	Skilled/ Semiskilled	Laborers
U.S.	450 (27.9%)	136 (14.3%)	157 (47.4%)	41 (50%)	116 (46.5%)
Britain	291 (18.0%)	133 (14.0%)	79 (23.8%)	12 (14.6%)	67 (26.9%)
Italy	130 (8.0%)	100 (10.5%)	15 (4.5%)	6 (7.3%)	9 (3.6%)
Poland	133 (8.2%)	117 (12.3%)	8 (2%)	1 (1.2%)	7 (2.8%)
Slovakia	303 (18.8%)	219 (23.0%)	42 (12.6%)	10 (12.1%)	32 (12.8%)
Other	304 (18.8%)	244 (25.7%)	30 (9%)	12 (14.6%)	18 (7.2%)
Non-British Immigrants	870 (54.0)	680 (71.6%)	95 (28.7%)	29 (35.3%)	66 (26.5%)
Total	1,611	949 (58.9%)	331 (20.5%)	82 (5.0%)	249 (15.4%)

Note: Britain includes England, Scotland, Wales, and Ireland (2 of total).

Source: Created by the author.

An examination of the ethnic breakdown of the mine workers by job category in tables 8.1 and 8.2 suggests potentially divisive problems for Nanty Glo's local unions. While U.S.-born (50.2%) and British Isle—English, Scottish, Welsh, and Irish (7.3%)—mine workers made up 57.5 percent of the total, they were only 38 percent of the tonnage miners. They held 63.4 percent of the skilled and semiskilled jobs and 81.5 percent of the laborer jobs. When ethnicity based on father's place of birth is examined instead of place of birth, American (27.9%) and British Isle (18.0%) mine workers made up 45.9 percent of the total mine workers and 28.3 percent of the tonnage miners. Their percentage of the laborers was 73.4 percent, and of the skilled and semiskilled workers was 64.6 percent. While a disproportionate percentage of the laborer, skilled, and semiskilled daywork jobs were held by American- and British-origin miners, non–British Isle immigrants and to a greater extent their sons, did have access to these job categories. Two job categories not included above were solidly controlled by American and British Isle mine workers. Of the thirty-three men employed by the coal companies who were listed as a foreman or an assistant foreman, seven were at least second-generation Americans (21%) and eighteen were either from the British Isles or had fathers born in the British Isles (55%). American and British Isle mine workers totaled 76 percent of the foremen. Only two foremen (6%) were from Nanty Glo's Slovak, Polish, Italian, Lithuanian, or Finnish communities. Three foremen were German and the other three were from other Western European countries.

The UMWA clearly recognized the need to appeal to the non-American and non–British Isle miners. Three UMWA District 2 representatives resided in Nanty Glo during the 1920 census. William Welsh, an elected Board Member, was born in England; Dominick (Gioletta) Gelotte, a district organizer, was born in Italy; and Joseph Foster, a district organizer, was born in Hungary. However, eight of the thirteen checkweightmen, union representatives elected by the local miners, were born in the United States (62%); four were born in the British Isles (31%); and one was born in Germany. Of the eight American-born checkweightmen, three had fathers born in the United States and five in the British Isles. None of the elected checkweightmen were drawn from Nanty Glo's Slovak, Polish, Italian, Lithuanian, or Finnish communities. The domination of coal company foreman positions and of the local union by American and British Isle mine workers potentially created an ethnic wedge that coal operators could use to undermine class solidarity among the Nanty Glo miners.

Longevity, or rootedness in Nanty Glo, was another potential source of tension between ethnic groups during times of crisis, as different ethnic communities tried to deal with the effects of strikes, lockouts, and evictions during the 1920s, and as the mine workers battled to control the municipal government. While the 1920 census does not report longevity in a community, it does provide some clues for ascertaining a group's commitment to remain and struggle. For example, in 1920, 17 percent of the Nanty Glo mine workers owned their own homes; 33 percent were renters, generally from the coal companies; 23 percent were boarders; and 27 percent were relatives living in households (fathers, sons, brothers, and in-laws). A fair assumption is that boarders are the most mobile group of mine workers, homeowners the least, while relatives and renters are somewhere in the middle. Percentages of mine workers in each category varied by ethnic group. Twenty-four percent of the British Isle mine workers were homeowners and 38 percent were renters. Only 8 percent were listed as boarders. The rest, 30 percent, were living in households with relatives. Among Italian immigrants, 17 percent were owners, 33 percent were renters, 6 percent were living in households with relatives, and 41 percent were boarders. Fifty-two percent of Polish immigrants and 30 percent of Slovak immigrants were boarders. While only 7 percent of the Poles owned their own homes, 21 percent of the Slovaks did.

Control of the Nanty Glo borough government was of crucial importance to local mine workers. During open-shop drives, it meant that municipal police and courts would protect the right to strike and picket, ensure that some measure of due process was followed before evictions from company housing, and that private Coal and Iron police respected the civil liberties and property rights of striking mine workers. Citizenship, required to vote, became a key factor in the defense of workers' rights in Nanty Glo (see tables 8.3 and 8.4). Control over municipal affairs by Nanty Glo mine workers was weakened if large numbers of mine workers were noncitizens. For a particular immigrant group, noncitizenship also meant that its concerns were less likely to be addressed. In 1920, only 44 percent of the tonnage rate miners were listed as citizens. Of these, 78 percent (331 out of 422) were either U.S. born or naturalized citizens from the British Isles. Eighty-two percent of the non–British Isle immigrants were not citizens, including 95 percent of the immigrants from Poland, 88 percent of the immigrants from Slovakia, and 86 percent of the immigrants from Italy.

Another potential source of division for Nanty Glo's UMWA locals was that ethnic groups were not evenly distributed among the borough's major mines. While it is not possible to tell definitively where specific miners worked, the census does make educated guesses possible. The 149 mine-workers living at Lincoln Mine and on Lincoln Road most likely worked for the Lincoln Mining Company. Thirty percent of these miners were born in the United States, but of these, 62 percent were the children of immigrant fathers. Only 22 percent of the miners were either second-generation or more Americans or descendants of immigrant fathers from the British Isles. Seventeen percent of the mine workers were Italian, 15 percent were Polish, and 31 percent were Slovak; a total of 116 of the 149 mine workers (78%) were non–British Isle immigrants or their children. Only 11 of these 94 non–British Isle immigrant mine workers (12%) were citizens.

Table 8.3. Citizenship of Coal Miners

	U.S.-born	Naturalized	Total Citizens	Noncitizens
Total Miners	300 (32%)	122 (13%)	422 (44%)	531 (56%)

Source: Created by the author.

Table 8.4. Citizenship Rates for Coal Miners from Different Nationalities

Nationality	U.S. Citizen	Noncitizen
Total Miners	44%	56%
U.S.-born	100%	—
British Isle	53%	47%
Italy	14%	86%
Poland	5%	95%
Lithuania	18%	82%
Russia/Poland	7%	93%
Finland	36%	64%
Hungary	35%	65%
Slovakia	12%	88%
Belgium/France	58%	42%
Other	17%	83%
Non-British Immigrants	18%	82%

Source: Created by the author.

The areas in close proximity to the Springfield mines had a significantly higher percentage of American and British Isle mine workers and immigrants who had become naturalized citizens. Of the 317 mine workers living on Chestnut, Springfield, Ivory Hill, Baker Row, and Railroad Streets, 145 (46%) were second generation in the United States or the children of immigrant father's from the British Isles. Eleven percent of the miners were Italian, 10 percent were Poles, and 14 percent were Slovak; a total of 172 of the 317 miners (54%) were non–British Isle immigrants or their children. Twenty-nine of these 147 non–British Isle immigrant mine workers (20%) were citizens. Downtown Nanty Glo also tended to have a significantly higher percentage of American and British Isle miners and immigrants who had become naturalized citizens. Of the 178 miners living on Elder, Third, Fourth, Hill, and Fifth, 77 (52%) were second generation in the United States or the children of immigrant fathers from the British Isles. Twelve percent of the miners were Italian, 13 percent were Lithuanian, and 18 percent were Slovak; a total of 85 of the 178 miners (48%) were non–British Isle immigrants or their children. In this neighborhood, 21 of the 76 non–British Isle immigrant mine workers (28%) were citizens. Heisley

#3 and Webster miners lived in close proximity in the area south and west of Blacklick Creek and are difficult to separate. The 147 miners living on Tile and in New Town most likely worked at the Heisley #3 mine. Twenty-eight of these miners (19%) were born in the United States, but of these, 71 percent were the children of immigrant fathers. Only 12 percent of the miners were either second generation or more Americans or descendants of immigrant fathers from the British Isles. Twenty-three percent of the miners were Polish and 41 percent were Slovak; a total of 128 of the 147 miners (87%) were non–British Isle immigrants or their children. In this area, only 6 of the 123 non–British Isle immigrant mine workers (5%) were citizens.

Chapter 9

Nanty Glo versus the Open Shop

In 1924, bituminous coalminers in the District 2 town of Nanty Glo were in a relatively strong position to resist the coal operator's open-shop drive. They had a long history of effective labor organization and lived in an open town where a local Labor Party shared political power, so operators were unable to deny basic civil liberties to miners and their families. British Isle, Eastern European, and Southern European miners were all well-established in Nanty Glo; had invested in the town; and the union locals and miners had ethnic, civic, and religious organizational ties to nonminers in the area. The leadership of the local miners was experienced, capable, and working-class conscious. They helped build Nanty Glo locals 1386 and 1347, District 2, and the town itself. John Brophy developed his ideas on unionism while a miner in Nanty Glo. Much of the Miners' Program reflected the values of Nanty Glo miners and had been debated in their union hall for almost two decades. Nanty Glo coal miners had a history of helping organize nonunion mines in the area. In fall 1919, they supported the Johnstown, Pennsylvania, steel strike and helped organize Bethlehem Steel's captive mines. In 1922, they were the backbone of the Somerset campaign. Many Nanty Glo miners acted as official or unofficial union organizers while others helped process relief supplies for the families of strikers. When the Cleveland CCF contract was signed in 1922, Nanty Glo miners refused to work for over a month because it permitted local mining interests to sign a union contract for a mine in Nanty Glo while continuing to operate nonunion in neighboring Revloc (*Johnstown Tribune*, November 1–4, 1919; *Johnstown Leader*, November 8, 1919; Marcus 1992).

Despite these experiences, Nanty Glo coal miners were defeated by open-shop forces during two years of intense class conflict. Ultimately, the same industrial conditions that laid the basis for increasing class-consciousness among Nanty Glo workers, and galvanized their struggles, undermined their ability to resist the open-shop forces in a fight at the local level. By 1926, the most militant trade unionists in Nanty Glo were leaving the town to seek work in other coalfields or industries, rather than return to the local mines as scabs. The collapse of the UMWA in Nanty Glo pinpoints the cruel dilemma that UMWA insurgents could not resolve. Circumstances increasingly demonstrated that their analysis of conditions in the industry and their program for alleviating the hardships of the bituminous coal miner made more sense than the business-unionist strategy of the international office. However, the same events that stimulated the miner's receptiveness to class-conscious ideas undermined the miner's ability to organize to achieve them. The development of working-class consciousness paralleled the collapse of trade union organization in the coalfields, and with it, the miner's increasing inability to preserve the Miner's Freedom and achieve the Miners' Program. Isolated from the main industrial centers, trapped in a declining industry, and confronted by a national open-shop campaign determined to rid America of trade unionism, the insurgent miners' movement was defeated and the miners' working-class conscious ideals were threatened.

While Nanty Glo is not typical of mining towns in District 2 or in other union fields, there are advantages for choosing it for more detailed local study. It was the hometown of John Brophy and his brother-in-law William Welsh. Local 1386 in Nanty Glo was one of the strongest in District 2 and many miners active in the struggles of the 1920s continued to live in the town through the Great Depression, World War II, and the collapse of the bituminous coal industry in the 1950s. In 1920, Nanty Glo, Pennsylvania, with a population of 5,208, was the largest coal town in Cambria County and in District 2. The town housed a number of mining companies and the miners tended to be better organized than the operators. Under the leadership of Brophy, Welsh, Dominick Gelotte, and Harry Carnahan, who was elected borough Burgess, local miners won control of the municipal government. The local press was also sympathetic to the miners and reported on their activities. These conditions contributed to an atmosphere where rank-and-file miners had the freedom to develop their ideas and institutions. Further, because Nanty Glo is located on the border of Cambria and Somerset counties, it was a major outpost in the 1922 campaign to organize nonunion miners in Somerset and key to District 2's resistance to the open-shop drive with labor educators and union organizers continually passing through the town (Pennsylvania Census Manual, 1929: 456–57; U.S. Department of Commerce, 1924: 16, 69; *Nanty-Glo Journal*, August 14, 1968).

Ku Klux Klan

The open-shop drive in the Nanty Glo region was preceded by a period of intensive Ku Klux Klan activity that was part of the national resurgence of the Klan in the 1920s. In 1924, there were a reported 100,000 Klan members in western Pennsylvania and there may have been as many as 250,000 by 1926. Locally, the Klan operated out of Johnstown and tried to drive a wedge between Protestant and Catholic miners. District 2 officials suspected that Klan activities were secretly sponsored by the bituminous coal operators. Local political and union officials viewed the first reported Klan incidents in September 1923 as harmless pranks. Work was slack, and some of the younger Protestant men and teenage boys paraded up hills to burn crosses. Local Catholics countered by founding the Society of the Burning Circle. They responded to cross burnings with circle burnings on neighboring hills (Jenkins, 1986: 121–33; Singer, 1982: 217–19; Singer, 1988a: 60–62; *Nanty-Glo Journal*, September 6, 1923; Interview, Clair Cook, 1976).

Nanty Glo, with a large population of Protestant miners, was a logical target for Klan organizers. Robed Klansmen paraded into the town's Protestant churches during services and made contributions to the congregations. The Klan also sponsored picnics and social events and invited Protestant families to attend. Ku Klux Klan activities offered Protestant Nanty Glo miners an alternative value system that challenged District 2's efforts to develop working-class conscious ideals as harmless pranks evolved into anti-union attacks and in January 1924, the local Klan began a campaign against "pro-labor" newspapers (Interviews, Spider Bill Ray, Paul Martin, 1976; *Nanty-Glo Journal*, November 23, 1923; January 24, 1924; *Johnstown Tribune*, August 14, 1922, April 1, 1924).

After a long winter of short work in 1923–1924, District 2 miners were restless and tension erupted into violence in the Central Pennsylvania town of Lilly. Two Italian miners, suspected members of the Society of the Burning Cross, were arrested on charges of shooting into the home of the Minister of the Lilly Lutheran Church. Italian miners dominated the Lilly UMWA local and responded to the arrests by suspending six Protestant miners suspected of Klan membership. The Klan decided to make a show of strength in Lilly to intimidate the Italian population. It rented a special train in Johnstown and 450-armed Klansmen descended on the town. They paraded up an overlook, burned a cross, and exploded dynamite. As the Klansmen marched back to the train the townspeople of Lilly turned hoses on them and the Klan opened fire. A bystander, a member of the Lilly Lutheran Church, and two Catholic miners were killed, and twenty people were wounded. On the train back to Johnstown, twenty-four Klansmen were arrested for carrying concealed weapons. Eventually, thirteen Lilly miners and twenty-six Klansmen were tried for murder. Tension in the region continued to flare when one thousand miners marched at the funerals in Lilly. Later, twenty thousand pro-Klan marchers paraded in Johnstown when one of the jailed Klansmen died of pneumonia while awaiting trial. A special judge was brought to Johnstown from Philadelphia to preside over the joint trial while the Klan demonstrated outside the courthouse. After eighteen Klansmen and ten Lilly miners were sentenced to two years in jail, four hundred Klansmen marched in Somerset County and the Klan disrupted the Nanty Glo Columbus Day celebration with a cross burning. Cambria County Labor Party leaders charged that Republican candidates were inciting the Klan in order to win local elections (Singer, 1982: 217–19; *Nanty-Glo Journal*, April 10; April 17; May 1; June 19; July 3, 1924; *Johnstown Tribune*, April 7–8, 1924; *Ebensburg Mountaineer-Herald*, April 7; 17; May 1; June 12; July 3; September 4; October 16, 1924).

Violence also broke out in Nanty Glo. Weaver interests were shifting coal orders to their nonunion Revloc mine and operating their Heisley #3 mine on short shifts. The miners suspected that the management of the Heisley #3 mine was sponsoring local Klan activities in preparation for breaking with the union. Some miners also suspected that Samuel Chilton, the newly elected Local 1347 president, was a Klan member. Chilton, listed as age forty-seven in 1920, migrated to the United States from England as a child in 1880, and became a citizen in 1896. He lived with his wife, two sons, and three daughters in Heisley Company housing. Chilton was also rumored to have been a management spy at the Springfield mine where he previously worked but was fired after sending the company president a report attacking the local mine superintendent. Chilton's son and son-in-law helped him secure a job at the Heisley #3 mine and engineered his election to the local's presidency in a bitter campaign that divided English-speaking and non-English-speaking miners.

The local exploded when Chilton violated union bylaws refusing to defend an Eastern European checkweightman suspended by the company on charges of intoxication on the tipple. Fuses were short after the Lilly murders and an argument broke out at the next local meeting between Chilton's supporters and friends of the checkweightman. Chilton started a fight and he his son Albert were arrested. In response to developments in Lilly and Nanty Glo, a citizen's committee representing sixteen civic and ethnic organizations met at Nanty Glo's Slovak Hall. They condemned violence by masked organizations and opened membership to all creeds and beliefs. District 2 and Local 1386 sided with the checkweightman and the Eastern European miners. The district seized Local 1347's treasury and Local 1386 barred Chilton and his supporters from Nanty Glo's Miner's Hall. District 2's suspicion that local operators were sponsoring the Klan and Chilton were confirmed when the J. H. Weaver company took advantage of the unsettled situation in Local 1347 to announce its plan to close Heisley #3 mine indefinitely. When the company started evicting striking miners in June 1925, both sides sought redress in court. Chilton and a group of the "American" miners helped Heisley secure an injunction against 104 local union activists forbidding pickets near company owned property. The union protested and won a reversal of the order securing the right of miners to picket peacefully. The closing of Heisley was quickly followed by the closing of Nanty Glo's Lincoln mine (Singer, 1982: 217–19; Singer, 1988a: 56–65; Marcus, 1992; Interview, Clair Cook, 1976; *Nanty-Glo Journal*, April 17, 1924; 19; July 3; September 4; January 8, 1925).

Following the lockout, District 2 officials mounted a counteroffensive against the Klan and the operators in an effort to reunite Nanty Glo miners. A labor chautauqua was held in the town in August, and William Welsh and Paul Fuller addressed a large Labor Party rally in September. Local miners responded by supporting the local Labor Party and overwhelmingly voted for the 1924 Progressive Committee slate against Lewis. Gradually the situation among the miners improved and Local 1347 was reinstated under new leadership (*Nanty-Glo Journal*, July 17, 1924; September 18; October 30; December 11; January 8, 1925).

The struggle in Nanty Glo took a new turn in January 1925, when Heisley #3 and Lincoln announced plans to reopen as nonunion mines and pay the 1917 wage scale. Weaver brought in a large contingent of Coal and Iron police to protect the mine and began importing scabs. In April, sixty-five Nanty Glo men, primarily skilled American daymen, signed yellow-dog contracts pledging to return to work nonunion. The operators moved these men and their families to an isolated block of company houses for protection. Under the leadership of William Welsh and Harry Carnahan, miners picketed the mines and paraded through Heisley company housing threatening the scabs. When Heisley secured a warrant against Carnahan and the leaders of the union locals, the town council deputized the miners and assigned them to protect the rights of strikers. The new deputies represented all the ethnic groups that made up the Nanty Glo mining population. A second labor chautauqua was organized in May 1925, to rally the entire region to support the Nanty Glo miners. Bands and entertainers flocked to Nanty Glo from neighboring South Fork, Gallitzin, Portage, and Broad Top. Speakers included UMWA Vice President Philip Murray, Pennsylvania State Federation of Labor President James Maurer, longtime socialist Kate O'Hara of the International Ladies Garment Workers Union, Brophy, Fuller, Welsh, and local foreign-language speakers (Singer: 63; *Nanty-Glo Journal*, January 8, 1925; February 19; April 30; May 7; May 14; May 21; May 28, 1988a; Interview, Clair Cook, 1976; Plaintiff's Bill, June 1925; *Illinois Miner*, October 31, 1925).

Heisley started evicting striking miners in June 1925, and a full-scale war broke out. Strikers pelted scabs with sticks and bricks, Chilton's house was stoned, and the families of scabs were cursed and isolated from community life. The municipal government barred private police from public property and arrested nine Coal and Iron policemen for trespassing. The company retaliated by stepping up efforts to intimidate the union miners. It mounted a beacon on a hill overlooking the town and at night the light swept the streets and flashed through the windows of the homes of strikers. Guards patrolled the bony piles, chasing children searching for coal scraps and a pregnant woman was beaten for stealing two lumps of coal to use as cooking fuel. The battle heightened when strike leader William Welsh was kidnapped, beaten, and dumped in another town. Strikers began assigning regular patrols to protect his home and family. When the company increased its force of Coal and Iron police to 200, the town responded by increasing the number of labor deputies to 100 (Singer, 1988a: 63; *Nanty-Glo Journal*, May 21; June 11; September 17, 1925; *Illinois Miner*, October 31, 1925; Plaintiff's Bill, June 1925; Interview, Katherine Welsh Martin, 1976).

Spirits remained high among Nanty Glo miners as a second winter approached and the town remained a bulwark of District 2's battle to stem the open-shop drive. The district built barracks and supplied strikers with tents and foodstuffs and some of the men worked at local mines that continued to pay the union scale. Other men secured work on state road building gangs. In November 1925, the Labor Party candidates were endorsed by local Democratic and Republican Parties and swept the municipal elections (*Nanty-Glo Journal*, June 11; July 2; September 17; November 5, 1925; *Illinois Miner*, October 31, 1925; Interview, Clair Cook, 1976).

The Nanty Glo miners and their families won many victories. They withstood Klan activities and two years of deprivation. They remained united and their hold on the municipal government increased. But at the start of 1926, the mines paying the 1924 union wage scale locked out their workers. This proved to be the last straw. The miners realized that with the depressed state of the industry, the companies were prepared to hold out indefinitely, retooling and meeting their orders from nonunion mines and many strikers started to drift away from Nanty Glo. Defeat of the Nanty Glo miners foreshadowed the defeat of the rank-and-file movement's challenge to Lewis and its efforts to redirect the UMWA. The operators had avoided a national strike in 1924. Instead they isolated the Central Competitive Field by attacking the Miner's Freedom and union locals in the outlying fields. The open-shop drive proved the accuracy of the opposition's critique of the business-unionist ideas and strategy of the international office. The union could not survive in an industry divided between union and nonunion fields, especially when capacity exceeded demand. Unfortunately for the opposition forces, the open-shop attack was particularly destructive of the rank-and-file movement, undermining some of the most class-conscious elements in the union. The same conditions that contributed to the development of the rank-and-file miner's class-consciousness overwhelmed the ability to resist. They left Lewis in firm control of what remained of the UMWA as membership plummeted (Interviews, Clair Cook and Katherine Welsh Martin, 1976).

Part 4

Save the Union

Chapter 10

1926 UMWA Presidential Campaign

By 1926 the open-shop forces had decimated the miners' union in the outlying fields. Labor practices that had been abandoned since the nineteenth century were reinstituted. Convict labor was put to work in Missouri and Alabama coal mines. In Oklahoma and West Virginia mine explosions increased as inexperienced nonunion workers feared to report gaseous conditions to their supervisors. In nonunion West Virginia, entire sections of the state were closed to outsiders. Peddlers were arrested as trespassers for plying their wares in company towns. Only a temporary surge in export demand caused by a British coal strike saved the UMWA from total collapse. When the British strike was settled, the market returned to its normal depressed state and nonunion operators launched a new round of wage reductions (*Illinois Miner*, January 30, February 6, February 20, February 27, March 27, 1926; *Federated Press*, January 6; January 20; August 25; November 17; December 8, 1926; January 19, 1927).

On March 10, 1926 John Brophy wrote Powers Hapgood describing the conditions in the bituminous coalfields.

> I don't know of a time since the middle nineties that conditions were as gloomy as they have been during the present and there is no prospect of improvement in sight. Scores of mines in the district have been shut down for a year and others are working a day or two a week. . . . In addition to this, injunctions, evictions, and all the paraphernalia of the strike have been employed by companies against us. Local strikes, of which we have quite a number, are deadlocked, hopelessly without decision. This year

> I expect will be worse than last year. (Hapgood Papers, Series
> 1, Box 4)

The union appeared powerless to stem the open-shop tide. In District 2, many miners accepted offers from small operators of steady work at the 1917 scale. A strike dragged on in the Anthracite field as operators insisted on the right to reorganize production. In March 1926, the UMWA international office canceled organizing efforts in every West Virginia county except Fairmont. The miners were advised to secure work as best as they could (*Illinois Miner*, January 30, March 6, May 1, May 22, July 3, July 10, 1926; *Federated Press*, February 3, 1926).

Increasingly operators turned their attention toward ousting the union from the Central Competitive Field. In District 5 (Western Pennsylvania) operators laid off day men. Miners were denied support services and forced to perform unpaid dead work. In Illinois, Peabody Coal and other unionized mining operations began to close and in March 1926, Peabody announced it would sell nonunion coal from its Kentucky mines in Illinois markets. The company purchased seven new nonunion mines in Kentucky, and reopened eight mines on a nonunion bases. In April, Old Ben, one of the largest operators in District 12, closed ten of its twelve union mines and began importing nonunion West Virginia coal to fulfill its contractual obligations. The New Orient #2 mine, a heavily mechanized underground factory and the largest mine in the world, was closed indefinitely. It employed 1,200 union miners and had set production records the three previous months. In Zeigler, Illinois, violence broke out when rank-and-file miners, led by members of the Progressive Committee, protested an unpopular contract signed by Springfield subdistrict officials. Seven miners were sentenced to one to fourteen years in prison for rioting and assaulting the subdistrict president (Singer, 1982: 233–34; *Federated Press*, March 17, 1926; September 1, 1926; *Illinois Miner*, January 2, January 16, March 6, March 13, April 3, April 10, May 22, 1926).

Business unionists in the UMWA international office offered miners no solution to the deteriorating condition of the union. Instead of battling open-shop operators, they concentrated on securing their hold on the union machinery by suppressing opposition. In response to rank-and-file pleas for organization, Lewis postponed the next UMWA convention until after the expiration of the Jacksonville CCF contract in 1927. When miners protested, Lewis renewed his assault on his opponents in the union.

In April 1926, the International Executive Board attempted to end the rank-and-file challenge by declaring the Workers' (Communist) Party dual to the UMWA. Membership or participation in party activities, including distribution of the *Daily Worker*, was made grounds for expulsion from the UMWA. Lewis also maneuvered against Frank Farrington. He exposed a personal contract between Farrington and the Peabody Coal Company and forced Farrington to resign from the District 12 presidency (*Illinois Miner*, October 10, 1925, April 24, 1926; Dubofsky & Van Tine, 1927: 125–26; UMWA MA K. C. Adams File).

Throughout 1926, conflict in the UMWA mounted. Miners in the Workers' Party and remnants of the Progressive Committee attempted to revitalize the rank-and-file opposition, weakened by three years of purges and operator blacklists. They coalesced with John Brophy and the remaining District 2 insurgents in support of District 2's version of the Miners' Program. Under the banner, "Save the Union," they launched a unified challenge to Lewis and business unionism that rallied demoralized miners and nearly succeeded in capturing control of the international office and the union. Lewis countered by channeling the remaining resources of the union to defeat his opponents. After a bitter fight that further devastated the rank-and-file miner's ability to resist the open-shop forces, Lewis retained control of the shell of the former union. The architect of the Save the Union coalition was Powers Hapgood. Hapgood encouraged Brophy to join with the remnants of the Progressive Committee and the Workers' Party in a national challenge to Lewis and the international office. In Hapgood's view the communists were "the most sincere, hard-working, and intelligent group in the labor movement" (Brophy, 1964: 213–18; Hapgood Papers, July 26, 1926, Series 1, Box 4).

The communists initially planned to run candidates in the December 1926 UMWA elections using the Progressive Committee version of the Miners' Program. However, after years of purges and a renewed anticommunist assault by Lewis, it was unlikely they would be able to field a slate of officers. They were prepared to support a prominent opposition leader with an acceptable program who had a better chance of unseating Lewis and to remain in the background if necessary during the campaign. In early July, Jay Lovestone of the Workers' Party approached Powers Hapgood during a conference in Pittsburgh, and asked him to sound out John Brophy as a potential candidate for UMWA president. Hapgood and a small group of Brophy supporters discussed Lovestone's proposal with Brophy, who refused to commit himself, despite the communist pledge to endorse the District 2 version of the Miners' Program during the election campaign (Hapgood Papers, July 2/3, 5, 10, 26, 1926, Series 1, Box 4; Bussel, 1999: 90).

Powers Hapgood continued to press Brophy, and in August he forwarded him a letter from Albert Coyle that detailed Lewis' illicit relationship with coal operators. In the letter, Coyle discussed meeting with a former general manager of the Consolidation Coal Company's Kentucky properties. The man claimed he was chairman of a 1922 slush fund committee selected by West Virginia operators to raise $100,000 for Lewis and Philip Murray. In return, Lewis pledged not to run an organizing drive in the West Virginia field. The Coyle letter finally convinced Brophy. On August 6, he declared his candidacy for UMWA president. He recruited William Brennan, former president of District 1 (Anthracite) and William Stevenson of District 24 (Michigan) as candidates for secretary-treasurer and vice president on what came to be known as the Save the Union slate. Neither man was affiliated with the Progressive International Committee or the communists. Joe Tumilty, who was projected as the presidential candidate on the original communist-endorsed slate joined the Brophy ticket as their candidate for the District 12 (Illinois) presidency (Hapgood Papers, August 4, August 12, 1926, Series 1, Box 4; *Federated Press*, September 1, 1926; Brophy, 1964: 214–18; Dubofsky & Van Tine, 1977: 127–28; Brophy Papers, August 8, September 24, 1926, Series 1, Box 3).

Brophy opened the Save the Union campaign by presenting his program and ideas through a press release and an open letter to union miners. These were followed by a detailed fifteen-page statement titled *A Larger Program for the Miners' Union*. In general, these presented the three-part Miners' Program developed by District 2 and the Nationalization Research Committee based on the 1919 Cleveland convention resolutions—nationalization of the mines, organization of the unorganized and formation of a Labor Party (Brophy, November 1926).

Brophy explained as follows:

> With the fight for 100% unionism must go the movement for public ownership of the coal industry, with democratic management, which means the workers, through their union, having a share with the public in the control of the industry. . . . The drive for public ownership will give new life to all our union activities. It will put the union on the offensive and the operators on the defensive. It will answer the operator's cry that he

cannot afford to pay decent wages under a competitive system. The answer is that if he cannot the public can. (Press Release, August 6, 1926, Brophy Papers, Series 1, Box 3)

The longer document denounced Lewis and the business unionist strategy for the union and detailed district-by-district losses in membership. It analyzed the failure of Lewis' policy of salvaging the CCF contract by permitting companies to continue nonunion operation in the outlying fields. The platform also heavily criticized the international office's operation of the union and the suppression of union dissidents. It offered District 2's educational program as a model for building a democratic union that encouraged open debate and rank-and-file participation (Brophy, 1964: 214–15; Brophy, November 1926).

While Brophy was publicizing the program, communist miners and the Workers' Party mobilized the campaign in the field. Within a month they secured eighty-six nominations from local unions to put Brophy on the UMWA ballot. Twenty-nine nominations were from District 12 locals, fifteen from District 2, and fourteen from District 5. Only twenty-seven locals, over half from machine strongholds in Indiana, sent in Lewis nominating petitions (UMWA MA Save the Union File; Bussel, 1999: 88–91).

At the start of the UMWA presidential campaign the international office faced a damaging split among Illinois business unionists that threatened Lewis' reelection drive. Interim District President Harry Fishwick, heir to the Farrington machine, was battling Lewis ally International Executive Board member William Sneed for the District 12 presidency. Both candidates were vulnerable to Tumilty's Save the Union candidacy. Fishwick was tainted by the exposure of Farrington's contract with Peabody Coal and Sneed was suspected by foreign miners of ties to the Ku Klux Klan (*Illinois Miner*, September 11, 1926).

All sides recognized the crucial nature of the Illinois contest. Albert Coyle, a key Brophy adviser, was negotiating with Oscar Ameringer, editor of the *Illinois Miner*, to win support for the opposition slate. He wrote Hapgood that Fishwick might permit the paper to report on the Brophy candidacy and endorse him because of the fight with Sneed and Lewis. Lewis feared that a Fishwick-Sneed bloodbath in Illinois would elect Tumilty and damage his own reelection chances, especially if the *Illinois Miner* publicized the Brophy campaign. He decided to reach a settlement with Fishwick and assigned international organizer Samuel Pascoe of Kentucky to work out a compromise. Eventually the warring factions agreed to run a joint slate and

Sneed was appointed acting vice president for District 12. This agreement secured the support of the Illinois machine for Lewis, unified the business unionists against the Brophy challenge, and closed the *Illinois Miner* to opposition candidates. During the ensuing election campaign, the paper completely blacked-out the Save the Union ticket (*Illinois Miner*, September 18, 1926; UMWA MA Save the Union File).

Lewis, recognizing the strong appeal of the Brophy candidacy to rank-and-file miners, used the international office to promote his own candidacy and undermine the Save the Union ticket. On September 10, 1926, the international office published a list of nominating petitions filed by union locals. According to the list Lewis outdistanced the Brophy slate by 789 to 84. However, most of the Lewis petitions were from the "blue-sky" locals in the Appalachian field. Rather than electoral support, these petitions represented the mobilization of the union's international organizers to secure a Lewis landslide. In the months preceding the election the international office assigned fifty-seven organizers to work on his reelection campaign, including five in District 2. These organizers worked against Brophy, blaming the District 2 office for the collapse of the union in Central Pennsylvania and accusing Brophy of sacrificing District 2 miners to aid a communist plot to foment revolution in the United States. They also maneuvered to have pro-Brophy candidates disqualified and to inflate the Lewis vote. The UMWA organizers consciously broke laws and systematically perpetuated fraud. They stole Save the Union correspondence and forwarded copies to union headquarters. They planted shills at Save the Union rallies to disrupt speakers. In District 31, Van Bittner was issued fifty extra ballot return sheets and an "official" list of eligible voters in West Virginia locals. At the time there were only six functioning locals in the state (UMWA MA 1926 Election File).

Lewis was prepared to destroy the remnants of the union in District 2 to undermine Brophy at his home base. UMWA organizers inflamed local disagreements in an attempt to split the district into warring factions. The Save the Union campaign was seriously weakened, locally and nationally, when international organizers succeeded in exacerbating a dispute between Brophy and longtime supporters John Kerr and Faber McCloskey. Kerr and McCloskey of Gallitzin Local 1056 had argued with Brophy over the value of investing the district's limited funds in the labor chautauqua movement. In November 1925, they circulated petitions demanding that the district cut its educational budget and sent the protest to the International Executive Board. District 2 International Executive Board member John Ghizzoni, a

Lewis supporter, convinced McCloskey and Kerr to openly oppose Brophy. Kerr's defection was especially damaging to the Save the Union campaign because Powers Hapgood was a member of the Gallitzin local and Kerr had helped protect his UMWA membership. Hapgood used the Gallitzin local as his mailing address in District 2 and Kerr had access to his mail. Kerr gave Ghizzoni letters from Albert Coyle to Hapgood and Ghizzoni forwarded them to Phillip Murray. One letter from Coyle to Hapgood was particularly damaging to the Save the Union campaign. In the letter Coyle proposed that Hapgood become the nominal editor of a new periodical, the *National Miner*, which would publicize the Save the Union campaign and program. Vern Smith, former editor of *Industrial Solidarity*, would actually run the paper, but Coyle and others did not want Smith's name on the masthead because of his close ties to the Workers' Party (Brophy, 1964: 214–18; Hapgood Papers, September 24, 1925, November 17, December 2, 1926, Series 1, Box 4; District 2 Papers, November 26, 1925, September 30, 1926, Series 1, Box 6; UMWA MA Save the Union File; Bussel, 1999: 92; Dubofsky & Van Tine, 1977: 128).

Red Scare

Lewis used the Coyle-Hapgood letters to claim-communist domination of the Save the Union campaign and pressured the District 2 Executive Board to disavow Brophy. Ghizzoni succeeded in either convincing or forcing District Vice President James Mark, Secretary-Treasurer Richard Gilbert, and seven of the nine subdistrict board members to endorse Lewis and run an anti-Brophy slate in District 2. The new slate was headed by Mark and Gilbert and included Faber McCloskey as its candidate for District 2 vice president. John Kerr was chosen to run for chairman of the district auditor's committee. The slate issued a statement attacking Brophy for his ties to Coyle and Lovestone and charged, "The outside influences who are supporting the candidacy of President Brophy have done an unpardonable injury to our union." The international office's success in dividing District 2 forced the national Save the Union campaign to divert time and manpower to the district election. Hapgood organized a ticket headed by Pat McDermott, a coal miner and Labor Party representative to the Pennsylvania state legislature. However, the pro-Lewis majority on the District Executive Board ruled that McDermott and most of the Save the Union slate were ineligible for office on a series of technicalities. Brophy supporters cited similar violations by pro-Lewis candidates, but they were ignored (Singer, 1982: 241–243; UMWA MA Save the Union File; Press Release, District 2 Papers, September 30, 1926, Series 1, Box 6; Flyer, Petition to District 2 Executive Board, Brophy Papers, 1926, Series 1, Box 3; Dubofsky & Van Tine, 1977: 128).

The international office assigned an organizer to investigate Powers Hapgood's career in an effort to disqualify him as a Save the Union candidate for UMWA delegate to the AFL convention. International organizer Silas Houck discovered that in 1921 the Nanty Glo Local 1386 secretary had not recorded a transfer card from the District 27 (Montana) local where Hapgood joined the UMWA. Based on this evidence, a committee of Gallitzin Local 1056, selected by Faber McCloskey, ruled that Hapgood was never properly initiated into the UMWA and thus was ineligible for union office. The committee decision was reversed by the union local, but Lewis managed to keep Hapgood off the ballot pending further investigation (Singer, 1982: 243; UMWA Powers Hapgood file; Hapgood Papers, December 3, 12, 1926, Series 1, Box 4; Bussel, 1999: 92–94).

While the international staff attacked the opposition in the districts, Lewis and Philip Murray campaigned through the press. They accused the Save the Union ticket of ties to both an international communist conspiracy to seize the American Labor movement and to the nonunion operators. At the October 1926 AFL Convention, Lewis released the Coyle-Hapgood letters and charged Alexander Howat was instructed to found the Save the Union Committee during a summer trip to Moscow. The November 1 issue of the *UMWA Journal* ran a front-page cartoon of a wide-eyed Bolshevik trying to blow up the UMWA fortress while a gleeful scab operator looked on. An accompanying article accused Albert Coyle of connections with the TUEL and Workers' Party, and through his job as editor of the Brotherhood of Locomotive Engineers newspaper, with the Coal River, West Virginia Collieries. In the December 1 issue of the *UMWA Journal*, Murray accused Brophy of signing contracts with companies that operated nonunion in other fields (Dubofsky & Van Tine, 1977: 128; *New York Times*, October 13: 1, 3; October 16: 7, 1926; *UMWA Journal*, November 1, December 1, 1926).

Brophy and Hapgood tried to answer Lewis' accusations in open letters to the UMWA membership. In his first letter Brophy attempted to redirect debate to a discussion of the issues in the campaign. Brophy wrote, "I have become a candidate for international president of the miners' union in response to the desire on the part of a large group of the membership who believe in the principles which I have long advocated. . . . It is because of this program, and this only, that I am a candidate" (Open Letter, Brophy papers, October 15, 1926, Series 1, Box 3; Singer, 1982: 245). However, the Lewis campaign, especially in District 2, continued to focus on charges that Brophy was pro-communist and pro-operator. In a second open letter, Brophy sharply rebutted the pro-Lewis District 2 Executive Board's attack on his record as district president. He charged, "their cohorts have not attempted to discuss such issues, however, and their contributions have been on irrelevant matters, attacks on personalities, and pure unadulterated lies" (Brophy, December 2, 1926; Singer 1982: 245).

In Hapgood's letter he answered his denunciation by Lewis with accusations of his own. He charged that the press was playing up Lewis' claim that Moscow was trying to seize the American Labor movement in an effort to discredit rank-and-file activism in the miners' union and the American working class. He also tried to expose Lewis' use of international organizers to discredit the Save the Union ticket. Hapgood wrote,

> I am not now, and have never been, a member of the Communist Party, because I have not been convinced of the necessity of all their methods. . . . I can't stand for all the deliberate and malicious lies that have been told not only by the capitalists, but also by some of our own leaders about them. . . . Because I will not be part of this unwarranted persecution on some of the best fighters for good conditions we have in the trade union movement, and because I have criticized the international officers. . . . I am having the axe turned on me. (Hapgood Papers, October 20, 1926, Series 1, Box 4; Singer, 1982: 245)

Lewis' red scare tactics undermined the Save the Union Committee's ability to communicate its ideas to the miners and the general public. The scandal over the Coyle-Hapgood letter forced the committee to remove Hapgood's name from its newspaper. It also made it difficult to secure donations from liberals and noncommunists. The major national press services ignored Save the Union press releases, leaving only the Federated Press to actively publicize the campaign (UMWA MA 1926 Election File; *UMWA Journal*, December 1, 1926; *Coal Miner*, November 1, 1926).

Vote Fraud

Despite the virulent anticommunist attacks, the press silence, and the misuse of international staff, rank-and-file miners wanted the alternative presented by Brophy and the Miner's Program. The collapse of the UMWA during the open-shop drive had discredited Lewis and the business-unionist ideology. Ultimately, Lewis depended on vote fraud to keep his hold on the union. In December 1926, the International Executive Board declared Lewis the election winner by a vote of 173,323½ to 60,661½. However, tellers, required by the UMWA constitution to release figures for each union local by January 15, 1927, announced that the report would be delayed until after the union's convention (Brophy, 1964: 217–18; *Illinois Miner*, December 25, 1926; *UMWA Journal*, March 1, 1926; Brophy, June 15, 1927).

While Brophy and the other Save the Union candidates were suspicious of the delay, the surprisingly high voter turnout, and the overwhelmingly pro-Lewis vote, they decided to accept the results and concentrate on challenging Lewis' policies at the UMWA convention. In a press release Brophy evaluated the reasons for the election loss and the future course of the Save the Union Committee. Brophy argued the following:

> The trade resulting from the British strike and the storing of coal to have on hand when the contract expires have created a delusive and temporary feeling of prosperity. A short-lived period of employment is being experienced which the *United Mine Workers Journal* represents as a permanent condition. . . . This greater employment likewise temporarily checked the wage reduction policy of the employers, so that in the non-union fields there are in general as high wage rates as in the union fields. . . . The attempt of the national administration to represent these temporary wage increases and greater employment as permanent gains due to their policy is leading the miners to close their eyes to facts. (*Federated Press*, June 15, 1927; Singer, 1982: 247; Press Release, Brophy Papers, January 10, 1927, Series 1, Box 3)

In an effort to rally his supporters he wrote, "The international convention is the next great opportunity for progressive action. This may well be the most important convention of our union. Every local should see that its delegates understand the impending struggle and the fundamental nature of the resolutions progressives will have to fight for in the sessions of the convention" (Singer, 1982: 247; Press Release, Brophy Papers, January 10, 1927, Series 1, Box 3).

In preparation for the UMWA and district conventions, the Save the Union Committee lobbied in friendly locals to have its supporters appointed as delegates. In District 2 these delegates caucused and decided to press for a new district election because the Save the Union ticket had illegally been thrown off the ballot. Meanwhile the Lewis group organized to thwart the Save the Union plans. International staff members were appointed delegates from blue-sky locals. All suspected Workers' Party members were summarily banned as dual unionists. The District 2 Executive Board ruled that Powers Hapgood was a nonmember of the union and banned his appointment as a delegate. Then, in case Hapgood and other Save the Union delegates failed to understand that they were not welcome at the convention, Hapgood was beaten in his hotel two days before the start of the proceedings. The physical intimidation proved to be unnecessary. Lewis and his supporters were well organized and in firm control of the 1927 convention. The decimation of union locals and mining communities by the open-shop drive and Lewis' purge of his opponents had its impact. The 1926 Save the Union election effort represented the last wave of rank-and-file insurgency in the UMWA, rather than a secure base for continued organization. In the midst of the collapse of the union, a rubber stamp convention confirmed the wisdom of Lewis' leadership and business-unionist ideas. Lewis and Murray reported to the convention that the union was as firmly entrenched as ever, and critics were ignored. Brophy, still officially president of District 2, was denied a committee assignment, while his opponents in the district were placed on key committees (Hapgood Papers, 1927, Series 1, Box 4; Singer, 1982: 247–48; *Federated Press*, February 2, 1927; Bussel, 1999: 93; Brophy 1964: 225–28; UMWA Proceedings, 1927: 26, 234, 294, 345; *Illinois Miner*, February 5, 1927; *Coal Age*, February 3, 1927: 200).

Lewis was able to use his pliant convention majority to purge "socialist" ideas from the UMWA constitution and program. His presidential address denounced nationalization of the mines in favor of Hooverian volunteerism. While the delegates voted to reaffirm eventual nationalization, they also voted to abandon the idea of an independent Labor Party and approved an amendment to the union constitution that eliminated the demand that miners receive "the full social value of the product." It was replaced by a more moderate request for "an equitable share of the fruits of their labor." Neutral delegates and noncommunist progressives were intimidated by the Lewis show of strength. A Resolutions Committee proposal that the convention bar communists from union membership was vigorously debated. However, when the chair requested a standing vote on the issue, only twenty delegates were prepared to risk identification as "pro-Communists." The convention also voted to raise Lewis' annual salary from eight thousand dollars to twelve thousand dollars, and it granted the international officers significant new powers when it voted them the unlimited authorization to levy new assessments on the membership (UMWA Proceedings, 1927: 345; Dunne, 1927; Singer, 1982: 247–49; *Illinois Miner*, February 5, 1927; Dubofsky & Van Tine, 1977: 129; *Coal Age*, February 3, 1927: 200).

Lewis' domination of the international convention served as a model for the district conventions that followed. The District 2 Executive Board used the excuse of contract negotiations to postpone the convention. The delay meant that new District President James Mark chaired the meeting instead of Brophy. At the convention Brophy was allowed to deliver a final Presidential Message but was denied seating as a delegate. The Committee on the Officer's Reports recommended nonconcurrence, charging that Brophy was dredging up controversial issues that were damaging the union, and debate was closed before Brophy supporters could effectively respond. The committee's recommendation was then upheld by the convention (Brophy, 1964: 226–28; UMWA District 2, Proceedings, 1927: 274).

The long-delayed Teller's report on the December 1926 election was withheld until May 1927. When it was finally released, Brophy and the Save the Union Committee yelled fraud. In a flyer titled "An Appeal to the International Executive Board for Honesty and a Square Deal in the Vote Count," they compared vote totals with membership roles in a number of districts and documented "gross irregularities, self-evident fraud, and vote stealing." The committee claimed that their analysis of the Teller's report showed " 'Save the Union' candidates were duly elected the international officers of the union." In District 30 (Eastern Kentucky) there were no dues-paying members, yet 2,686½ votes were cast, all for Lewis. In District 31 (West Virginia), 377 dues paying members submitted 14,164 ballots. In District 19 (Tennessee), 482 dues paying members cast 3,977 votes, all but fifteen for Lewis. Save the Union poll watchers had reported a light turnout in Districts 1 and 7 (Anthracite). The Teller's report showed between 80 and 100% of the miners in those districts voting. In comparison with these districts, Illinois, a functioning district with a hotly contested local election, the voter turnout was approximately 70 percent. In Illinois, a spot check of pro-Brophy locals showed that the reported results had been changed. Lewis was credited with 986 more votes than the locals reported, while Brophy was docked 477 votes. Nationally, the Teller's report showed 163,627 miners voting or approximately 10,000 more miners than the union's dues-paying membership in December 1926. Evidence in the UMWA files that Bittner filed false election totals in West Virginia, supports the Save the Union claim that Brophy actually out-polled Lewis. The remnants of the class-conscious rank-and-file movement in the UMWA had repudiated Lewis and the business unionists. However, they were unable to force Lewis to surrender control of the union to its membership. Through his grip on the international office machinery, Lewis declared his reelection and stacked the UMWA convention to confirm his position (Brophy, 1927, June 15: 1; UMWA MA, Save the Union File).

Despite the virulent anticommunist attacks, the press silence, election fraud, and the misuse of international staff as Lewis campaign workers, the 1926 UMWA election demonstrated that communist and noncommunist activists could garner broad support among rank-and-file coal miners. The Lewis campaign had guaranteed that every miner who voted for Brophy and the Save the Union ticket knew that it was running with communist support. Yet it was only Lewis' grip on the international office machinery that allowed him to declare his reelection and stack the UMWA convention to confirm it. Unfortunately for bituminous coal miners, the Save the Union campaign also underscored the difficulty involved in dislodging Lewis as long as the coal companies in the remaining unionized fields continued to recognize him as UMWA president. The Workers' Party and the TUEL were in no position to appeal for justice to Lewis, the coal operators, or to the American Federation of Labor, which was now headed by William Green, a former Lewis lieutenant in the UMWA. Furthermore, as a result of his defeat in the election, John Brophy, one of the few noncommunists in the labor movement willing to coalesce with the TUEL and the Workers' Party, had lost his position as District 2 president and was isolated from his former liberal allies. The only alternatives left for rank-and-file activists were continuing to organize miners to challenge the Lewis regime from within the UMWA or to leave the UMWA and form an actual dual union (Brophy, 1964, 220–33).

Contract Negotiations

With the UMWA's three-year Jacksonville Central Competitive Field contract scheduled to expire March 31, 1927, Lewis called for a new joint-wage conference to extend the pact. He argued that renewed cooperation between union operators and the miners would rebuild the industry and save the $7.50 day in the Central Competitive Field. John Brophy and the other Save the Union Committee members anticipated the failure of the wage negotiations. Instead of cooperating with the operators, they demanded that the UMWA prepare for a nationwide bituminous coal strike in both the union and nonunion fields and the group began organizing miners in the collapsed outlying districts to push for a walkout. Lewis and the International Executive Board staunchly opposed the idea of a nationwide strike. They no longer had any standing among miners outside the Central Competitive Field, and they were afraid to jeopardize their hold on the international office by working with the Save the Union Committee to organize unorganized miners (*Federated Press*, January 19, February 23, March 23, 1927; Brophy, June 25, 1927: 4; Singer, 1982: 252).

In February 1927 operators from Districts 5, 6, 11, and 12 agreed to meet with the union in Miami, Florida. However, many of the companies attending the conference were already committed to nonunion operation. With the depressed state of the industry, and the weak position of the union, they did not believe a strike was likely, or had the potential to damage operations. At the conference the operators delayed, waiting for Lewis to offer them favorable terms. Finally, with the Jacksonville expiration date approaching and no CCF agreement on the horizon, the IEB authorized individual districts to sign contracts using the 1924 Jacksonville accord as a guideline. It also announced limited strikes in the CCF. These strikes permitted operators willing to pay the 1924 wage scale to continue mining coal until a full settlement was reached. These decisions by Lewis and the IEB effectively suspended the UMWA as a national union. Union leaders justified them as efforts to prevent nonunion operators from making inflated profits during a prolonged strike. However, the strategy continued the business unionist's mistake of overestimating the willingness of CCF operators to cooperate with the union. Once the threat of a nationwide strike was shelved, the CCF operators, following the pattern established during the 1924 open-shop drive in the outlying fields, shifted production to their nonunion mines and waited for the UMWA to die (*Illinois Miner*, January 22; February 12; February 19; February 26; March 5; April 2, 1927; *Federated Press*, March 23, 1927; Brophy, June 25, 1927: 4).

In district after district the union tottered on the brink of extinction. In District 5 (Western Pennsylvania), the Jones and Laughlin mines went nonunion after twenty-five years of union operation. In District 6 (Ohio), operators locked out and evicted union miners. In the southern part of the state, desperate miners organized a dual union that signed a five dollars a day scale. In District 12 (Illinois), Peabody Coal fenced in its mines in preparation for reopening as an open shop. It was later charged that Peabody hired agent provocateurs to incite wildcat strikes and justify nonunion operation. The UMWA appealed for public support in an effort to quell the open-shop assault. Lewis published a proposal for a permanent joint conference board to resolve labor-management disputes. In the proposal he offered to join operators in a presentation to the Interstate Commerce Commission to secure a more favorable tonnage rate for the CCF, and he pledged the UMWA to help maintain the profitable operation of unionized mines (*Federated Press*, April 13, April 20, June 22, 1927; *Illinois Miner*, April 16; September 10, 1927; Lewis, May 14, 1927).

The CCF operators were not interested in a general settlement with the union. A district-wide joint scale conference in Illinois collapsed when the companies insisted on signing contracts mine by mine. It was not until the middle of August that District 12 had sufficient mines under contract to resume dues collection and strike-relief payments. A second joint conference in Illinois was scheduled for September, but talks broke off when the operators demanded that District 12 withdraw from the UMWA. In October 1927, with the approach of the peak order season, the Illinois operators finally agreed to extend the Jacksonville CCF wage scale through spring 1928. In return, the union conceded management's right to the unlimited use of coal cutting and loading machines, the reassignment of miners, and the reorganization of work. These were costly concessions. The union bartered away important elements of the traditional "Miner's Freedom" in exchange for less than six months of work (*Illinois Miner* June 18; July 9; August 20; September 3; September 24; October 8; November 5, 1927).

The wage extension in Illinois enabled the UMWA to secure similar arrangements in Iowa, Indiana, Missouri, and Kansas. These states joined Michigan, Montana, Wyoming, and Washington as the only districts with union contracts. However, in an unanticipated development, desperate union miners flooded these states looking for jobs. District relief rolls swelled to the bursting point while the strike was crippled in other CCF fields. In December 1927, Secretary of Labor James Davis tried to arrange a joint conference to extend the truce into the other fields. The operators refused, telling Davis, "So far as we are concerned that organization is entirely out of the picture." Meanwhile, in the Pennsylvania and Ohio fields, Districts 2, 5, and 6 mines operated nonunion if they operated at all. The American Federation of Labor estimated that in January, 200,000 miners were working nonunion in West Virginia, Pennsylvania, and Ohio. In these states open-shop operators were supported by state and federal courts. An Ohio state judge threatened to deport any immigrant found guilty of violating an antistrike injunction. In District 2, courts issued sweeping injunctions barring picketing and upholding evictions from company housing. In District 5, the Pittsburgh Terminal Coal Company instituted a 1.5-million dollar suit against the UMWA, charging that the 1927 strike was a "conspiracy in restraint of trade" in violation of the Sherman Anti-Trust Act and Interstate Commerce Commission regulations. In support of the suit, a federal judge made an initial ruling enjoining legal aid to miners who violated court orders. Industry and government agencies also assisted the open-shop drive against the Central Competitive Field. General Motors, the Pennsylvania Railroad, the Baltimore and Ohio Railroad, and the New York Central Railroad all refused to use union coal. Bethlehem Steel and the U.S. Steel Company armed their captive mines to protect nonunion operation. Mellon-controlled railroads tried to bar union coal. The Interstate Commerce Commission, after years of upholding discriminatory shipping rates against the union-ized Ohio and Pennsylvania fields, agreed to lower shipping rates now that the mines in Pennsylvania, Ohio, and Kentucky were operating nonunion (*Illinois Miner*, August 27; September 24; October 8; October 15; November 19; November 26; 1928, January 28; February 25; March 10; March 17; June 23, 1927; *New York Times*, December 10: 9; December 11: 28, 1927; *Federated Press*, October 6, November 17, November 24, 1927; Dubofsky & Van Tine, 1977: 146–47).

By January 1928, the operators had gained a completely free hand in these fields. When Mellon companies started a new round of wage reductions, Coal and Iron police used machine guns to silence opposition and evict malcontents. Symbolic of the total route of the UMWA, the Mellon companies continued to deduct union dues and the checkweight-man's salary from the miner's wages, though there was neither a union nor a checkweightman. In February 1928, the Mellon interests defended their actions in a full-page advertisement in the *Pittsburgh Post-Gazette*. The ad flatly stated that the company recognized no obligation to hire union members or operate a closed shop. In a biting rejoinder to union charges of corporate duplicity, they pointed out that the 1924 Jacksonville CCF accord permitted them to operate both union and nonunion mines, and they were only bound to pay the Jacksonville wage scale in unionized mines. The company claimed the right to decide which mines to operate union and which to operate nonunion, and if union members chose to work in the nonunion mines at the nonunion wage scale, those were the conditions of employment. The Consolidation Coal Company seconded Mellon's open-shop determination. After a year of record setting production in its nonunion mines, Consolidation recommended that the rest of the industry follow this path. Open-shop operation allowed the company to pay lower "fair market" wages, close inefficient units, eliminate unnecessary miners, and reorganize work (*Illinois Miner*, January 21; January 28, 1928; Ringer, 1929: 139–40; *Federated Press*, March 29, 1928; Brophy Papers, June 9, 1928, Series 1, Box 3).

By the spring of 1928, there was virtually no miners' union outside of Illinois. As the Jacksonville extension neared expiration, District 12 President Fishwick sought to avoid a strike. The district office organized a "Buy Illinois Coal" booster campaign and offered to "permit" any mine willing to pay the union scale to continue working. However, only fifty-three mines were interested, and these mines would only sign temporary agreements while they waited for a wider settlement. Northern Illinois operators, unable to compete because of thin coal seams, broke with the union and posted a lower wage scale. In July, Fishwick asked the IEB for authorization to negotiate a contract for less than the $7.50 day. The IEB responded with instructions that the districts secure the best possible agreements. Illinois settled for a $6.10 day and more job concessions. Operators were given the right to switch machine miners from tonnage rates to hourly wages. Once Illinois accepted the reduction Indiana signed for the $6.10 day, Iowa for $5.80, and in District 21 (Arkansas) and in Ohio, the remnants of the union settled for a $5.00 scale (*Illinois Miner*, March 24; April 7; April 14; May 5; May 19; June 23; July 14; July 21; September 1; September 8; September 29; October 6; October 27, 1928).

Chapter 11

Save the Union Committee

When the International Executive Board ruled out a national bituminous coal strike in 1927, Save the Union Committee members tried to rally support for a strike in the outlying fields. Powers Hapgood and Anthony Minerich, a communist miner, campaigned across Somerset County in District 2, but they found rank-and-file miners embittered by past UMWA betrayals and unwilling to support the union. Another problem was that the Save the Union Committee never developed a permanent organizational structure. Ostracized by the UMWA international office and unable to motivate the besieged rank-and-file of the union, the leadership of the 1926 election campaign dispersed. John Brophy, politically isolated in District 2 after the election of the Mark-McCloskey slate, moved to Pittsburgh. During the summer of 1927, he traveled to the Soviet Union with a group of American union officials and labor activists. When he returned to Pittsburgh, he helped set up a labor school and spoke to groups of UMWA dissidents in District 5. Powers Hapgood attempted to organize a labor newspaper with Brophy as editor. Hapgood wrote Norman Thomas and other former supporters of District 2's educational programs trying to raise money, but noncommunist progressives and socialists were frightened by Lewis' red-baiting and disapproved of communist ties to the Save the Union Committee. When Hapgood was unable to secure funding, the project fell through. Blacklisted in the coalfields, Hapgood moved to Massachusetts, where he joined the Socialist Party's committee to save Sacco and Vanzetti, married Mary Donovan, a Socialist Party activist, and worked in her campaign as the Party's candidate for governor of Massachusetts (Singer, 1982: 258–59; Brophy, 1964: 220–29; Bussel, 1999: 99–100; Singer, 1991: 143–47; Hapgood Papers, 1927, Series 1, Box 4).

During this period, communist miners worked to keep the ideas of the Miner's Program alive in the coalfields, however Workers' (Communist) Party leaders were divided over what direction to pursue. The union had declared the Party a dual organization and miners who participated in its activities risked expulsion by their locals. Further, the 1926 results showed that it was unlikely that Lewis could be dislodged as UMWA president as long as the American Federation of Labor recognized his election, and the remaining union operators were willing to bargain with the international office. A sizable faction in the Party argued that the communist miners should suspend work in the UMWA and concentrate on the organization of a new union to reach the thousands of miners in fields abandoned by Lewis. They were opposed by William Z. Foster, the Party's leading labor organizer, who defended the Party's strategy of organizing within the established unions (Singer, 1991: 132–57).

During 1927 and 1928, the members of the Workers' Party and communist miners debated the formation of new, essentially dual, miners' unions. With the death of Workers' Party Secretary C. E. Ruthenberg in March 1927, the faction supporting new unions emerged as the dominant group among the communists. Their position received important support from the Soviet Union when the Red International of Labor Unions called for the formation of new revolutionary unions. However, because of Foster's stature among American workers and communists and the risk of splitting the Party after Ruthenberg's death, no changes were made in the Party's labor union policy at its fall 1927 convention. To end the stalemate in the Party, Foster decided to strengthen his position in favor of working existing unions by endorsing the reorganization of the Save the Union Committee as a permanent committee to lead rank-and-file opposition in the UMWA. In December 1927, Foster met with John Brophy and Powers Hapgood to secure their support in organizing noncommunist miners. A second, larger meeting was scheduled for January 4, 1928, to plan a Save the Union Conference for April in Pittsburgh to coincide with the expiration of the 1927 Jacksonville CCF contract extension. Brophy, Hapgood, and communist miner and organizer Pat Toohey signed a "Call for Coal Miner's National Save the Union Conference" (Foster, April: 195–200, June: 323, July 1928: 399; Swabeck, 1928: 622; Nyden, 1977: 69–101; Brophy, 1964: 229–30; Hapgood Papers, 1928, Series 1, Box 4).

In the April 1 issue of the Workers' Party magazine, *Labor Unity*, William Z. Foster outlined the Save the Union strategy to revitalize the UMWA and win control of the international office. Key was rebuilding the 1922 alliance between the union and nonunion fields. The committee planned to concentrate on organizing support for a strike in the nonunion Pennsylvania coalfields of Somerset, Fayette, Westmoreland, and Greene Counties, and in District 12 (Illinois). It hoped that strike momentum in the nonunion fields would convince other Illinois miners to walk out, and that this would produce a domino effect on the rest of the bituminous coal industry. District conferences were planned to support the national April 1 conference, prepare for the strike, and create a permanent structure for the committee (Foster, April 1, 1928: 1–4).

While John Brophy continued as chairman of the Save the Union Committee, communist miners and their ideas on organizing dominated the revitalized coalition. A comparison of the first edition of the committee's newspaper, *The Coal Digger*, with 1926 Save the Union Committee press releases shows major changes in tone and some subtle differences in philosophy. Where Brophy had a tendency to provide lengthy explanations, *The Coal Digger* was strident and sloganeering. In 1926, Brophy refused to personally attack Lewis, while in 1928 *The Coal Digger* directly attacked Lewis, listing his salary and expenses and exposing nepotism in the international office. In 1926, ideological disagreements between Brophy and the communists were resolved when the communists agreed to accept Brophy's version of the Miner's Program as the campaign platform. In 1928, disagreements about class conflict, the role of a Labor Party, and a plan to nationalize the coal mines remained; however, slogans replaced detailed proposals and disputes were glossed over. The strategy discussed by Foster in the *Labor Unity* article reflected this change. Brophy was a trade unionist who believed in building a stable and class-conscious labor movement. His entire career focused on long-term educational programs and organization. Foster and the communists were committed revolutionaries probing for weaknesses in American capitalism. The national strike was their weapon; it would hopefully produce a catharsis capable of winning control over the UMWA and the labor movement and securing their support for a revolutionary anticapitalist program (*The Coal Digger*, February 1, February 15, March 19, 1928; *The Coal Miner*, November 1, 1926; Singer, 1982: 261–62).

The shift in the committee reflected a reduction in the number of noncommunist rank-and-file activists willing to challenge the Lewis regime for control of the UMWA. Brophy no longer had an established base of support. The strongest union miners had left District 2 and the other outlying fields. The remaining union miners in these fields and the CCF clung desperately to jobs and feared expulsion from the union and unemployment if they worked with Brophy or the communists. During a February tour of Districts 5, 6, and 12 to publicize the Save the Union Conference, Brophy was forced continually to defend the committee as a coalition independent of the Workers' Party. District 1 (Anthracite) was the only field where a significant number of noncommunist rank-and-file miners supported the Save the Union Committee. It was a working unionized field and the rank-and-file turned to the committee for support around serious local grievances. The district office, allied with operators, was accused of using terrorism to impose a hated subcontract system on anthracite miners. Homes were bombed and four insurgent leaders were murdered. A fifth, Sam Bonita, was charged with manslaughter after killing a hired thug who attacked him. Powers Hapgood helped organize a Progressive Convention in the district in February 1928, to tie the local struggle into the national campaign against Lewis and the international office and to recruit delegates to the April Save the Union Conference (*Pittsburgh Sun and Telegram*, February 27, 1928; Brophy, 1964: 228–29; Federated Press, March 22, 1928; Hapgood & Donovan, March 14, 1928: 293–94).

On April 1, over 1,000 miners assembled in Pittsburgh for the Save the Union Conference. Most of them represented areas that had been on strike for over a year with little support from the international union. The largest group was a delegation of over 350 strikers from District 5. Brophy's campaign in District 6 attracted approximately 150 delegates from Ohio. Anthracite, Illinois, and District 2 (Central Pennsylvania) all sent contingents of just under 100 miners each. Brophy spoke at the conference and was warmly received, and he and Hapgood were both elected to a newly constituted national board of the Save the Union Committee. However, Brophy was given no organizational responsibilities and was treated primarily as an elder statesman. Communist miners held the key posts in the conference and on its committees. James Watt of Illinois was selected permanent chairman of the convention and Pat Toohey was chosen national secretary of the Save the Union Committee. A majority of the national committee was also affiliated with the communist group (Lee, May 1928: 3–6; Save the Union Minutes, 1928: 2, 3, 9, 10).

On April 16, 1928, Hapgood and Anthony Minerich launched the Save the Union Committee organizing drive in the nonunion fields with a mass rally in Westmoreland, Pennsylvania. Initially over sixteen thousand miners rallied to the strike call. However, a fundamental flaw emerged in the committee's strategy. Most of these miners were already hopelessly engaged in long-term strikes at mines that had switched to open-shop operation. These strikers had little prospect of securing union contracts. Basically, they turned to the Save the Union Committee hoping for strike relief. The committee also underestimated Lewis' resolve to fight back and his tenacious hold on the remnants of the union. While the conference was still in session, families of Curtisville, Pennsylvania, Local 2242 miners attending the conference were evicted from UMWA strike barracks and denied relief (*Pittsburgh Sun and Telegram*, April 17, 1928; *The Coal Digger*, May 7, 1928; Lee, May, 1928: 3–6; *Labor Unity*, May 1, 1928: 2; Save the Union Minutes, 1928: 5; Sukle, 2003: 249).

On April 24, 1928, John L. Lewis declared the Save the Union Committee and an allied organization, the Pennsylvania-Ohio Relief Committee, to be dual unions. The Save the Union Committee was charged with "creating mistrust, confusion, turmoil and dissension within our ranks," as well as fomenting Soviet communism, destroying children's "faith in God," taking payoffs from nonunion operators, and receiving funds from Moscow. In June 1928, the *UMWA Journal* instructed all locals to purge Save the Union Committee members. Lewis' counteroffensive destroyed any possibility of the Save the Union Committee organizing as an opposition force inside the UMWA. In District 1, the union identified Save the Union Committee members to the operators and they were fired and blacklisted. In Districts 5 and 6 the union forced striking miners to sign yellow-dog contracts barring participation in Save the Union activities. Violators forfeited strike benefits. In Illinois, the District 12 office red-baited and Jew-baited the committee, and forty committee organizers were expelled from the union or placed under investigation for participating in Save the Union activities. District Secretary-Treasurer Walter Nesbit ruled petitions for a district convention automatically invalid because they were on Save the Union Committee stationery. Locals were warned that signing a Save the Union Committee petition was sufficient grounds for suspension. The committee went ahead with its plans for a district convention anyway. On May 19, the District 12 Save the Union convention voted to remove Fishwick and his supporters from office, set up a new district office, and called on District 12 locals to send the new office their dues (*Federated Press*, April 26, 1928; *UMWA Journal*, June 15, 1928; *The Coal Digger*, April 14, May 7, 1928; *Illinois Miner*, May 5, May 19, June 16, 1928; Dubofsky & Van Tine, 1977: 130; UMWA MA Save the Union File; Singer 1991: 148).

The decision by the Illinois Save the Union Committee to set up a parallel structure that requested dues from district locals effectively established the committee as a dual union and signaled the failure of the Workers' Party's

Save the Union strategy to oust Lewis from control of the UMWA. Lewis succeeded in denying the legitimacy of the Save the Union committee, and it was not strong enough to force the operators to negotiate with them. The 1922 alliance between the CCF and the outlying and nonunion fields could not be rebuilt. During the intervening six years the open-shop drive had demoralized and impoverished bituminous coal miners, undermined their sense of class-consciousness and solidarity, and left the UMWA at the margin of the industry. The union and its international office survived in a shaky alliance with operators, when it served the purposes of the companies. Most miners potentially interested in the Save the Union Committee were already engaged in hopeless strikes. Working miners knew committee affiliation meant unemployment and blacklisting with too many hungry men waiting for their jobs for them to take the risk.

Brophy Resigns

John Brophy recognized the failure of the strike strategy and the communist drift toward dual unionism, and in May 1928, he resigned from the Save the Union national committee. Publicly, Brophy blamed his decision on poor health, however, in an exchange of letters with Powers Hapgood, he explained his disagreements with the communists. Brophy argued that there was "no sign of mass opposition" among the miners and "no solid support for a new union." He accused Foster and the communists of being "creatures of chance" who were unwilling to lay the strong foundation necessary to rebuild the union. In a second letter he wrote, "We were victims of our own propaganda." Rhetorically he quizzed Hapgood, "I don't understand how the communists don't see this. Are they playing blind chance on the hope something will turn up?" (Brophy, 1964: 230; Singer, 1991: 148; *Pittsburgh Gazette-Post*, May 8, 1928; Hapgood Papers, June–July 1998, Series 1, Box 4; UMWA MA Save the Union File).

For their part, the Workers' Party and the communist miners saw no alternative to creating a new miners' union. Workers' Party members and supporters were already expelled from the UMWA. The only alternative to creating a new union was to surrender the bituminous coal industry and the miners to Lewis and the business unionists. Propelled by events in the coalfields, the Workers' Party finally announced its decision to form new unions in the mass production industries, and at a June 12, 1928 meeting, George Voyzey, Luke Coffey, Dan Slinger, Freeman Thompson, James

Watt, and Pat Toohey signed a call for a September conference to found the National Miners Union. Anthony Minerich corresponded with Brophy and Hapgood, trying to convince them to support the decision. Minerich claimed that Illinois, Kentucky, and West Virginia were on the verge of rebellion from the UMWA and fertile ground for a new organizing drive (Myerscough, 1928: 1–3, 26–27; Foster, July 1928: 387, 399; Singer, 1991: 148; Hapgood Papers, 1928, Series 1, Box 4).

Brophy answered that while he accepted the legitimacy of a new organization to continue the communist struggle in the coalfields, he was convinced it would never become a genuine union. He argued that the communist evaluation of the situation continued to be unrealistic and concluded, "I only regret that there is no sound basis for such a move at this time. It will give a few individuals a sense of activity—nothing more." Hapgood agreed with Brophy and decided not to associate his name with an openly dual movement. He doubted the new union could negotiate contracts unless it agreed to lower the wage scale and underbid the UMWA (Hapgood Papers, 1928, Series 1, Box 4; Singer, 1991: 149).

The organizing convention for the new union in Pittsburgh ended up as a battleground between the communists and 200 to 300 pickets paid by the UMWA. The police allowed the pickets to attack the convention, and then arrested 120 of the delegates for rioting. Hapgood and Brophy tried to attend as observers but were unable to enter because of the fighting. Finally, the new union was forced to move the meetings out of Pittsburgh (*Pittsburgh Gazette-Post*, September 9–10, 1928; Hapgood Papers, September 26, 1928, Series 1, Box 4).

During the convention Brophy decided to make public his position on the formation of a new union. In a September 13 press conference, Brophy explained that he considered the formation of a new union a mistake. "It is to be regretted that many of the Save the Union group among the coal miners have decided to set up a new union. Dual unionism is contrary to the original purposes of the Save the Union forces in the United Mine Workers, and means splitting and weakening the progressives in the industry." He continued, blaming Lewis' policies for provoking the dual union. "John Lewis, in addition to pursuing a labor policy that finally wrecked many districts, brought low wages to the miners and lost 300,000 members in the last five years, through his corrupt machine, nullified the democratic provisions of the organization, stole elections at will, and sought to silence all opposition by expulsion and intimidation. Yet the withdrawal of the progressive forces into a new union with extremely doubtful chances of success, surrendered completely the United Mine Workers or what was left of it to the forces of reaction" (*Pittsburgh Gazette-Post*, September 13, 1928).

The communists responded by branding Brophy a coward. Hapgood tried to defend Brophy and in a letter to communist organizer Ella Reeve "Mother" Bloor, he explained his own views in detail.

> I think the present move of dual unionism is the logical thing for the Communist Party to do. It will have a good effect on building it. Whatever they can do in the mining industry, they can use to good affect as propaganda in the needle trades, the textile industry, and vice versa. Individuals can also, and will use it, as a means of building themselves in the Communist Party. But I'm not sure if the affect of dualism will be helpful to the workers. Of course if one believes that the C.P. is the only real hope for the emancipation of the working class, then it naturally follows that what is good for the C.P., and helps to build it, is for the best interests of the workers whether it helps them at the moment or not. If I could be convinced that it was the only hope, I would be with you 100% on anything that would help build the C.P., but no one has convinced me yet. (Singer, 1991: 149; Hapgood Papers, September 26, 1928, Series 1, Box 4)

Communists and Coal Miners

William Z. Foster and the American communist movement made a major investment of time and manpower during the 1920s, supporting the organization of coal miners to challenge the leadership of the United Mine Workers of America. But agents of the Workers' Party did not infiltrate the UMWA. Militant rank-and-file coal miners and their indigenous leadership turned to communists for help, frequently after they had already been red-baited or suspended by union officials. UMWA dissidents were attracted to the TUEL and the Workers' Party because they brought structure, coordination, a general ideological framework, and outside organizational and financial support. In return, these militant miners were the communist movement's organic intellectuals, class-conscious coal miners who were a conduit between the left-wing party and the working class. They expanded the political content of trade union struggles and by their undaunted determination to organize under the most difficult circumstances they earned the Workers' Party legitimacy in an important sector of the American working class.

Charges that communist organizers precipitated dual unionism are unfair. John L. Lewis and his business unionist supporters in the UMWA international office, red-baited and charged dual unionism indiscriminately, in order to isolate dissidents that they perceived as threats to their control over the union. Where a tendency toward dual unionism did exist, it was not a product of communist organizing, but a normal feature of internal UMWA union politics. Entrenched bureaucratic machines were organized to maintain their control over the union. They refused to run fair union elections or open conventions. Dissident factions were forced to create parallel political structures to challenge these machines. Whether intended or not, these structures had the potential to become dual organizations.

One of the most controversial issues in the early history of the American Communist Party was its decision in 1928 to shift its labor policy from organizing inside the American Federation of Labor to building new revolutionary unions affiliated with its own labor federation, the Trade Union Unity League. The conflict between working within established unions and creating independent revolutionary unions was part of the tradition of American labor radicalism that included the nineteenth-century Knights of Labor and the Industrial Workers of the World. Support for these positions was in a constant state of flux. In the coalfields, the decision to form a new union reflected the debate among communist miners over the conditions in the industry and possibilities for change in the UMWA. It was contingent on the interplay between earlier choices and new events. It was not a simple response to ideological dictates from either the international communist movement or the American party leadership.

The National Miners Union initiative as a labor union essentially ended in August 1930, when a Pittsburgh convention was able to attract only a few dozen miners. Although communist organizers continued to have some success recruiting African American coal miners in the Pittsburgh area, agitating in the Pennsylvania anthracite fields, and were active in Harlan County, Kentucky, in 1931. Worker Party organizers seem to have finally accepted the unfeasibility of a new union in January 1931. Steve Nelson, a chief organizer in Anthracite, wrote, "The NMU, which never had much of a foothold in the region, was smashed and retained only a small group of CP members and sympathizers." However, the NMU lingered on paper until it was officially dissolved in 1935 (Nyden, 1977: 101; Stamm, 1930: 2; Howard, 2001: 118; Howard, 2005).

William Z. Foster, the TUEL, the Workers' Party, and communist miners made serious mistakes. Sometimes they antagonized potential allies unnecessarily. They overestimated the revolutionary potential of the miners because they wanted to believe that a mass strike would snowball and win broad support for their trade union work and communist ideology. John Brophy's assessment of the virtual impossibility of building a new union in the coalfields proved to be correct. Certainly, UMWA officials were also correct when they claimed that American communists had revolutionary goals and were affiliated with an international movement. However, revolutionary goals and international affiliation do not in themselves make communist trade union activity illegitimate or establish that the communists were manipulating the concerns of American workers to serve outside interests. Whatever their mistakes and limitations, communist miners were indigenous rank-and-file organizers who energized coal miners in some of America's bitterest battles against an antilabor government and open-shop employers during the 1920s. And it was dogged organizing by communist miners who kept unionism alive in many coalfields during the early years of the Great Depression. The groundwork that they laid throughout this period helped prepare the way for rebuilding the UMWA, when new conditions made possible the labor upsurge of the 1930s (Draper, 1972, 371–92; Bernstein, 1960, 358–90; Bernstein, 1971, 41–66).

Part 5

Revival and Collapse

Chapter 12

New Deal and World War II

The class-conscious rank-and-file movement that developed in the bituminous coalfields after World War I was defeated by 1929. During the preceding ten years, open-shop operators routed the United Mine Workers of America in both the outlying fields and large sections of the Central Competitive Field. Open-shop drives effectively pushed the UMWA out of Central Pennsylvania's bituminous coalfields. Between 1923 and 1926, dues-paying membership in Central Pennsylvania District 2 declined from about 40,000 to 17,000, and in Western Pennsylvania District 5 from 39,000 to under 19,000. The union fared even worse in neighboring West Virginia. Coal companies were able to take advantage of expanded production during World War I, capacity no longer needed in the postwar era, mechanization, internal divisions within the union, and ethnic divisions among miners, to shift production to nonunion fields and weaken the UMWA (Brophy, 1964: 227; Hardman, 1928: 173–85; Dix, 1988: 126).

On March 13, 1929, John L. Lewis delivered a "confidential and privileged address" to the UMWA International Executive Board on conditions in the bituminous industry. Lewis reported,

> The industry seems to be cursed with an inability to regulate its affairs in accordance with modern practice, and the man who works in a coal mine in the nation today is made responsible for the economic defects of the industry and the lack of intelligence and co-operation upon the part of those who purport to manage the industry. . . . (W)ith the waning and dissolution of our union in certain coal fields of America today, there is coming

back into those coal fields the same injustices and the same evil practices that prevailed in the days of our boyhood. . . . Our union is not gone so long as its membership can retain courage and hope for the future and confidence in their fellow man. Labor has always had these cycles in its history in our country, it has had its triumphs, and it has had its reverses, and it always will. Progress has come in cycles. (UMWA MA International Executive Board File, March 13, 1929)

The decade-long open-shop drive succeeded, in a large measure, because operators eradicated the network of strong UMWA union locals that were the backbone of the union. Employers were then free to lower wages and to mechanize and reorganize production without effective opposition. The shift away from traditional patterns of work undermined the "Miner's Freedom," the ideological source of the rank-and-file miner's class-consciousness; as a result, the UMWA and the rank-and-file movement in the union were undercut at their roots.

In an article for the *Federated Press* labor news service in 1929, John Brophy reported on the collapse of the UMWA struggle against open-shop operators in the bituminous coalfields. While the article focused on an individual strike, it reflected Brophy's general evaluation of the situation in the industry. Brophy wrote, "The tremendous loss of membership by the United Mine Workers is not the worst feature; there is a loss of morale that has no parallel in the 38 years of U.M.W.A. history. The miners have been defeated in other strikes but never with such devastating results to the spiritual and moral resources of the miners" (Brophy, 1929). By 1929, the UMWA no longer was a national union. The average monthly membership was approximately 86,000 miners, a decline from a peak of over 384,000 in the bituminous coalfields in 1921. Sixty-two percent of the unionized miners in 1929, over 53,000, were working in District 12 (Illinois). In 1921, the states of Pennsylvania and West Virginia had the second and third most UMWA members. By 1929 there were virtually no union miners working in either state. The UMWA completely disappeared in North Dakota, Oklahoma, Montana, Arkansas, Missouri, Kentucky, Alabama, Tennessee, Virginia, and Maryland. Only skeletal organization remained in Ohio, Colorado, and Michigan. Indiana operators, after signing a union contract in 1928, continued to lower wages (*Illinois Miner*, February 2; October 26, 1929).

Despite this assault on the union, John L. Lewis and business unionists in the UMWA international office remained committed to a program of cooperation between labor and management to rationalize production in the industry. Instead of combating open-shop operators, they concentrated on maintaining control over the union machinery by suppressing dissidents, and on efforts to convince Republican administrations in Washington, DC, to sponsor a settlement in the industry. In a radio broadcast to West Virginia miners, Lewis ally Van Bittner presented the official UMWA explanation for the collapse of the industry. Bittner defended the union's international office and its commitment to the 1924 Jacksonville CCF contract. He claimed that the pact gave "the operators time to put their house in order and allow both miners and operators to cooperate in settling the problems of the industry." According to Bittner, the Jacksonville agreement failed because operators permitted the evils of the industry to continue and refused "to take their medicine" (Lewis, March 13, 1929; Bittner, May 5, 1929).

With the onset of the Great Depression, conditions in the bituminous coal industry worsened. In 1932, as coal's share of the energy market slumped below 50 percent, bituminous coal miners mined less coal than at any time since records started being kept in 1904. The market was so weak that employed miners averaged only 146 working days a year. Because of changes in energy use and desperation for work, the tonnage rate for bituminous coal miners, which averaged between $2.00 and $4.00 before the start of the Great Depression, fell to $1.31 a ton in 1932, and the day rate dropped precipitously. One-third of working miners earned less than $2.50 a day and in some regions the rate was as low as $1.00 a day (Johnson, 1979: 125).

From 1929 through 1933, Lewis and the business unionists in the UMWA international office, with support from the AFL and occasionally from operators who feared coal miner militancy, staved off challenges from the National Miners Union, from remnants of the district autonomy coalition, from localized dual movements among disenchanted miners, and from a major effort to unseat him by the leadership of District 12 (Illinois). By the end of this period, Lewis held undisputed control of what remained of the UMWA in the coalfields, with his last remaining opposition in Illinois in retreat (Parker, 1940: 72–79; *Illinois Miner*, April 6, April 13, June 15. July 20, October 5, October 12, October 19, October 26, 1929).

Labor Resurgence

In 1933, when the promises of Franklin Roosevelt and the New Deal helped renew the spirit of unionism in the coalfields, John L. Lewis was in position to rebuild the UMWA consistent with his vision of the role of the union. He centralized all authority in the international office, denying union democracy and the rights of opponents. Later in the 1930s, Lewis and the UMWA business unionists used their position as leaders of the most powerful industrial union in the United States to dominate the American Federation of Labor's Committee for Industrial Organization and in attempts to direct the new Congress of Industrial Organizations (Bernstein, 1971: 40–66; Davis, 1980, 124: 43–84).

From 1929 until 1933, as the Great Depression deepened, the UMWA and most of the American labor movement floundered. In 1931, John L. Lewis testified before the Senate La Follette Committee that "unless we recognize squarely and deal intelligently with these new forces and movements in modern industry and finance, our existing troubles will grow in volume and intensity, and that the future will be filled with recurrent disasters" (Brophy, 1964: 235; Lewis, December 4, 1931: 624–45).

After the election of Franklin D. Roosevelt in November 1932, the miners and the American working-class exploded in an electric surge of union organization. Class-conscious coal miners, who had been beaten down since 1919 by the economic collapse of the industry, open-shop operators, and by Lewis' ruthless efforts to dominate the union, rose up to demand the right to unionize and in a few short months they rebuilt the UMWA. In December 1932, when the Springfield mine in Nanty Glo announced a wage reduction, miners went on strike and reorganized Local 1386. Despite stalled negotiations, over 1,000 coal miners rejoined the UMWA, and by June 1933, Nanty Glo miners were nearly 100 percent unionized. Irving Bernstein, in *Turbulent Years*, argued that the passage of Section 7(a) of the National Industrial Recovery Act in June 1933 with provisions protecting the right of workers to organize was the spark that rekindled the union movement, but in the coalfields and communities like Nanty Glo, organizing preceded passage of the law (Lester, 2004; Rottenberg, 2003; Marcus, 1995; *UMWA Journal*, January 15, 1933; Bernstein, 1971: 41–43).

The 1935 National Labor Relations Act greatly expanded the move toward a pro-union, high-wage political environment, sparking massive increases in the number of workers represented by a union. Overall union membership among American workers doubled between 1936 and 1938. Bernstein credited John L. Lewis with anticipating the upsurge and committing the union's treasury and organizers to the drive. Lewis had a similar interpretation. On October 15, 1933, the *UMWA Journal* published an official union circular that explained, "Previous to the enactment of the National

Industrial Recovery Act and for a period after its adoption, the United Mine Workers of America waged an intensive organizing campaign in the non-union and partially-organized bituminous coal fields of the country. This campaign of organization was successful beyond expectations. Local unions were established at every bituminous coal mine, embracing in membership all the mine workers employed in or about the mines" (Bernstein, 1971: 41–43; *UMWA Journal*, October 15, 1933: 11).

On June 17, the day after the NIRA passed, a UMWA organizer in the Ohio coalfields reported that 80 percent of the local miners had signed up as members. By June 19, anti-union Logan County, West Virginia was completely organized. A UMWA representative from Kentucky wrote the following to the central office on June 22, "The people have been so starved out that they are flocking into the union by the thousands. . . . I organized 9 Locals Tuesday." By the end of June, there were 128,000 new union members in the Pennsylvania bituminous coal fields. The July 1 issue of the *UMWA Journal* reported "A tidal wave of enthusiasm for the United Mine Workers of America is sweeping over the entire country, with the result that mine workers everywhere are joining the union by the tens of thousands. So tremendous is this ground-swell that it is almost impossible to keep track of it. In every coal mining field in America the campaign of organization is going forward by leaps and bounds never before witnessed." John Brophy described what happened as the miners "moved into the union en mass. . . . They organized themselves for all practical purposes." While Lewis took credit for the surge in UMWA membership, Brophy's assessment is probably more accurate. In an industry with a strong union tradition based on activist locals and with deep-rooted working-class consciousness, bituminous coal miners had organized themselves (Bernstein, 1971: 41–45; UMWA MA CIO Files; Brophy, 1964: 236; *UMWA Journal*, July 1, 1933: 3).

On September 21, 1933, after seven weeks of negotiations, the UMWA and Appalachian region bituminous coal operators, working with the New Deal National Recovery Administration, signed a contract covering UMWA Districts 2, 3, 4, 5, 6, 17, 19, 30, and 31 (Pennsylvania, Ohio, West Virginia, Maryland, Virginia, and parts of Kentucky and Tennessee). It established maximum hours, standard pay rates, the right to a checkweightman, and included safety provisions. The operators and the union declared it the "greatest" agreement ever in collective bargaining and "the beginning of a new era in the task of stabilizing and modernizing the economic processes of this basic industry." The agreement, cosigned by NRA administrator Hugh Johnson and President Franklin D. Roosevelt, impacted on the annual production of about 95 percent of bituminous coal tonnage and affected 340,000 miners. The *New York Times* declared the agreement, scheduled to go into effect on April 1, 1934, a major victory for the UMWA. The next day, striking District 5 western Pennsylvania miners announced that they would march into West Virginia where they would sign-up nonunion miners into the UMWA. On September 23, 8,000 Pennsylvania coal miners marched to the state line where they were stopped by Pennsylvania and West Virginia state police; however, West Virginia miners were permitted to join them there and the group agreed to meet again to plan future action. Of significance for future organizing efforts, while Pennsylvania coal miners were overwhelming white, the leader of the West Virginia miners was African American. District 5 coal miners next turned their attention to the Pittsburgh region steel industry where companies refused to recognize or negotiate with unions. On September 26, hundreds of miners on "holiday" picketed outside of a Carnegie Steel factory. They targeted Carnegie because its subsidy, the H. C. Frick Coke Company, had refused to sign the new coal contract. Class-consciousness, which dissipated under the onslaught of the 1920s open-shop drive, now reemerged with a vengeance (Stark, 1933: 1; *New York Times*, September 22: 4, 5; September 23: 5; September 24: 28; September 27, 1933: 36).

The bituminous coal miners were among the earliest, but they were not the only American workers to battle depression conditions and oppressive employers in this period. While in 1932 there were only 841 strikes, involving a total of 324,000 workers in the United States, in 1933 there were 1,695 strikes, involving more than one million workers. The American Federation of Labor responded to pressure from this labor upsurge and decided to establish Federal locals that could enlist unskilled and semiskilled workers in the mass production industries. John L. Lewis, who had battled against UMWA rank-and-file movements during the 1920s, recognized the strength of the organizing surge, while remaining committed to a business unionist approach. As miners poured into the UMWA, he cautioned them to wait while the union negotiated a new union contract for the CCF and the southern coalfields. Meanwhile Lewis reestablished the union's infrastructure in the reorganized fields creating provisional district offices under his control. Lewis was able to claim success for his strategy in September 1933. when, with President Roosevelt's encouragement, the bituminous coal operators and the UMWA announced an Appalachian Agreement that covered over 90 percent of the bituminous coal mined in the United States. The contract established an eight-hour day and forty-hour week in the coalfields and checkoff but did not provide for a union shop. In January 1934, Lewis reported at the UMWA convention "The United Mine Workers of America has substantially accomplished the task to which it has been dedicated . . . through the forty-four years of its history. It has at last succeeded in bringing into the fold . . . practically all the mine workers in our great North American continent" (Preis, 1972: 12–18; Bernstein, 1971: 45; Laslett, 1996: 117–19).

Nanty Glo

Between 1920 and 1940, Nanty Glo coal mining families lived through the failed 1922 Strike for Union, open-shop drives shifting production from union to nonunion mines, mechanization of the mines, Klan activity in the region, mine closings, the collapse of the CCF contract and with it UMWA membership, and the Great Depression. By 1940, with the United States on the brink of entering World War II, national coal production was up and the local mines were acting at full capacity.

According to the fifteenth census of the United States taken in 1930, between 1919 and 1929, the number of bituminous coal mines in the United States declined by 32 percent, the number of mine workers declined by 16 percent, and mine wages declined by 15.8 percent. The value of the bituminous coal produced declined by 15.6 percent nationwide. Despite this, the population of Nanty Glo rose by 11 percent—from 5,028 in 1920 to 5,598 in 1930—and by 9 percent—to 6,217 in 1940. While the overall population grew, there were some significant demographic changes in Nanty Glo. The percentage of single adult men rose from 55 percent in 1920 to 64 percent in 1940, which probably reflected an influx of unattached miners as production increased and job opportunities expanded in the area's coal mines at the end of the 1930s. The immigrant population fell during this period from 27 percent of the total to 17 percent, which most likely reflected changes in national immigration policy during the 1920s (U.S. Department of Commerce Bureau of the Census, 1931: 941; 1933: 256; 1942: 915).

Census data suggests community stability despite adversity. The average population aged slightly, but not dramatically, as might be expected if young people of child-rearing age had left the community. On the 1940 census, respondents were asked if they lived in the same place that they had five years previously. While coal production and work in the mines was picking up in 1940 as the nation geared for war, 1935 was in the midst of the

Great Depression and local mines were barely operating. Yet over 85 percent of the population of Nanty Glo in 1940, not counting the youngest children, lived where they had five years earlier. Another 13 percent had lived in another part of Cambria County or in one of the neighboring counties (U.S. Department of Commerce Bureau of the Census, 1942: 915).

A Nation at War

John L. Lewis had a history of endorsing candidates for office, including presidential candidates, based on his own personal objectives. He supported Herbert Hoover for reelection in 1932, Franklin Delano Roosevelt in 1936, but broke with Roosevelt and endorsed the Republican presidential candidate in 1940. Lewis claimed that Roosevelt had "broken faith" with American workers, most likely by blocking Lewis' own presidential ambitions when he decided to seek a third term. In an October 1940 radio address, Lewis denounced Roosevelt and New Deal for "thoughtless and sadly executed experimentation" that had not solved the problems of the Great Depression and for unnecessarily moving the nation toward war. Lewis' actions during the final stage of the 1940 campaign set the stage for intense conflict between Lewis and the CIO, which supported Roosevelt; Lewis and Roosevelt; and the UMWA and the federal government during the war years (Dubofsky & Van Tine, 1977: 341–45; Preis, 1972: 79–81; *UMWA Journal*, November 1, 1940: 4–6; Laslett, 1996: 133–37).

Increasing U.S. involvement in wartime preparation benefited bituminous coal miners as it revitalized heavy industry. It also forced the nation, the labor movement, and the UMWA to reevaluate possibilities and strategies for the future. The UMWA initially resisted what John L. Lewis considered restrictive labor policies put in place prior to an official declaration of war. When CIO leadership cooperated with the Roosevelt administration, the *UMWA Journal* declared, "The United Mine Workers will not accept the defeatist attitude of some weak-kneed union leaders." Bituminous coal miners struck briefly in April 1941, when the national contract expired, and in September the union supported a strike by 45,000 miners working in captive mines owned by steel companies. The October 1941 issue of the *UMWA Journal* announced, "President Lewis and his co-workers feel . . . that if there ever was a time in American history when it was imperative for labor to assume the aggressive and complete the job of organizing American working men that time is now." The federal government intervened in the captive mine strike forcing suspension of the walkout for thirty days while the National Defense Mediation Board attempted to resolve the dispute. When mediation failed, the strike resumed on October 25 (Lichtenstein, 2003: 59–69; *New York Times*, April 6, 1941: 1, 33; Pressman, 1958: 201–3, 315; Zieger, 1986: 71–74; Preis, 1972: 127–31; Davis, 1980, 124: 73–77; Laslett, 1996: 137–40).

Roosevelt appealed to Lewis to cancel the strike because "in this crisis of our national life there must be uninterrupted production of coal." Lewis replied, "If you would use the power of the state to restrain me, as an agent of labor, then sir, I submit that you should use that same power to restrain my adversary in this issue, who is an agent of capital." When the government threatened military intervention to end the strike, Lewis responded, "If the soldiers come, the mineworkers will remain peacefully in their homes, conscious of the fact that bayonets in coal mines will not produce coal." The Roosevelt administration finally agreed to appoint a three-member arbitration board that approved a union shop in the "captive mines" (Laslett, 1996: 138–139; *UMWA Journal*, September 1, 1941; Preis, 1972: 127–31; Lichtenstein, 2003: 69–70; Dubofsky & Van Tine, 1977: 397–404).

On December 16, following a formal declaration of war with Germany and Japan, Lewis and the UMWA agreed to a "no-strike" pledge with a National War Labor Board (NWLB) to mediate all disputes. The *UMWA Journal* declared, "the President's (Roosevelt's) letter represents a guarantee, . . . by which American labor can be assured of the preservation of its rights as prescribed under American law. Labor always has been willing to do its part in any hour of peril; now that we have an understandable labor code, by which labor can seek redress from managerial stupidity and arrogance, it behooves labor leaders everywhere to conform to the tenets of the program and refrain from agitating or promoting any work stoppages whatsoever" (Laslett, 1996: 138; *UMWA Journal*, January 1, 1942: 3).

In 1942, the UMWA joined the rest of the American labor movement exhorting members to aid the war effort and to set production records. The UMWA *Journal* declared, "We must produce more coal, we must buy more bonds, we must cooperate and do everything possible to contribute to victory for the Allied nations. Because this is a war for survival, we cannot, we must not at any time content ourselves with the thought that we may be doing our part; we must constantly strive to do more" (Laslett, 1996: 139; *UMWA Journal*, July 15, 1942: 3; Zieger, 1986: 85–90).

While Lewis was critical of federal policy "that runs to the premise of rewarding and fattening industry and starving labor," miners observed the "no-strike pledge" until a December 1942 wildcat strike by 20,000

Pennsylvania anthracite miners. The anthracite strike, led by anti-Lewis insurgents, was precipitated by a 50 percent hike in UMWA dues. Always pragmatic, Lewis called for an end to the work stoppage as an unauthorized strike, but he also publicly sympathized with the plight of the miners and their families and pointedly did not attack them for breaking the union's "no-strike" pledge. It wasn't until the end of January 1943 that Lewis threatened to use his authority as UMWA president to expel the protest leaders. The anthracite strike appears to have convinced Lewis that coal miners would be willing to engage in job actions with the expiration of the UMWA contract in March 1943 (*UMWA Journal*, March 15, 18, June 1, 1943: 17; Preis, 1972: 174–76; Lichtenstein, 2003: 157–60; Dubofsky & Van Tine, 1977: 415–40; Zieger, 1986: 87–96).

In March 1943, the UMWA opened negotiations with operators for a new bituminous coal contract with demands for portal-to-portal pay and a two-dollars-a-day raise. In a preemptive move, the union dismissed coal companies that "smugly hope the government will chastise the mine worker for daring to make known the miserable facts of his existence" and accused the Roosevelt administration of pursuing policies that "inflame the workers in industries who know that their rights are being withheld from them by this strange combination of government and industry." The coal operators countered by refusing to negotiate a contract they claimed would violate federal wartime regulations, and the NWLB insisted it was required to enforce a presidential decree that controlled wage agreements. The UMWA responded that it was the NWLB, not the UMWA that had violated the "no-strike pledge." "Labor representatives did not agree to accept any set formula, nor arbitrary method, upon which mass production adjudication of labor controversies could be handled." At the end of April, coal miners in Western Pennsylvania District 5 and Alabama went out on wildcat strikes, and by April 28, over 40,000 bituminous coal miners were refusing to work. On May 1, 1943, the NWLB suspended hearings on the new contract. With 60,000 coal miners already out on strike, the Board refused to consider "any cases when strikes, walkouts or lockouts are in progress" (*UMWA Journal*, March 15, 1943: 3, 9; Preis, 1972: 177; Dubofsky & Van Tine, 1977: 421–24).

In 1943, during the summer and early fall, the Roosevelt administration put the coal industry under federal control in an effort to maintain essential wartime fuel supplies and to halt the strikes. When strikes resumed in October, the federal government seized control over the mines again. Negotiations resumed and a settlement was reached that was approved by the NWLB. In important ways the wartime strike wave backfired against the UMWA. In 1943, conservative forces in Congress overrode a Roosevelt veto and passed the Smith-Connally War Labor Disputes Act, presaging anti-union legislation in the postwar era. For the miners striving to make a living in the bituminous coalfields, the strikes also had mixed results. The miners' average weekly wage only rose from $54.50 under the 1941 contract to $57.06, which was considerably less than the union's initial demands, and most of the raise resulted from a negotiated extension to the workweek. To secure the agreement, UMWA miners risked alienation from the nation and continued isolation from the rest of the organized labor movement (Lichtenstein, 2003: 157–69; Preis, 1972: 177–90, 193–96; Dubofsky & Van Tine, 1977: 427–40; *UMWA Journal*, June 1, 1943: 10; Zieger, 1986: 91, 95–96; Wechsler, 1944: 249–52).

In May 1943, Nanty Glo miners in Local 1386 voted to remain on strike in defiance of Lewis' promise to end work stoppages and the federal government. Although they returned to work after a week, Nanty Glo miners went out on strike again in June. A May 1943 *Life* magazine photo essay on the Nanty Glo, Pennsylvania coal miners was sympathetic to miners regarding their living and working conditions. However, the article also attacked the strikers for lending support to the Axis powers and argued, "As they confusedly obeyed Lewis, the miners did not realize that his disruptive tactics were serving only to turn the whole country against labor, start a congressional stampede for more stringent curbs on labor's rights." An editorial in the *Nanty-Glo Journal* also condemned the miners for refusing to work while the nation was at war. However, other articles argued that bituminous coal miners had received a bad deal from the federal government and condemned the War Labor Board (Marcus, 1995; *Life*, May 10, 1943b: 25; *Nanty-Glo Journal*, May 20, 1943).

In the midst of all of this, organized labor's pro-war response and petty jealousy exacerbated tension between Lewis and Philip Murray, a former UMWA vice president and Lewis lieutenant who was now president of both the Congress of Industrial Organizations and the United Steel Workers Union. Lewis banned Murray from UMWA membership and office, precipitating a schism between the UMWA and the CIO that led to the miners' union withdrawing from the umbrella organization and negotiating to return to the AFL (Laslett, 1996: 134–40).

Chapter 13

Aftermath

Communities in Distress

World War II temporarily revitalized the bituminous coal industry in the United States and secured better wages for coalminers. But just as after World War I, in the postwar period, the demand for coal declined. The collapse in the coal industry and its impact on miners was more serious this time as energy production continued to shift to other fossil fuels. As in the late 1920s, working-class consciousness eventually declined along with the industry (Bowden, 1946: 165–74).

In 1942 and 1943, bituminous coal supplied over half of total United States energy needs and almost all of that coal was produced by over 320,000 coal miners working in underground mines. According to the Bureau of the Mines, in 1943 bituminous coal accounted for 50.2 percent of the country's energy consumption; domestic and imported petroleum accounted for 28.6 percent; natural gas, 11.9 percent; anthracite coal, 5 percent; and waterpower, 4.2 percent. But there already were indications that coal miners faced trouble. Coal output accelerated as companies used increased demand and federal price guarantees to introduce more mining machinery. Between 1938 and 1945, the number of mobile coal-loading machines employed in American bituminous coal mines more than doubled from 1,405 to 2,950, and the number of self-loading conveyors almost quadrupled from 346 to 1,383 (Fishman & Fishman, 1952: 391–96).

A 1946 labor agreement in the coalfields hammered through by President Harry Truman was supposed to end labor unrest, protect jobs, and provide lifetime health-care benefits for miners. As part of the agreement, the UMWA accepted further mechanization of the mines. By 1949, mechanical coal-loading equipment accounted for 67 percent of all coal mined underground in the United States and the percentage reached 90 percent in 1960. At the same time, the production of bituminous coal declined by 36 percent from 631 million tons in 1947 to 412 million tons in 1959. As productivity per man hour increased because of the expanded use of machinery, the number of workers employed by coal companies declined even more precipitously from 436,000 in 1948 to 168,000 in 1959. During roughly the same period, the sources for U.S. energy consumption radically shifted, contributing to the declining demand for coal (see table 13.1). By 1960, coal provided only 21.7 percent of U.S. energy needs; natural gas, 27.5 percent; petroleum, 44.1 percent, and other sources, 6.6 percent. With these changes, the Miner's Freedom, the underpinning for the bituminous coal miner's working-class consciousness, had basically ceased to exist (Lester, 2004; Rottenberg, 2003; Brown, 2017; Adams, 1961: 1081–86).

The decline in coal mining continued into the twenty-first century. The number of mining jobs, both underground and open pit, was approximately 175,000 in the mid-1980s, 70,000 in 2000, and by 2020 only about 40,000. The situation was even direr for Pennsylvania miners. In 1933, the state produced about a quarter of United States bituminous coal; in 1974, it was down to 13 percent as western strip mining replaced underground mines. In 1940, there were 900 operating coal companies in the state; in 1976, there were 280 (Buckley, 2021: A1; Hoffman, 1978: 351–63).

In 1950, Cambria and Somerset County coal mines employed 21,300 workers. In 1977, Bethlehem Steel announced it would start closing its Cambria County coal mines, affecting 1,800 workers at eight mines, and contributing to a 17 percent unemployment rate in the county. The coal companies also vigorously fought any attempts by the UMWA to organize workers in operating nonunion mines, suing District 2 and union locals for interfering with operation of their mines during a 1977–1978 strike. The Johnstown area's steel factories were also closing at the same time. The city had the highest rate of unemployment in the state, ending the era of blue-collar industrial work in Central Pennsylvania. The Heisley mine, which was sold to a Bethlehem Steel subsidy in 1948 and renamed Bethlehem Mine 31, ceased operation in the early 1980s. The mine, which opened in 1915, had been the largest and most profitable in Nanty Glo, and it was the last operating coal mine in the borough. By 2000, only 1,280 miners were still employed in local coal production and most of the area's coal came from above ground strip mines using giant scoops that peeled off surface earth to expose the coal layers (Kennedy & Oravec, 2019; C & K COAL CO. v. UMWA, 1982; *New York Times*, October 16, 1977: 64; Serrin, 1982: 28; Park, 2018).

In the second half of the twentieth century and into the first decades of the twenty-first century, Central Pennsylvania miners and their families suffered a series of economic and social catastrophes, including renewed anti-union activities by coal companies, mine closings, exodus of young people, debilitating medical issues, and the opioid epidemic. Institutions that contributed to the Miner's Freedom and militant working-class consciousness in the 1920s and sustained Nanty Glo miners and their families through dark times in earlier decades, their work, union, and community, had diminished or disappeared. For Central Pennsylvania bituminous coal miners, like other working-class Americans, their jobs were central to their identity. Until the 1970s, union membership was another major component. However, in the United States since the 1970s, union membership and the availability and permanence of blue-collar work have declined, first impacting on African American males and then contributing to what economists Anne Case and Angus Deaton (2020) describe as an epidemic of "deaths of despair" among displaced white male workers. Case and Deaton built on the pioneering work of sociologist William Julius Wilson, who in *The Truly Disadvantaged* (1987) and *When Work Disappears* (1996) attributed the increase in crime and drug abuse and the deterioration of families and neighborhood institutions in inner-city Black communities to the disappearance of well-paying meaningful jobs. Case and Deaton document how declines in economic growth rates in the United States since the 1960s and deepening income inequality led to opioid abuse, alcoholism, and higher suicide rates in white working-class communities, a growing epidemic that emerged in public view starting in the 1990s. Their loss fed a sense of malaise in those who remained in blue-collar communities that led to anger at betrayal and a profound shift in political allegiance (Case & Deaton, 2020: 150–56).

Table 13.1. U.S. Energy Consumption (in Quadrillion BTUs)

Source	1945	1950	1955	1960
Coal	16.0	12.3	9.7	9.8
Petroleum	10.1	14.4	17.3	19.9
Natural Gas	3.9	6.0	9.0	12.4

Source: Created by the author.

The UMWA reorganized after World War II, tried to maintain membership numbers by organizing workers in other occupations, including health-care workers, corrections officers, and public employees. Districts were enlarged geographically, so that District 2, which historically was exclusively Central Pennsylvania, included the entire northeastern United States and parts of eastern Canada. In 2016, fewer than 10,000 of the UMWA's 67,440 dues-paying members were working coal miners. The changes fundamentally transformed the nature of what for over 100 years had been a coal miners' union (Maher, 2014: B1).

Meanwhile Central Pennsylvania coal miners and retirees were plagued by Black Lung disease caused by a lifetime of inhaling coal dust. In 1976, Paul Bichko, a Bethlehem Mine 31 miner, union committeeman, and president of the Pennsylvania Black Lung Association, testified at a United States Senate hearing on the Black Lung Benefits Reform Act (157–62). In his testimony, Bichko described his work as a coal dumper and his exposure to coal dust.

> I worked as a car dumper outside from 1941 to about, well in between the time of going into military service, I have about 28 years outside. When I dumped coal, I used to dump coal cars one at a time. Their weight averaged approximately anywhere from 1½ tons to about 4 tons. And they were driven up an incline with a chain. A brakeman was there. They called the brakeman to slow down the cars going to the dump, and I handled the cars going to the dump and I dumped the coal into the tipple at which time the tipple separated all different types of coal in 1 inch to 1¾ inches, dust, rock and what have you. It was nothing more than a separation plant. While I operated this dump, I operated for 7¼ hours a day, I worked two shifts. It did not matter whether the wind was blowing, whether it was cold and whether it was warm I worked in dust atmosphere that I could not see my hand in front of me. In fact the only way that I knew that I could not go anywhere more, I would stock up seven cars in the kickback. We had a kickback and cars would go back down and go down an incline. I could not get cars in the dump no more. We had to raise one car up, hold it, place six cars on the track and start again. We had to wait before the dust cleared before we could do that. (Bichko, 1976: 159)

Bichko also reported on a number of local miners who had died from Black Lung–related conditions, including his brother, Joe Bichko.

> I had a brother, Joe who had 38 years in the coal mines. He came home from the third shift one night. He had three children. They were grown up. One is a priest. These were sitting around eating breakfast, talking, discussing, and he says to his wife, I think I will go up and lie down awhile. He goes up to lie down, this was about 10 o'clock in the morning, in 1969. I do not know the exact date. Anyhow, he went to lie down. In the meantime my sister-in-law is ironing clothes from 10 o'clock until about one. She does not hear no stirring upstairs or anything. She had compiled quite a few pieces of material that she has ironed and she was going up in the bedroom to put them away. She went into her husband's bedroom, and she seen his hand lying down over the bed. She dropped the clothes she had. She reached for the hand and raised it up, and said my God, Ken, Ken, something has happened to Dad. He checks his father, and he says, "Mom, father is dead." (Bichko, 1976: 159)

In 2000, the population of Nanty Glo was 3,054, and by 2010 it had fallen to 2,734 people, a decline of over 10 percent. In 2010, it was an aging population; the median age was forty-two years old—five years older than the median age in the United States overall. It was also an increasingly female and poorer population. For every 100 females over the age of eighteen, there were only 84 males. Per capita income was $14,184 in Nanty Glo, compared to over $26,000 for the United States as a whole. Almost 15 percent of the population and almost a quarter of the borough's children lived in households below the official poverty line. Home ownership in Nanty Glo was almost 10 percent above the national average, which is one reason people remained in the borough. But homes tended to be old, an average of seventy-four years old compared to an average of forty years in the United States as a whole, and their value was far below the national average, $32,000 compared to $231,200. These conditions left Nanty Glo and Cambria County at grave risk for the twenty-first-century opioid epidemic; at the time, Cambria County ranked second in Pennsylvania for opioid overdoses (Wikipedia; Nanty Glo Population History; BestPlaces. net; DEA, 2016).

Conditions in Nanty Glo and Cambria County transformed an area once noted for working-class consciousness and militancy into conservative political strongholds. While the United Mine Workers of America did not support any presidential candidate in either 2016 or 2020, in both presidential elections, Cambria County, Pennsylvania, and Nanty Glo voters cast their ballots heavily for the Republican Party candidate Donald Trump. In 2016, Donald Trump, the first Republican presidential candidate to carry Pennsylvania since 1988, took Cambria County by 66 percent (42,258) to 30 percent (18,867). In the two Nanty Glo election districts, Donald Trump led Hillary Clinton 62% to 35% and 69% to 26%. In 2020, Cambria County, Pennsylvania, and Nanty Glo voters went even more heavily for President Trump. In Cambria County, Donald Trump received 48,085 votes (68%) to Joe Biden's 21,730 (30.7%). In Nanty Glo, Donald Trump led Joseph Biden 68 percent to 32 percent and 75 percent to 25 percent (Pesto, 2020; Bloch et al., 2018; Park et al., 2021; WBOY 12, 2020; Cambria County, n.d.).

In the lead-up to the 2020 presidential election, Reuters interviewed Pennsylvania coal miners about their views on the candidates. Twenty-five out of the twenty-six interviewees said that they supported Donald Trump's reelection bid. Most expressed fear that Biden's commitment to clean-energy meant his election would be the final death blow to the bituminous coal industry. Coal miners remained loyal to Donald Trump, despite his failed promise to revive the coal industry. U.S. coal production and coal miner jobs steadily declined after 2008 as over 250 coal-fired power plants closed between 2010 and 2020, including more than 60 during Trump's presidency. During the first three years of the Trump administration, the number of bituminous coal miners in the United States fell by more than 6,000, including a decline in Pennsylvania from 4,559 in 2017 to 3,979 in 2019. This was despite the appointment of a former coal industry lobbyist as the head of the Environmental Protection Agency and the relaxation of Obama-era environmental rules that limited power-plant emissions and protected local land and water from coal waste (Rhys & Garner, 2020; Nark, 2020).

After the 2020 election, many of Cambria County's Republican voters supported Donald Trump's claim that the election was stolen. A *New York Times* article quoted a retired truck driver from Nanty Glo who called Joseph Biden a "total fool," Kamala Harris a "very scary woman," and argued that a Biden presidency would be illegitimate and disastrous. Other people from the region had similar attitudes (Gabriel, 2020: 10).

While it is both impossible and illegitimate to condense an entire community's experience into the persona of one individual, an individual's life can serve as a metaphor for the impact of the changes affecting the people of Nanty Glo in the decades after World War II. A November 2017 article in the online magazine *Politico* declared that Pam Schilling of Johnstown, Pennsylvania, is the reason Donald Trump was elected president of the United States. Pam Schilling grew up in Nanty Glo, "the daughter and granddaughter of coal miners. She once had a union job packing meat at a grocery store, and then had to settle for less money at Walmart. Now she's 60 and retired, and last year, in April, as Trump's shocking political ascent became impossible to ignore, Schilling's 32-year-old son died of a heroin overdose. She found needles in the pockets of the clothes he wore to work in the mines before he got laid off." Donald Trump held a campaign rally at the Cambria County War Memorial arena in Johnstown on a rainy night on October 21, 2016, before a crowd of 5,000. Desperate for change, people like Schilling, once reliable Democrats, "responded enthusiastically to what Trump was saying—building a wall on the Mexican border, repealing and replacing the Affordable Care Act, bringing back jobs in steel and coal." A year after Trump's election, in an interview for the *Politico* article, Schilling declared, "I think he's doing a great job, and I just wish the hell they'd leave him alone and let him do it. He shouldn't have to take any shit from anybody" (Kruse, 2017; Gilliland, 2016).

Commentators across the political spectrum offered explanations for Donald Trump's election as president in 2016, and continued support from his political base after his defeat in 2020. White working-class voters, particularly voters without a college degree, and especially white men from rural areas, turned against traditional Republican candidates and a Democratic Party they once supported, because they felt abandoned by changes sweeping through the country, especially in their communities. The death of the bituminous coal mining industry meant the virtual death of Nanty Glo and towns like it. Class consciousness based on work, union, and community that had once sustained radical resistance to coal operators dissolved with the diminution of these institutions over the course of decades, leaving ethnic identification and anger producing a swing to a very different kind of political behavior (Montanaro, 2016; Lempien, 2020; Page & Elbeshbishi, 2021).

Bibliography

Abstracts (1911). *Abstracts of reports of the Immigration Commission with conclusions and recommendations and views of the minority, vol. 1, presented by Mr. Dillingham, December 5, 1910*. Washington DC: Government Printing.

Adams, Robert. 1961, October. "Technology and productivity in bituminous coal, 1949–59," *Monthly Labor Review*, vol. 84, no. 10.

Albertson, Dean, ed. 1955. *The reminiscences of John Brophy, 1944*. New York: Columbia University Oral History Project.

Alinsky, Saul. 1949. *John L. Lewis: An unauthorized biography*. New York: Putnam.

American Experience. n.d. "The mine wars: Women in the mine towns," *PBS*, https://www.pbs.org/wgbh/americanexperience/features/minewars-women/# (accessed January 17, 2022)

American Labor Yearbook, 1926, VII. "Workers' education and health." New York: Rand School.

American Mining Congress. 1928. *Yearbook on coal mine mechanization for the year 1928*. Washington, DC: American Mining Congress.

Angle, Paul. 1992. Bloody Williamson: A chapter in American lawlessness. Urbana IL: University of Illinois Press.

Baker, Christina and Page, Myra. 1996. *In a generous spirit: A first-person biography of Myra Page*. Champaign, IL: University of Illinois Press.

Baratz, Morton. 1955. *The union and the coal industry*. New Haven: Yale.

Beik, Mildred. 1996. *The miners of Windber*. University Park, PA: Pennsylvania State University Press.

Bernstein, Irving. 1966. *The lean years, a history of the American worker 1920–1933*. Baltimore, MD: Penguin.

Bernstein, Irving. 1971. *Turbulent years, a history of the American worker, 1933–1941*. Boston: Houghton Mifflin.

BestPlaces.net. https://www.bestplaces.net/housing/city/pennsylvania/Nanty-glo (accessed January 27, 2022).

Bichko, Paul. 1976. "Testimony," *Black lung benefits reform act, 1976: hearings before the Subcommittee on Labor of the Committee on Labor and Public Welfare,*

United States Senate, Ninety-fourth Congress, second session, on H.R. 10760 and S. 3183. Washington DC: U.S. Government Printing Office, 1976.

Bittner, Van. 1929, May 5. "Coal—The human equation," transcript of WMMN Fairmont, West Virginia, radio broadcast, Brophy Papers.

Blankenhorn, Heber. 1922, May 17. "Liberty and union in the coal fields," *The Nation.*

Blankenhorn, Heber. 1922, May 24. "Questions for coal barons," *New Republic.*

Blankenhorn, Heber. 1924. *Strike for union; a study of the non-union question in coal and the problems of a democratic movement.* New York: Wilson.

Bloch, Louis. 1931. *Labor agreements in coal mines.* New York: Russell Sage Foundation.

Bloch, Marc. 1953. *The historian's craft.* New York: Knopf.

Bloch, Matthew, Buchanan, Larry, Katz, Josh, and Quealy, Kevin. 2018, July 25. "An extremely detailed map of the 2020 election," *New York Times.*

Booth, Stephane. 1996. "Ladies in white: Female activism in the southern Illinois coalfields, 1932–1938," in Laslett, John, ed. *United Mine Workers of America: A model of industrial solidarity?* University Park, PA: Pennsylvania State University Press.

Bowden, Witt. 1946, August. "The changing status of bituminous-coal miners, 1937–46," *Monthly Labor Review*, vol. 63, no. 2.

Braverman, Harry. 1974. *Labor and monopoly capital.* New York: Monthly Review Press.

Brinton, Jasper, ed. 1914. *Labor laws of Pennsylvania.* Harrisburg PA: Commonwealth of Pennsylvania.

Brody, David. 1965. *Labor in crisis, the steel strike of 1919.* Philadelphia: Lippincott.

The Brookwood Review. 1923, March 2; 1923, March 20; 1924, January 1; 1925, January 1; 1925, April 5.

Brophy, John. 1921. *The Miner's Program.* Altoona, PA: UMWA District 2.

Brophy, John, Mitch, William and Golden, Christopher. 1922a. *Compulsory information in coal.* Altoona, PA: Nationalization Research Committee.

Brophy, John, Mitch, William and Golden, Christopher. 1922b. *How to run coal.* Altoona: Nationalization Research Committee.

Brophy, John. 1922a, March. Report to the 1922 District 2 Convention.

Brophy, John. 1922b, March 25. "Nationalization of Coal Miners—The Miner's Program," *The Survey Graphic,* vol. XLVII no. 26, 1026–1029.

Brophy, John. 1924, March 11. Report to the 1924 District 2 Convention.

Brophy, John. 1926, November. *A larger program for the miners' union.* Clearfield, PA.

Brophy, John. 1926, December 2. "Answer to enemies of the Save the Union Program," Open Letter.

Brophy, John. 1927, June 15. "Brophy claims presidency of miners' union," *Labor Unity.*

Brophy, John. 1927, June 25. "Miners must change strategy to win strike, says Brophy," *American Appeal.*

Brophy, John. 1929. "1929 bleak year in Pittsburgh coal fields," *Federated Press Eastern Weekly Newsletter, n.d.*

Brophy, John et al. n.d. *Principles of a labor party*. Altoona, PA: UMWA District 2.

Brophy, John. n.d. *The miner's program*. Altoona, PA: UMWA District 2.

Brophy, John. 1964. *A miner's life*. Edited by John O. P. Hall. Madison: University of Wisconsin.

Brown, Dylan. 2017, April 11. "Mining union faces 'life-and-death' test," *E&E News reporter*.

Buckley, Cara. January 2, 2021. "Peak pillaged for coal gets solar upgrade," *New York Times*.

Bussel, Robert. 1999. *From Harvard to the ranks of labor: Powers Hapgood and the American working class*. University Park PA: Pennsylvania University Press.

C & K COAL CO. v. United Mine Workers of America. 1982, March 17. 537 F. Supp. 480. United States District Court, W.D. Pennsylvania.

Calhoun, Arthur. 1928. "Labor's new economic policy" in J. B. S. Hardman, ed. *American labor dynamics*. New York: Harcourt Brace. 320–328.

Cambria County. n.d. *2020 general election*. http://elections.cambriacountypa.gov/Elections.Webclient/.

Carr, Edward H. 1961. *What is history?* New York: Random House.

Case, Anne and Angus Deaton, Angus. 2020. *Deaths of despair and the future of capitalism*. Princeton, NJ: Princeton University Press.

Central Pennsylvania Coal Producers' Association. 1921, December 6. "Minutes," District 2 Papers, Ebensburg, PA.

Central Pennsylvania Coal Producers' Association, 1923, "Minutes," District 2 Papers, Ebensburg, PA.

Central Pennsylvania Coal Producers' Association and the Association of Bituminous Coal Operators of Central Pennsylvania. 1923. *Brief to the United States Coal Commission*. Altoona, PA, District 2 Papers.

Christenson, C. L. 1962. *Economic redevelopment in bituminous coal*. Cambridge, MA: Harvard University Press.

Cole, G. D. H. and A. W. Filson, ed. 1967. *British working class movements, Selected documents, 1789–1875*. New York: St. Martin's.

Coleman, McAllister. 1943. *Men and coal*. New York: Farrar and Rinehart.

Davis, Mike. 1980, November/ December. "The barren marriage of American labour and the Democratic Party," *New Left Review*, 124.

DEA. 2016, July. "Analysis of drug-related overdose deaths in Pennsylvania, 2015," *DEA Intelligence Report*.

Dillingham Commission. 1911. *Reports of the Immigration Commission, Immigrants in Industries (in Twenty-five Parts), Part 1: Bituminous Coal Mining* (in Two Volumes: Vol. I) Senate Document No. 633, 61st Congress, 2nd session. Washington: Government Printing Office.

Dix, Keith. 1977. *Work relations in the coal industry, the hand-loading era, 1880–1930*. Morgantown WV: Institute for Labor Studies.

Draper, Theodore. 1957. *The roots of American communism*. New York: Viking.

Draper, Theodore. 1972, Spring. "Communists and the miners, 1928–1933," *Dissent*.

Dropcho, John, and Cashdollar, Donna. 2005. *Life in the valley—Streams of coal*. Indiana PA: Indiana University of Pennsylvania.

Dubofsky, Melvyn and Van Tine, Warren. 1977. *John L. Lewis, a biography*. New York: Quadrangle.

Dunne, William. 1927, March. The thirtieth convention of the United Mine Workers of America," *The Communist*, vol. 1 no. 1.

Ebensburg *Mountaineer-Herald*. 1924, April 7, 17, May 1, June 12, July 3, September 4, October 16, 23.

Eldridge, H.O. 1934, May 17. "As others see us," *Nanty-glo Journal*.

Evans, Christopher. 1918. *History of the United Mine Workers of America*, vol. 1. Indianapolis IN: United Mine Worker of America.

Everling, A. Clark. 1976. "Tactics over strategy in the United Mine Workers of America: Internal politics and the question of nationalization of the mines, 1908–1923." Ph.D. dissertation, Pennsylvania State University.

Eyerman, Ron. 1981. "False consciousness and ideology in Marxist theory," *Acta Sociologica*, vol. 24, no. 1/2.

Federated Press. 1921, June 4, 1931, July 31.

Fishman, Leo and Fishman, Betty. 1952, January. "Bituminous coal production during World War II," *Southern Economic Journal*, vol. 18, no. 3.

Foster, William Z. 1923, July. "The Progressive Miners' Conference," *Labor Herald*, vol. 2, no. 5.

Foster, William Z. 1928, April. "Tasks and lessons of the miners' struggle," *The Communist*, vol. vii, no. 4.

Foster, William Z., 1928, April 1. "A show-down in the mining industry," *Labor Unity*, vol. ii, no. 3.

Foster, William Z. 1928, July. "Old unions and new unions," *The Communist*, vol. vii no. 7.

Foster, William Z. 1947. *American trade unionism*. New York: International.

Fritz, Wilbert and Venstra, Theodore. 1935. *Regional shifts in the bituminous coal industry with special reference to Pennsylvania*. Pittsburgh: Bureau of Business Research.

Fuller, Paul. 1925, May 29. "Workers' education in mining industry," *Justice*.

Fuller, Paul. 1926, March. "Miners' educational work," *American Federationist*.

Gable, John. 1926. *History of Cambria County Pennsylvania, Volume Two*. Topeka, KS: Historical Publishing Company.

Gabriel, Trip. 2020, November 9. "In Pennsylvania, voters for Trump are a ways from accepting defeat," *New York Times*.

Gagliardo, Domenico. 1941. *The Kansas industrial court*. Lawrence KN: University of Kansas Press.

Galloway, R. L. 1898. *Annals of coal mining and the coal trade*. London: The Colliery Guardian Co., Ltd.

Giardina, Denise. 1987. *Storming heaven*. New York: Random House.

Gilliland, Donald. 2016, October 21. "Donald Trump speaks at a rally in Johnstown," *Tribune Live*.

Golden, Clinton. 1925, October 31. "Pennsylvania miner's Chautauqua is great success in first year," *Illinois Miner*.

Goodrich, Carter. 1925. *The miner's freedom, a study of the working life in a changing industry*. Boston: Marshall Jones.

Grayson, Carmen. 1975. "W. Jett Lauck: Biography of a Reformer," unpublished doctoral dissertation, University of Virginia.

Green, William. 1921, September 20. *Secretary-Treasurer's Report to the International Convention of the United Mine Workers of America*. UMWA Archives.

Greene, Janet. 1990. "Strategies for survival: Women's work in the southern West Virginia coal camps," *West Virginia History, vol. 49*.

Gutman, Herbert. 1976. *Work, culture and society in industrializing America*. New York: Knopf.

Hamilton, Walton and Wright, Helen. 1926. *The case of bituminous coal*. New York: Macmillan.

Hapgood, Powers. 1921, August–September. *In non-union mines, the diary of a coal digger*. New York: Bureau of Industrial Research.

Hapgood, Powers. 1923. *Non-union coal: Report to the U. S. Coal Commission*. Altoona, PA: UMWA District 2.

Hapgood, Powers and Donovan, Mary. 1928, March 14. "Murdered miners." *The Nation*, vol. 126, no. 3271.

Hardman, J. B. S., ed. 1928. *American labor dynamics*. New York: Harcourt, Brace.

Hayes, Arthur Garfield. 1922, June14. "Report on Vintondale (Pennsylvania)." *New Republic*.

Henderson, D. and Kleiner, D. 1976. "Coal and lignite mining," *Handbook of Texas Online*. Austin, TX: Texas State Historical Association.

Hinrichs, Albert F. 1923. *The United Mine Workers of America and the non-union fields, Studies in history, economics and public law*. New York: Columbia University.

Hirshfield, David. December 1922. *Statement of facts and summary of the committee appointed by Honorable John F. Hylan of New York to investigate the labor conditions at the Berwind-White Company's coal mines in Somerset and other counties, Pennsylvania* (New York).

Hoffman, John. 1978, October. "Pennsylvania's bituminous coal industry: An industry review," *Pennsylvania History: A Journal of Mid-Atlantic Studies*, vol. 45, no. 4.

Howard, Walter. 2001. "The National Miners Union: Communists and miners in the Pennsylvania Anthracite, 1928–1931," *The Pennsylvania Magazine of History and Biography*, vol. 125, no. 1/2.

Howard, Walter. 2005. *Forgotten radicals: Communists in the Pennsylvania Anthracite, 1919–1950*. Lanham, MD: University Press of America.

Illinois Miner. 1923, February 3, 1929, October 26.

Jenkins, Philip. 1986. "The Ku Klux Klan in Pennsylvania, 1920–1940," *Western Pennsylvania Historical Magazine*, vol. 6. No. 2.

Johnson, James. 1979. *The politics of soft coal, the bituminous industry from World War I through the New Deal.* Urbana, IL: University of Illinois Press.

Johnstown Democrat (Pennsylvania), 1922.

Johnstown Tribune (Pennsylvania), 1919–1922.

Kennedy, Jon and Oravec, Stephen. 2019, June 17. "When coal was king," *Nanty Glo Homepage.*

Kenny, R. and Tyron, F. 1926, December 16. "Machine loading gains rapidly in last three years," *Coal Age*, vol. 30.

King. Clyde L., ed. 1924, January. The price of coal, anthracite and bituminous. Philadelphia, PA: *Annals of the American Academy of Political and Social Science,* vol. CXI.

Kopald (Selekman), Sylvia. 1924. *Rebellion in labor unions.* New York: Boni and Liveright.

Korson, George. 1943. *Coal dust on my fiddle.* Philadelphia: University of Pennsylvania.

Kruse, Michael (2017, November 8). "Johnstown never believed Trump would help. They still love him anyway," *Politico.*

Labor Unity. 1928, May 1. "The miners spread their strike," *Labor Unity*, vol. ii, no. 4.

Laslett, John. 1970. *Labor and the left.* New York: Basic Books.

Laslett, John, ed. 1996. *United Mine Workers of America: A model of industrial solidarity?* University Park, PA: Pennsylvania State University Press.

Lauck, Rex. 1922. "Railroad revenue and expenses, vol. 5," *Subcommittee of the United States Senate Committee on Interstate Commerce, 67th Congress, 1st Session.* Washington, DC: Government Printing.

Lauck, Rex, ed. 1952. *John L. Lewis and the international union.* Washington, DC: UMWA.

Lempien, Edward. 2020, December 7. "Despite drift toward authoritarianism, Trump voters stay loyal. Why?" *Berkeley News.*

Lee, Jack. 1928, May. "The Save-the-Union Conference," *Labor Unity*, vol. ii no. 4.

Lester, Jeff. 2004, November 16. "UMWA membership declined as production trends changed," *Coalfield.com.*

Lewis, John L. 1924. *Attempt by communists to seize the American labor movement. Congressional Record, 68:1, Document 14.* Washington, DC: Government Printing Office.

Lewis, John L. 1925. *The miners' fight for American standards.* Indianapolis: Bell, 1925.

Lewis, John L. 1927, May 14 "The coal miner's proposal," *Information Service.*

Lewis, John L. 1929, March 13. "Address before the Executive Board of the United Mine Workers of America," UMWA Papers.

Lewis, John L. 1931, December 4. "Statement of John L. Lewis, President United Mine Workers of America," *Hearings before a Sub-Committee of the Committee on Manufactures United States Senate.* Washington DC: United States Government Printing Office.

Lesher, C. E. 1922, April. "The position of the operators," *The Survey.*

Lichtenstein, Nelson. 2003. *Labor's war at home: The CIO in World War II.* Philadelphia PA: Temple University Press.

L.I.D. 1923, February–March. "More about coal," League for Industrial Democracy News Bulletin.

Life. 1943a. May 10. "Nanty-glo" *Life*, vol. 14 no. 19.

Life. 1943b May 10. "U.S. takes over the coal mines," *Life*, vol. 14 no. 19.

Maher, Kris. 2014, January 9. "Mine workers union shrinks but boss fights on," *Wall Street Journal.*

Marcus, Irwin. 1992. "Nanty-glo: A Worker's Town Under Siege, 1921–29," unpublished paper presented at the March 1992 meeting of the Popular Culture Association.

Marcus, Irwin. 1995. "Ferment in the coal fields, 1933–43: Nanty-glo, PA, a case study," unpublished paper presented at the April 1995 meeting of the Popular Culture Association.

Martin, William. 1968, August 14. "The history of Nanty-glo Local 1386," *Nanty-glo Journal.*

Merithew, Caroline Waldron. 2006. "'We were not ladies': Gender, class, and a women's auxiliary's battle for mining unionism," *History Faculty Publications, 51.* Dayton OH: University of Dayton.

Miliband, Ralph. 1971. "Barnarve: A case of bourgeois class consciousness," in Istaván Mészáros, ed. *Aspects of history and class consciousness.* New York: Routledge. 22–48.

Miliband, Ralph. 1977. *Marxism and politics.* Oxford: Oxford University.

Montanaro, Domenico. 2016, November 12. "7 reasons Donald Trump won the Presidential election," NPR.

Montgomery, David. 1979. *Workers' control in America.* Cambridge UK: Cambridge University.

Moore, Marat. 1996. "Women go underground," in Laslett, John, ed. *United Mine Workers of America: A model of industrial solidarity?* University Park, PA: Pennsylvania State University Press.

Morris, James O. 1979, Winter. "The acquisitive spirit of John Mitchell, United Mine Workers of America President (1899–1908)," *Labor History.*

Myerscough, Thomas. 1928, July. "Miners want a new union," *Labor Unity*, vol. ii no. 6.

Nanty-glo Journal. 1922, May 5, 1925, November 5.

Nanty-glo Journal. 1925, May 28. "Chautauqua has attracted large crowds."

Nanty-glo Journal. 1943, May 20.

Nanty-glo Journal. 1968, August 14. "Nanty-glo Borough Golden Jubilee."

Nanty-glo Population History, 1990–2019. https://www.biggestuscities.com/city/Nanty-glo-pennsylvania (accessed January 27, 2022).

Nark, Jason. 2020, October 21. "Trump didn't bring back coal in Pa. But that doesn't mean miners are backing Biden," *The Philadelphia Inquirer.*

National Cyclopedia of American Biography. 1951. New York: James T. White.

National Labor Tribune (Pittsburgh), 1924, August 21.

New York Times. 1889, June 1. "Hundreds of lives lost," *New York Times.*

New York Times. 1906, April 17. "Miners shot down in battle at jail," *New York Times.*

New York Times. 1906, April 18. "Miners awed by bayonets," *New York Times.*

New York Times. 1906, April 30. "Many miners wounded," *New York Times.*

New York Times. 1919, November 8. "Coal Operators' Chief Declares Russian Reds Are Financing Radicalism Among Unions Here," 1.

New York Times. 1922, February 2. "Miners seek union with rail workers," *New York Times.*

New York Times. 1922, February 3. "A dual alliance?" *New York Times.*

New York Times. 1922, February 23. "Union chiefs form alliance of miners and transport men," *New York Times.*

New York Times. 1922, April 3. "Pittsburgh non-union men in doubt," *New York Times.*

New York Times. 1922, April 4. "Coal miners' wages," *New York Times.*

New York Times. 1922, April 27. "Miner's Home Dynamited," *New York Times.*

New York Times. 1922, July 25. "Reopen Many Mines as Troops Stand By," *New York Times.*

New York Times, 1922, August 8. "Soft coal agreement near," *New York Times.*

New York Times, 1922, August 10. "Mark time at Cleveland," *New York Times.*

New York Times, 1922, August 13. "Split at Cleveland over arbitration," *New York Times.*

New York Times, 1922, August 16. "Agreement at Cleveland," *New York Times.*

New York Times. 1922, October 4. "Windber Mine Insists on Open Shop," *New York Times.*

New York Times. 1923, January 2. "Worse than slaves, Says Berwind Mine committee's report," *New York Times.*

New York Times. 1924, April 20. "Soft coal industry undergoes treatment," *New York Times.*

New York Times, 1925, May 12. "Pittsburgh company says it is not considering consolidation," *New York Times.*

New York Times, 1925, July 1. "Lewis threatens huge coal strike," *New York Times.*

New York Times, 1925, July 22. "Coal strike threat is wired to Hoover," *New York Times.*

New York Times, 1925, August 16. "Four more mines closed," *New York Times.*

New York Times, 1925, November 23. "Coolidge unlikely to act," *New York Times.*

New York Times, 1925, November 28. "Soft coal strike hangs on 54 mines," *New York Times.*

New York Times, 1926, August 30. "Farrington to resign as miners' leader to take $25,000 office in coal company," *New York Times.*

New York Times, 1926, October 13. "Red plot on labor moves federation to spurn Soviet," *New York Times.*

New York Times, 1926, October 13. "Repudiates link with Reds and says letter was taken from mails," *New York Times.*

New York Times, 1926, October 16. "Scouts letter by Coyle," *New York Times.*

New York Times. 1933, September 22. "Text of agreement on wages and hours in soft coal industry," *New York Times.*

New York Times. 1933, September 22. "Support pledged in executing pact; Operators and mine workers hail 'greatest' agreement in collective bargaining," *New York Times.*

New York Times. 1933, September 23. "Miners to march into West Virginia," *New York Times.*

New York Times. 1933, September 24. "Thousands vote for mine holiday," *New York Times.*

New York Times. 1933, September 27. "Steel workers urged to strike," *New York Times.*

New York Times. 1941, April 6. "Coal tie-up ended in 65% of the mines," *New York Times.*

New York Times. 1943, June 24. "Many Miner Locals Voting Against Returning to Work," *New York Times.*

New York Times. 1977, October 16. "Bethlehem is closing Pennsylvania mines," *New York Times.*

Nyden, Linda. 1977, Spring. "Black miners in Western Pennsylvania, 1925–1931, The National Miners Union and the United Mine Workers," *Science and Society.*

Olds, Leland. 1924, February 2. "Federated Press report," *Illinois Miner.*

Olds, Leland. 1925, June 10. "Business loads dice against bituminous coal miners," *Federated Press.*

Olds, Leland. 1925, July 8. "Miners' president writes about coal," *Federated Press.*

Olds, Leland. 1925, December 2. "Huge triple trap is set for mine union by owners and the state," *Federated Press.*

Olds, Leland. 1926, July 27. "Unionized central field holds its own in coal production in spite of non-union mine work," *Daily Worker,* reprinted from *Federated Press.*

Olds, Leland. 1927, May 4. "Steady work fails to give non-union miner lead in wages," *Federated Press.*

Page, Myra. 1986. *Daughter of the hills, A woman's part in the coal miners' struggle.* New York: The Feminist Press.

Page, Susan and Elbeshbishi, Sarah. 2021, February 21. "Defeated and impeached, Trump still commands the loyalty of the GOP's voters," *USA Today.*

Park, Alice, Smart, Charlie, Taylor, Rumsey, and Watkins, Miles. 2021. "An extremely detailed map of the 2020 election," *New York Times.*

Park, Minju. 2018, November 17. "When coal was king: Nanty Glo struggles to envision change," *Pittsburgh Post-Gazette.*

Parker, Glen. 1940. *The coal industry, A study in social control.* Washington, DC: American Council on Public Affairs.

Parton, Mary Field, ed. 1925. *Autobiography of Mother Jones.* Chicago, IL: Kerr & Company.

Pennsylvania Department of Mines. 1919. *Report of the Department of Mines of Pennsylvania. 1917 (part 2) Bituminous.* Harrisburg, PA: Kuhn.

The Pennsylvania Manual, 1929. Harrisburg, Pennsylvania: Department of Property and Supplies, Bureau of Publication, State of Pennsylvania.

Perlman, Selig. 1928. *A theory of the labor movement.* New York: Macmillan.

Pesto, Mark. 2020, November 24. "Cambria, Somerset certify election results," *Johnstown Tribune-Democrat.*

Phelan, Craig. 1994. *Divided loyalties: The public and private life of labor leader John Mitchell.* Albany, NY: SUNY Press.

Plaintiff's Bill, Court of Common Pleas. 1925, June. Cambria County, Pennsylvania.

Pressman, Lee. 1958. "Reminiscences of Lee Pressman," *Columbia University Center for Oral History.* New York: Columbia University.

Preis, Art. 1972. *Labor's giant step: The first twenty years of the CIO.* New York: Pathfinder Press.

Progressive International Committee of the UMWA. 1923, June. *Program.* Labadie Collection, University of Michigan.

Progressive International Conference. 1923, June. Minutes. Hapgood Papers. 1921–1923. Lilly Library, Manuscripts Department, Indiana University, Bloomington, Indiana.

Pruner, Robert ed. 1954. *Sesquicentennial of Cambria County, 1804–1954.* Ebensburg, Pa.: *Ebensburg Mountaineer-Herald.*

Putney, Bryan. 1935. "Stabilization of the bituminous coal industry," *Editorial research reports 1935* (Vol. II).

Rhys, Dane and Garner, Timothy. 2020, September 3. "In Pennsylvania coal country, miners forgive Trump for failed revival," *Reuters.*

Ringer, Strawder. 1929. "A history of the United Mine of America." M.A. dissertation, University of Pittsburgh.

Rosen, George. 1943. *The history of coal miners' disease.* New York: Schuman's.

Rottenberg, Dan. 2003. *In the kingdom of coal: An American family and the rock that changed the world.* New York: Routledge

Save the Union. 1926, September 24. "An Open Letter from the Save the Union committee," Brophy Papers.

Schneider, David. 1928. *The Workers' (Communist) Party and American trade unions. John Hopkins University Studies XLVI, no. 2.*

Schweinfurth, Stanley. 2003. "Coal—a complex natural resource: An overview of factors affecting coal quality and use in the United States," *U.S. Geological Survey Circular 1143*. Washington DC: United States Government Printing Office.

Searles, Ellis. 1922, June. "Giving stability to the coal industry." *Review of Reviews*.

Seldes, Gilbert. 1934, May 17. "City writer pictures Nanty-glo as horrible example," *Nanty-glo Journal*.

Serrin, William. 1982, October 3. "Steel industry woes weigh heavily on Johnstown," *New York Times*.

Sharfman, Isaiah. 1937. *The Interstate Commerce Commission*. New York: The Commonwealth Fund.

Shurick, Adam. 1924. *The coal industry*. Boston: Little, Brown.

Singer, Alan. 1982. "'Which side are you on?': Ideological conflict in the United Mine Workers of America, 1919–1928," unpublished doctoral dissertation, Rutgers University, New Brunswick, New Jersey.

Singer, Alan 1988a, Winter. "Class-conscious coal miners: Nanty-glo versus the open shop in the post World War I era," *Labor History*, vol. 29 no. 1.

Singer, Alan. 1988b Winter. "John Brophy's 'Miners Program': Workers' education in UMWA District 2 during the 1920s," *Labor Studies Journal*, vol. 13, no. 4.

Singer, Alan. 1991, Summer. "Communists and coal miners: Organizing mine workers during the 1920s," *Science & Society*, vol. 55 no. 2.

Soule, George. 1920. *History of the strike in Johnstown. Commission of Inquiry of the Interchurch World Movement*. New York: Bureau of Industrial Research.

Soule, George. 1947. *Prosperity decade. From war to depression, 1917—1929. Economic History of the United States,* vol. VIII. New York: Holt, Rinehart and Winston.

Stamm, Tom (Marsh). 1930, August 15. "The National Miners' Union Passes," *The Militant*, vol. iii no. 28

Stark, Louis. 1933, September 22. "Wage pact signed for 340,000 miners in non-union field," *New York Times*.

Stewart, Ethelbert. 1928, June. "Productivity of labor," *Monthly Labor Review*, vol. 26 no. 6.

Storey, Henry. 1907. *History of Cambria County, Pennsylvania*, vol. 1. New York: Lewis Publishing.

Stroup, Thomas. 1923, September. "Causes and growth of unionism among coal miners," *Mining and Metallurgy*, IV.

Strouse, L.K. 1923. "Reports and decisions of the Interstate Commerce Commission," *Interstate Commerce Commission*. Washington, DC Government Printing.

Sukle, R. S. 2003. *Bucket of Blood, The Ragman's War*. iUniverse.

Survey, The. 1922, April 8. "The lay of the land in the coal strike," *The Survey*.

Swabeck, Arne. 1928, October. "The National Miner's Union," *The Communist*, vol. vii no. 10.

Tryon, F. P. and McKinney, W.F. 1922, March 25. "The broken year of the bituminous miner." *The Survey.*

Tryon, F. P. and Hale, S. 1923. "Coal in 1919, 1920, 1921," United States Bureau of Mines, Mineral Resources of the United States, 1921, vol. 2, Non-metals. Washington DC: Government Printing.

UMWA Journal. 1923, April 1. "President Brophy's representative suggests a 20 per cent cut in the wages of mine workers," *UMWA Journal* vol. 34, no. 7.

UMWA District 2 (Central Pennsylvania). 1916–1927. *Proceedings of the Convention and Report of Officers.*

UMWA District 2 (Central Pennsylvania). 1921, December 6. Central Pennsylvania Coal Producer's Association, Confidential Memorandum.

UMWA District 2 (Central Pennsylvania). *Why the Miner's Program?* Clearfield PA: UMWA District 2.

UMWA District 2 (Central Pennsylvania). 1925–1926. *Salaries and expenses of officers and organizers and report of secretary-treasurer.* Altoona, PA.

UMWA District 12 (Illinois). 1920. *Proceedings of the convention and report of officers.*

UMWA Proceedings. *Proceedings of the convention, 1919–1927.*

U. S. Congress, Senate. Committee on Interstate Commerce. 1921. *The coal problem 67:1.* Washington, DC: Government Printing.

U. S. Congress, Senate. Committee on Interstate Commerce. 1922. *Railroad revenue and expenses 67:1 and 2.* Washington, DC: Government Printing.

U. S. Department of Commerce and Labor, Bureau of Census. 1913. *Thirteenth census of the United States taken in the Year 1910, Statistics for Pennsylvania.* Washington: Government Printing Office.

U. S. Department of Commerce, Bureau of Census. 1922. *Fourteenth census of the United States taken in the Year 1920, Volume III, Population 1920, Composition and characteristics of the population by states.* Washington: Government Printing Office.

U. S. Department of Commerce, Bureau of Census. 1924. *Fourteenth census—State compendium—Pennsylvania.* Washington, DC: Government Printing.

U.S. Department of Commerce, Bureau of Census. 1931. *Fifteenth census of the United States. Population,* vol. 1. Washington DC: Government Printing office.

U.S. Department of Commerce, Bureau of Census. 1933. *Fifteenth census of the United States. Mines and Quarries: 1929.* Washington DC: Government Printing office.

U.S. Department of Commerce, Bureau of Census. 1942. *Sixteenth census of the United States. Population,* vol. 1. Washington DC: Government Printing office.

U.S. Department of Commerce. 1949. *Historical statistics of the United States 1789–1945, A supplement to the statistical abstract of the United States,* "Series G 13–18. Fuels—Bituminous and Anthracite Coal, Production: 1807 to 1945." Washington DC: Government Printing.

U. S. Department of Commerce, Bureau of Census. 1975. *Historical statistics of the United States, Colonial times to 1970. 2 Vols.* Washington, DC: Government Printing, 1975.

U. S. Mine Bureau. 1921. *Mineral resources,* "Pennsylvania Production by County 1918–1920." Washington, DC: Government Printing.

U. S. Mine Bureau. 1927. *Mineral resources (Part 2 Non-Metals), 1921, 1923, 1925.* Washington, DC: Government Printing.

U.S. Senate Committee on Manufactures. 1921. *Publication of Production and Profits in Coal,* vol. 1. Washington DC: Government Printing Office.

Van Tine, Warren. 1973. *The making of the labor bureaucrat, Union leadership in the United States, 1870–1920.* Amherst, MA: University of Massachusetts.

Vorse, Mary Heaton. 1922, December 15. "Ma and Mr. Davis," *Survey, 49.*

Walkowitz, Daniel. 1978. *Worker city, Company town: Iron and cotton worker protest in Troy and Cohoes, New York, 1855–1884.* Urbana, IL: University of Illinois.

Warne, Frank. 1922. "Railroad Revenue and Expenses, vol. 3," *Subcommittee of the United States Senate Committee on Interstate Commerce.* Washington, DC: Government Printing.

Watkins, Thomas. 1921, May 4. "The coal problem," *Subcommittee of the United States Senate Committee on Interstate Commerce, 67th Congress, 1st Session.* Washington, DC: Government Printing.

Watkins, Thomas H. 1921, July 21. "T.H. Watkins says mine workers' pamphlet notable for misstatements and omissions," *Coal Age 20*(3).

WBOY 12. 2020, November 20. "United Mine Workers president issues statement on actions of Trump campaign," *WBOY 12.*

Weinberg, Carl. 2005. *Labor, loyalty, and rebellion: Southern Illinois coal miners and World War I.* Carbondale, IL: Southern Illinois University Press.

Weitz, Eric. 1989. *Conflict in the Ruhr: Workers and socialist politics in Essen, 1910–1925.* Boston, MA: Boston University.

Wechsler, James. 1944. *Labor baron: A portrait of John L. Lewis.* New York: William Morrow.

White, Jerome and Law, Samuel. n.d. *The story of coal in Cambria County.* Ebensburg, PA: Cambria County Historical Society.

Wickersham, Edward. 1951. "Opposition to the international officers of the United Mine Workers of America, 1919–1933." Ph.D. dissertation, Cornell University.

Wiebe, Robert. 1967. *The search for order, 1877–1920.* New York: Hill and Wang.

Wikipedia. Nanty Glo, Pennsylvania. https://en.wikipedia/wiki/Nanty_Glo_Pennsylvania (accessed January 27, 2022).

Williams, Bruce and Yates, Michael. 1976. *Upward struggle, a bicentennial tribute to labor in Cambria and Somerset Counties.* Johnstown, PA: Bicentennial Commission.

Wilson, William Julius. 1987. *The truly disadvantaged: The inner city, the underclass, and public policy.* Chicago IL: University of Chicago Press.

Wilson, William Julius. 1996. *When work disappears: The world of the new urban poor.* New York: Random House.

Yale Law Journal. 1935, December. "The Bituminous Coal Conservation Act of 1935," *The Yale Law Journal,* vol. 45, no. 2: 293–314.

Zeidel, Robert. 2004. *Immigrants, progressives, and exclusion politics—The Dillingham Commission, 1900–1927.* DeKalb, IL: Northern Illinois University Press.

Zieger, Robert. 1969. *Republicans and labor: 1919–1929.* Lexington, KY: University Press of Kentucky.

Zieger, Robert. 1986. *American workers, American unions.* Baltimore, MD: John Hopkins Press.

Oral Histories UMWA District 2 (Central Pennsylvania)

Braken, Dave. Nanty-glo, Pennsylvania. Interview, 1976.

Brushko, Frank. Nanty-glo, Pennsylvania. Interview, 1976.

Cook, Clair. Nanty-glo, Pennsylvania. Interview, 1976.

Halcovich, Cyril. Windber, Pennsylvania. Interview, 1976.

Hill, Johnny. Nanty-glo, Pennsylvania. Interview, 1976.

Hocevar, Frank. St. Michael's, Pennsylvania. Interview, 1976.

Martin, Katherine Welsh. Nanty-glo, Pennsylvania. Interview, 1976.

Martin, Paul. Nanty-glo, Pennsylvania. Interview, 1976.

Ray, William "Spider Bill." Nanty-glo, Pennsylvania. Interview, 1976.

Shulick, Joe. Colver, Pennsylvania. Interview, 1976.

Szekeresh, John. Nanty-glo, Pennsylvania. Interview, 1976.

Teeter, Russell. Nanty-glo, Pennsylvania. Interview, 1976.

Zankey, Charles. Windber, Pennsylvania. Interview, 1976.

Newspapers

Brookwood Review (Brookwood Labor College), 1923–1925.

Cleveland Plain-Dealer, 1922.

Coal Age, 1922–1927.

Coal Digger (Save the Union Committee), 1928.

Coal Miner (Save the Union Committee), 1926.

Communist (Workers' [Communist] Party*)*, 1928–1932.

Communist International (Executive Committee of the Communist International), 1928–1929.

Daily Worker (Workers' [Communist] Party), 1924–1928.

District 2 Bulletin (UMWA District 2), 1926.

Ebensburg Mountaineer-Herald (Pennsylvania), 1924–1925.

Federated Press (also known as *Federated Press Bulletin, Federated Press Daily Mail Service, Federated Press Labor Letter*), 1921–1929.

Illinois Miner (UMWA District 12), 1922–1929.

Johnstown Democrat (Pennsylvania), 1922.

Johnstown Tribune (Pennsylvania), 1919–1922.

Labor Herald (Trade Union Educational League), 1922–1924.

Labor Unity (Trade Union Educational League), 1927–1932.

Nanty-glo Journal (Pennsylvania), 1921–1926.

National Labor Tribune (Pittsburgh, Pennsylvania), 1924–1929.

New York Times, 1919–1928.

Penn-Central News (UMWA District 2), 1922–1923.

United Mine Workers Journal, 1900–1929.

Manuscript Collections

Heber Blankenhorn Papers (https://digital.library.pitt.edu/islandora/object/pitt%3AUS-PPiU-ais196615/viewer#aspace_ref16_m4e): Located in the University of Pittsburgh Library SystemArchives & Special Collections, Pittsburgh, PA. Series III and V (Folders 40–46, 51) include material on the 1922 Somerset Coal Strike.

John Brophy Papers, 1918–1963 (https://libraries.catholic.edu/special-collections/archives/collections/finding-aids/finding-aids.html?file=brophy): Located in the Special Collections of the University Libraries at The Catholic University of America, Washington DC (55 boxes and six oversized boxes). Series #1 includes Brophy's work on the Nationalization Research Committee, his 1926 challenge of Lewis for the UMWA Presidency, correspondence, speeches, clippings, official memos, reports, and three scrapbooks.

Powers Hapgood Papers, 1915–1951 (http://webapp1.dlib.indiana.edu/findingaids/view?doc.view=entire_text&docId=InU-Li-VAD6475): Located at the Lilly Library, Indiana University, Bloomington, Indiana. There are 4,286 items (11 boxes, 5 volumes, 3 folios). The papers include Hapgood's diaries from January 1, 1915 through June 15, 1925; drafts of his account of his trip around the world, 1924–1926, "Diary of an American Miner Abroad;" correspondence (series I, boxes 1–4) with members of his family, labor leaders, union members, persons interested in the labor movement; drafts of articles by Powers Hapgood; and pamphlets, periodicals, newspaper clippings, broadsides, posters, and maps; photographs. Newspaper clippings are either filed by year in boxes (series III, boxes 7 and 8) or mounted in five scrapbooks (series V) including one that focuses on the Somerset County coal strike of 1922 and one on the Lewis-Brophy campaigns for UMWA President. Correspondents on conditions in the bituminous coal industry include Hapgood's parents, especially his mother, Heber Blankenhorn, Ella Reeve Bloor, John Brophy, Frank Farrington, Harry Fishwick, Paul W. Fuller, Adolph Germer, Richard Gilbert, William Green, Mary Donovan Hapgood, Arthur Garfield Hays, Alexander Howat, John Kerr, Joe J. Kintner, John Llewellyn Lewis, Jay Lovestone, Faber V. McCloskey, James Mark, Anthony Minerich, Abraham John Muste, Thomas Myerscough, T.D. Stiles, and Pat Toohey.

John L. Lewis Papers, 1879–1969: Available on microfilm. Tamiment Institute, Bobst Library, New York University.

UMWA District 2 (https://www.iup.edu/library/departments/archives/manuscript-group-collections/index.html): Located in the Special Collections of Indiana University of Pennsylvania, Indiana, PA (489 boxes). Series I: Early Records, Boxes 1–15: Box 15, Somerset Strike of 1922; Series II: John Brophy, Boxes 16–49: Box 31, 41, 1922 Strike; Box 45, Save the Union Campaign.

UMWA Records (https://guides.libraries.psu.edu/c.php?g=443716&p=3026284): Located in the Eberly Family Special Collections Library of Pennsylvania State University. The collection includes International Executive Board records, Presidential correspondence organized by district, and photographs, and artifacts. Pennsylvania University Libraries is in the process of digitalizing the collection. The archive at the UMWA office in Triangle, Virginia (https://umwa.org/about/aboutaboutabouthistory/umwa-collection-archive/) has copies of every issue of the *UMW Journal* and meeting and session minutes of the International Executive Board.

Index

www.ingramcontent.com/pod-product-compliance
Lightning Source LLC
Chambersburg PA
CBHW032030090325
23169CB00009B/35